W9-BTR-810

# Strategic Change
# in Colleges and Universities

The Jossey-Bass Higher
and Adult Education Series

# Strategic Change in Colleges and Universities

## Planning to Survive and Prosper

DANIEL JAMES ROWLEY
HERMAN D. LUJAN
MICHAEL G. DOLENCE

Foreword by
GEORGE KELLER

Jossey-Bass Publishers • San Francisco

Copyright © 1997 by Jossey-Bass Inc., Publishers, 350 Sansome Street, San Francisco, California 94104.

Substantial discounts on bulk quantities of Jossey-Bass books are available to corporations, professional associations, and other organizations. For details and discount information, contact the special sales department at Jossey-Bass Inc., Publishers (415) 433–1740; Fax (800) 605–2665.

For sales outside the United States, please contact your local Simon & Schuster International office.

Jossey-Bass Web address: http://www.josseybass.com

Manufactured in the United States of America.

**Library of Congress Cataloging-in-Publication Data**
Rowley, Daniel James, date.
    Strategic change in colleges and universities : planning to survive and prosper / Daniel James Rowley, Herman D. Lujan, Michael G. Dolence. — 1st ed.
        p.    cm. — (The Jossey-Bass higher and adult education series)
    Includes bibliographical references (p. ) and index.
    ISBN 0–7879–0348–5 (cloth : alk. paper)
    1. Education, Higher—United States—Administration. 2. Universities and colleges—United States—Planning. 3. Strategic planning—United States. I. Lujan, Herman D. II. Dolence, Michael G. III. Title. IV. Series.
LB2341.R69 1997
378.1'07—dc20                                       96–25370

FIRST EDITION
*HB Printing*      10 9 8 7 6 5 4 3 2 1

# CONTENTS

In the past dozen years, hundreds of the 3,500 colleges and universities in the United States have launched efforts at strategic planning. Pushed by external changes in technology, demographics, family life, and financial support, and by political scrutiny, and pulled by fears of enrollment decline, by financial difficulty, and by outmoded academic programs, many campus leaders, faculty members, and trustees have struggled to find ways to make beneficial, strategic changes so that their colleges and universities can adapt to the rapidly shifting environment. These hundreds of efforts have had mixed success. A few institutions have transformed themselves dramatically. Others have been able to make important changes in parts of their operation by, for example, adding weekend programs, increasing distance learning through technology, cutting back on the types and numbers of programs offered, instituting new financial controls, offering innovative programs, and establishing new ties with industrial organizations. But many institutions have stumbled, dissolved into controversy, or lost their nerve. Exactly why some have succeeded while others have floundered is not clear. Few scholars have studied the many attempts at strategic change in higher education.

This book is a valiant effort to correct this scholarly neglect. It does so mostly by reporting candidly about what happened at one institution. The authors—a management professor, a university president, and a consultant—look at the strategic planning process from several perspectives. They offer some administrative theory and models. They describe vividly the land mines, barbed wire, and guerilla tactics of campus politics. They urge maximum consultation and involvement among university stakeholders but note that strong leadership and hard decisions are also imperative. And they confess that strategic change in an academic republic is very complex and difficult, often Sisyphean, with modernizers arduously rolling their stones up a steep incline. They have read the strategic planning literature, they have watched closely how the process actually unfolded at one university and studied how planning has fared at numerous other institutions, and they have drawn lessons for us.

Based on their observations, the authors gingerly offer advice on how others in higher education might or should proceed. Their prescriptions are wisely tentative and they are aware of the astonishingly diverse campus cultures at the many colleges and universities in the United States. The book reveals as much as it directs.

*Strategic Change in Colleges and Universities* is a major contribution to the continuing struggle to find an acceptable approach to strategic, foresighted improvements in higher education, a sector more comfortable with keeping its distance from the rest of society and with ancient traditions and prerogatives than with innovations and obligations to the young. Many of the tidy, highly rational business school schemes in management books are almost useless in academic circles. Except for a few strategists like Henry Mintzberg and James Brian Quinn, the business planning and management experts have provided little that colleges can use. Strategic planning has had to be invented anew in academia. This book is in part the story of one such invention.

Colleges and universities cannot escape from the imperatives of strategic change. Advanced learning and research constitutes one of the pistons of our new information society with its international connections. But a method for bringing about constructive adaptations, novel practices and structures, and fresh forms of learning in the traditionally conservative habitat dominated by professors is still being developed. The authors know the special attributes of professorial communities. They also know the necessity of strategic renovation in these communities. Out of their wide-ranging knowledge they have fashioned an instructive volume from which we can all learn.

George Keller
Editor, *Planning for Higher Education*

The old cliche "There is nothing as constant as change" applies today, perhaps more than ever, and that change is increasing at an exponential rate. The possibilities for reacting to change vary widely as organizations throughout the economy scramble to cope. Many hope that change will cease and that "the good old days" will return once again. That just is not going to happen.

For organizations that choose to address change in a straightforward manner, the future always represents an exciting set of opportunities as well as potential pitfalls. Over the past forty years, the methods of strategic management have emerged to address these issues, promising effective ways of dealing with change and the future. Yet strategic management and strategic planning (the process that develops strategic management) have been welcomed with varying levels of enthusiasm. First, the world of business began to experiment with its methods and technologies. Over time these methods improved and the groundswell of support began to grow. As more and more businesses found the key to success through applying strategic management principles, other organizations began to look at these methods as well. Soon strategic planning was a phenomenon that was also being tried out in not-for-profit and government organizations, as they began to feel the bite of change and intensifying challenges from their constituency bases. Within this emerging group of interested strategic planning experimenters, colleges and universities also began to show interest.

## The Scope of This Book

Unfortunately, the success of strategic planning experienced in the business sector has not been mirrored in the not-for-profit, government, or higher education venues. Upon analysis, there are several reasons for this. First and foremost is the reality that nonbusiness organizations are distinctly different from business organizations in character, governance, and scope, and many strategic planning enthusiasts in the nonbusiness sector have overlooked this plain and simple fact. Beyond that, however, is the impact on nonbusiness organizations of controlling forces from both inside and outside. This is a different condition than that addressed by the mission-driven, CEO-guided model that comes from the private business sector.

And so the dilemma reveals itself: Can nonbusiness organizations, such as colleges and universities (both public and private), engage a potentially powerful and promising model such as strategic planning and develop it effectively? Or are such institutions doomed to sit idly by as the world changes around them, perhaps leaving them behind? Unfortunately, this danger exists.

We have written this book because we strongly believe two things: (1) colleges and universities can engage in effective strategic planning processes that will lead to strategic management, and (2) they can use strategic planning to be proactive about their own futures and thus continue to play a critical role in the fast-changing world of which they are a part. *How* to proceed is the issue. With few models in place that work well, many strategic planning exercises in higher education have been unsuccessful if not downright hazardous to those who have tried to develop them. On several college and university campuses today, the term *strategic planning* is repugnant and tantamount to heresy. This is too bad, because the potential benefits of a properly initiated and implemented strategic planning process can have spectacular positive results on a campus.

There are several basic points about strategic planning in colleges and universities that we believe strategic planners need to consider. First, given the level of change that is occurring as we move from the industrial age to the information age, one real danger that colleges and universities face is that unrestricted commercialization could transform higher education, to its detriment, into an occupational training program unless effective new directions are identified. Witness the rise in workforce training mandates by the states and the federal government. Second, strategic planning seeks an approach to campus planning and management that is more comprehensive than traditional planning and, by not compromising knowledge as the foundation of higher education, addresses the diverse needs of a society growing evermore complex under severe economic and competitive restraints. Third, mission-based and CEO-driven planning may not work effectively in colleges and universities. We argue here that a statement of mission should be a derivative of planning rather than planning being a derivative of mission, and that a successful strategic planning process is marked by meaningful participation from across the campus. Fourth, there is no one model that can be applied like a cookie cutter to the strategic planning practices of all colleges and universities. Each campus must develop its own method of planning to match its own needs and characteristics. Fifth, strategic planning is a learning process. It is iterative; it involves the development of cognition; and it must be a formal method that will help prevent constituencies from becoming lost. Sixth, like learning, strategic planning is a continuing process that informs itself about the organization and its environments. And seventh, ongoing evaluation must be built into the process and be integral to it.

## Who Should Read This Book?

*Strategic Change in Colleges and Universities* is primarily aimed at those institutional leaders who are concerned with the strategic planning activities of the macroorganization. Presidents, chancellors, vice presidents, vice chancellors, governing board members, college and university planners, and systemwide administrators will gain a strategic planning perspective that should aid them in developing institution-wide strategic plans. Deans, department chairs, faculty leaders, and unit heads can also benefit from the material in this book, and in turn benefit the university, by using strategic planning to organize and reengineer the important academic (and nonacademic) components of the campus. Another group of potential readers are students of higher education and administration, who will find presented here a method of organizational management that identifies the current status of the art of institutional planning. And finally, all those who are involved in college or university strategic planning—faculty members, staff members, student body representatives, and outside representatives who have been asked to give of their time and talents to help organize and conduct a strategic planning process—will find here explanations of background and process that could help them to be more effective in their efforts.

## Organization of the Book

*Strategic Change in Colleges and Universities* develops a schema of strategic planning that has proved effective and useful on a variety of campuses across the United States and Canada. Though based in theory, the book also builds on practice and experience.

The book is organized into three parts. Part One presents the theoretical bases we used to develop our approach to strategic planning in colleges and universities. Chapter One looks at the general context and the imperative for doing strategic planning. Chapter Two considers the historical and traditional antecedents that have led to the present-day need to do strategic planning. Chapter Three discusses the major differences between strategic planning exercises in businesses and those in institutions of higher education and discusses the problems associated with mission-based planning. Chapter Four analyzes the general internal environments of colleges and universities, and develops a focus on some of the characteristics that strategic planners in higher education must consider as they develop their various campus strategic plans. Finally, Chapter Five examines the role of politics and political behaviors in colleges and universities and discusses several ways of working with, through, or around the realities of campus politics. Readers who want to know these contexts should read Part One in its entirety. Those who are only interested in certain parts of the strategic planning context may choose from among these various chapters those that will be of help to them.

Part Two develops several components of the strategic planning process in colleges and universities. Chapter Six presents a basic theoretical model for this process and describes the several major components that come together to help ensure an effective strategic planning experience. Chapter Seven provides a step-by-step method of constructing the planning process, beginning with the decision to do strategic planning and working through implementation, document writing, and mission identification. Chapter Eight is the first of several chapters that go deeper into the specific issues involved in carrying out strategic planning. Here the discussion focuses on "people issues"— what types of people should be involved, what they will be asked to do, and how they should be organized. It also examines "time issues"—how much time do various steps take and when should certain things happen. Chapter Nine looks at issues surrounding planning committees, including their structure, whether they must be created or whether the process can make use of committees already in place, and how planners can ensure a legitimate process and legitimate outcomes. Chapter Ten sets forth the importance of communication and participation in the strategic planning process and considers how planners need to establish from the very beginning a dialogue about how to improve the chances of approval for the plan as then various planning stages unfold. This chapter also points out the iterative nature of strategic planning and how planners can deal with those who do not understand or simply reject this important feature. Chapter Eleven focuses on key characteristics of planning, including enrollment management and academic planning, identifying both the methods of planning and related components that most colleges and universities need to consider. Finally, Chapter Twelve highlights the other major areas of planning, giving attention to resource planning, planning for information technology, and planning in service and support units that help ensure the quality and smooth operation of supplemental campus programs.

Part Three looks at how college and university strategic planners should implement the results of their planning efforts, and looks at where this planning is leading. Chapter Thirteen specifically addresses the integral components of a successful implementation strategy, including communication, support by top leaders, and the development of campuswide support. Chapter Fourteen identifies the major differences that must be understood when considering the differences in nature of individual campuses. It presents the differences between research and teaching institutions, between small and large campuses, and those that characterize public and private colleges and universities. Finally, Chapter Fifteen looks into the future and discusses some of the current thinking and trends that will shape higher education in the coming millennium.

## Bringing the Material to Life

To help the reader visualize how the activities and objectives of the strategic planning process work in practice, throughout the book we use examples in the form of vignettes and cases from colleges and universities that have become involved with strategic planning. Many of these examples and vignettes come from the University of Northern Colorado (UNC), a campus where the authors of this book collaborated at length on a successful strategic planning exercise. We believe that the examples from this particular campus, as well as examples from other colleges and universities, help demonstrate techniques that work and those that do not. These comparisons help explain why strategic planning has worked on some campuses and not on others.

As an aside, we understand that our statement regarding

successes and failures at UNC is arguable. Change is controversial on any campus. Some at UNC do not think that the process was beneficial or positive at all, while others have become involved in the changes that planning has continued to create. We claim success in the sense that strategic planning at UNC led to a more systematic way of recruiting and retaining students, a vastly improved information technology planning and implementation system, and a more focused and successful resource management system, and that it forced the beginnings of academic reform in an effort to fit the needs of the university's students with the strengths of the faculty. As a result of strategic planning, the university is better poised for its future, even though academic planning remains controversial. But that is the point. Academic and university planning priorities are now linked to the budget and its priorities. Budgets are no longer simply incremental, with bases essentially the same. Budget reallocation is now both driven and guided by strategic planning, allowing redistribution of 9.8 percent from the base over the last three years.

Those on the UNC campus who feel that strategic planning did not succeed argue that no major changes occurred during the process. They argue that it was not well understood by campus constituents, that it was not widely supported, and that the process was seriously flawed because it was not mission driven.

These concerns demonstrate the need for two things: (1) open and consistent communication, and (2) letting the campus know up front what strategic planning is and why it is different from traditional campus planning. We admit that at UNC we did not do a good job in either of these two areas, partially because we were developing the model. But these two problem areas caused the campus a tremendous amount of concern and confusion that led some people to the conclusion that the process was a failure.

One of our motivations for writing this book is to provide other campus strategic planners with important before-the-event knowledge that will help them avoid the mistakes we made and develop a more comprehensive and collegial approach to the process. At UNC, the future will be different than it otherwise would have been, in a positive way, because of strategic planning. And one more time for emphasis: that's the point. This is why we know that strategic planning is a success at UNC. On other campuses, the future will also be different from the present, and now is when campus leaders have a choice regarding what those differences will be. Either the future will dictate to the campus or the campus will position itself to take maximum advantage of the exciting changes that are just around the corner.

If conceived and implemented properly, strategic planning works (though perhaps never according to a perfect model), and it can work on nearly any college or university campus. Where experiments in strategic planning have not worked, a variety of good reasons explain how and why the processes went wrong. Regardless of outcomes, it is important to identify both those constructs that help support a successful planning process and those that work against it. With this knowledge, those who engage in strategic planning can better align their campuses with their environments and prepare their colleges and universities for the demands of the information age and the fundamental transformation that higher education is experiencing.

*December 1996*

Daniel James Rowley
*Greeley, Colorado*

Herman D. Lujan
*Evans, Colorado*

Michael G. Dolence
*Claremont, California*

DANIEL JAMES ROWLEY is currently a professor of management in the College of Business Administration at the University of Northern Colorado (UNC). From summer 1992 until fall 1995, he took a leave of absence from teaching to join the president's office at UNC to oversee the development of a university-wide strategic planning process. He worked directly with UNC's board of trustees to develop and approve strategic management policy for the university. During this time, he also served the university as chief of staff in the president's office and as secretary to the board of trustees, and helped formulate strategic priorities to guide the development of UNC's budgets. These efforts at UNC, which took Rowley beyond his experience in business strategic planning, were designed to uniquely fit the needs and characteristics of public higher education and resulted in growing national recognition for strategic planning in higher education.

In 1995 Rowley resumed his teaching, writing, and consulting activities. He currently works with other universities, school districts, and nonprofit organizations in their strategic planning efforts. He is cofounder and past president of the Institute of Behavioral and Applied Management, a national academic and professional organization for management professors, students, and practitioners. He is sole or lead author of a number of journal articles on the subjects of business management and strategic planning, and has given several national presentations on the same subjects. With UNC's current strategic planner, Donna Bottenberg, he has coauthored a chapter on strategic enrollment management published in 1996 in a scholarly casebook for the American Association of Collegiate Registrars and Admissions Officers.

Rowley received a B.A. degree (1969) in political science from the University of Colorado at Boulder. He earned an M.P.A. (Master of Public Administration) degree (1979) at the University of Denver, and a Ph.D. degree (1987) in organizational management and strategic management at the University of Colorado at Boulder. He and his wife, Barbara, are the proud parents of one daughter, Rebecca.

HERMAN D. LUJAN has been president of the University of Northern Colorado (UNC) since December 1991. During his tenure he has established UNC as a teaching university whose first priority is to serve Colorado with high-quality undergraduate programs while bringing new energy and direction to its role as one of twenty-nine Doctoral I universities in the United States. In 1992 he initiated a campuswide strategic planning process designed to identify and better focus campus resources to help the university build on its strengths and develop a stronger fit with the needs of Colorado and the Rocky Mountain Region. In addition, he has launched a series of programs to help increase and improve the diversity of UNC's faculty, staff, and student body.

Lujan's career in higher education began at the University of Kansas (KU), where he was a faculty member in political science and an administrator for thirteen years. He was the director of KU's Institute for Social and Environmental Studies from 1972 to 1979, and took a one-year leave from 1974 to 1975 to serve as director of the Division of State Planning and Research in the Kansas governor's office. Immediately prior to coming to UNC, Lujan spent thirteen years at the University of Washington as a faculty member and administrator. He served as vice president for minority affairs before becoming vice provost in 1988, a position he held until he came to UNC. Lujan has worked on more than thirty research grant projects and has published numerous scholarly articles and books. He serves on the board of directors of Bank One Greeley and is active in several other civic, educational, and charitable organizations both locally and nationwide, including the American Council on Education (ACE), the American Association of State Colleges and Universities (AASCU), and the National Association of State Universities and Land Grant Colleges (NASULGC).

Lujan is a native of Hawaii and holds an A.B. degree (1958) from St. Mary's College in California, an M.A. degree (1960) from the University of California at Berkeley, and a Ph.D. degree (1964) from the University of Idaho, all in political science. He and his wife Carla are the parents of three children, and grandparents of six.

MICHAEL G. DOLENCE is president of Michael G. Dolence and Associates. Formerly he served as strategic planning administrator for the California State University, Los Angeles; director of research, planning, and policy analysis for the Commission on Independent Colleges and Universities; founding director of the New York State Public Opinion Poll; and founding director of the Science, Engineering, and Research Campus Hook-up. While serving as strategic planning administrator at California State University, Dolence had the opportunity to implement a campuswide strategic planning process and to guide the development of an integrated planning and budgeting system.

Dolence consults nationally with higher education institutions, systems, associations, and vendors. He has worked with numerous institutions of higher education to develop campuswide strategic planning processes and strategic enrollment management programs with a special emphasis on crisis avoidance and intervention, and has had extensive experience in developing the tactical plans necessary to implement a strategic management system in a university of 22,000 students. His counsel is sought on strategies for responding to state and federal initiatives, as well as strategies for repositioning institutions for competitiveness. He has also worked with information system vendors in the development of state-of-the-art strategic enrollment and instructional management systems.

Dolence is a specialist in and nationally acclaimed keynote speaker on organizational transformation, strategic positioning, institutional strategic planning and management processes, and strategic enrollment management; in information technology planning and management linking planning and budgeting and linking academic planning and transformation; and in public advocacy and public relations. He has made many presentations before such national audiences as the Society for College and University Planning (SCUP), the American Association of Collegiate Registrars and Admissions Officers, the American Association for Higher Education, the College and University Systems Exchange, and the Interuniversity Communications Council. He is the author of numerous publications, and a member of *Who's Who Worldwide*, *Who's Who in American Education*, and the *Who's Who Registry of Global Business Leaders*. He and his wife, Maryann, have a son, Michael, and a daughter, Katie.

# PART ONE

# The Principles

# CHAPTER 1

# Higher Education— A System Under Fire

The chapters in the first part of this book develop the various contexts within which strategic planning takes place in colleges and universities. The central objective of strategic planning is to position the institution so that it can shape and exploit its environment. For this reason it is important to understand what exists within that environment that can be used or influenced to create the strategies that a strategic plan must consider.

This chapter looks at the context of the mounting pressures from the environment of higher education that are forcing change. It also develops the central questions that colleges and universities should address as they analyze their alignment with the environment, and ends with a list of the key vocabulary of strategic planning and the specific terms the authors use in this book.

## No More "Business as Usual"

Higher education is a system under fire. For decades, if not centuries, colleges and universities have enjoyed the status, prestige, reverence, and support that has helped them to become fonts of knowledge in both the generation and the sharing of knowledge within our society. This focal role is now undergoing significant change. The February 1996 Western Governors' Association conference report highlighted the change in this way:

> All western governors are feeling the press of increased demand on their state systems of postsecondary education. All recognize that the strength and well-being of both their states and the nation depend heavily on a postsecondary system that is visibly aligned with the needs of a transforming economy and society. At the same time, the states' capacity to respond to these challenges is severely constrained by limited resources and the inflexibility and high costs of traditional educational practices and by outdated institutional and public policies [Western Governors' Association, 1996, p. 1].

The challenges posed by the twenty-one governors who issued this report are not just problems for publicly funded colleges and universities. Private institutions of higher education face exactly the same challenges, perhaps only from different sources. Following on the heels of the landmark study *A Nation at Risk* (National Commission on Excellence in Education, 1983), the governors' alarm bell is a clear example of the growing concerns and criticisms that confront today's colleges and universities both in the United States and around the world.

## The Disquieting Challenges of Change

As the twentieth century draws to a close and the twenty-first century dawns before us, those of us who have dedicated our careers to the pursuit of academic excellence in the classrooms and laboratories of America's colleges and universities find that the massive changes that are occurring in the world around us are intruding into the academic realm as well (Leslie and Fretwell, 1996; Kaufman, 1993; Bollinger, 1990; Shirley, 1988). Criticism is increasing from politicians, government officials, and others about the time we spend in the classroom, the value of our research, the quality and preparedness of our students, and our role as experts in the emerging global society (Horne, 1995). Even accreditation bodies have joined the debate (Thompson, Johnson, Warren, and Williams, 1990). Much of this criticism is new, and surprisingly serious. Even some within the academy, such as Louis Menand (1991), question whether or not we are properly preparing students for the world they are about to enter. Botstein (1991) tells us that many who analyze higher education consider the general education program of colleges and universities to be "artificial, arbitrary, tendentious—even imposed and essentially dispensable" (p. 10).

Marshall and Palca (1992) tell us that as federal and state governments begin to follow their criticisms with reductions in support, or as private companies seek greater accountability for the use of their grants for academic projects and research agenda, all colleges and universities are feeling new operating pressures and resource cutbacks. Mercer (1993) advises that there is even growing concern among legislators, parents, and students about the amount of tuition that higher education is charging, and this concern is causing campus leaders to seek new ways of keeping costs in line to reduce the need for tuition increases, and/or to find other sources for funding.

These criticisms, resource cutbacks, and demands for new accountability are perceived by many within U.S. educational systems as severe threats (Houston and Schneider, 1994; St. John, 1991). While many outside the academy perceive these events as problems, too many campus constituents still believe that their institutions are insulated from harm. For the most part, however, according to the National Commission on Excellence in Education (1983), there is a growing feeling that something must change, that colleges and universities need to improve their relationships with those who criticize them, with those who threaten to withhold or reduce funding, or with those who take even stronger negative actions. This opinion has also been expressed more recently by Johnstone (1994) and Tornquist and Kallsen (1994).

The future could become an unpredictable and chaotic set

of surprises and fallbacks that could potentially change the nature of higher education, with which faculty, administrators, staff, and students have become very comfortable. As MacTaggart (1996) has suggested, the major challenge that higher education faces is to regain its credibility through reforms that allow it to meet the higher expectations of its publics.

To address these issues, one inevitably must wrestle with a word that most academic faculty and administrators honestly do not like: *change.* Yet as one looks at the general issue of change in colleges and universities, it is important to observe that these institutions change more slowly than other institutions and do not have a legacy of reacting happily or speedily to pressures to change. They are governed by traditions stretching back to the medieval days in European history. The color and formality of academic regalia reflect that heritage. Regalia aside, however, according to Birnbaum (1991), the common response to change on many campuses is to turn to the politics and procedures that have been invoked from time immemorial.

However, as Birnbaum further suggests, those who would pursue change on the campus must contend with strong resistance, or inertia, which takes the form of laborious process and review and is at the core of campus politics in both faculty and administrative circles. Because reactiveness, as opposed to proactiveness, is the normal response of campus leaders, politics has been used to keep things from happening, from changing.

The power of campus politics lies in a group's ability to veto change directly or to surround it with procedure and ritual that confounds, dilutes, or smothers it. Unfortunately, the resulting inertia tends to be a typical response to external pressures for change and, as a result, change seems to move at the proverbial snail's pace.

## Why Colleges and Universities Need to Do Strategic Planning

"Business as usual" is no longer acceptable to the taxpaying public, the business leaders, and the other laypersons who sit on governing boards (Gardner, 1995). And as students pay more of the cost of their education, their desire to voice their interests will reemerge. As Lipset (1993) suggests, the old codes of conduct and the rules of how the academic game is played have gone the way of history. This shift from the university as the primary creator and provider of knowledge to a global society potentially more capable of such innovation challenges how we develop and disseminate knowledge.

Further, the move of the country since the 1980s toward more conservative politics, whether temporary or not, is signaling a diminution of the days of government largesse, especially in national funding of research, state-supported growth, and the subsidy of tuition. Under the umbrella of accountability and efficiency, governments are increasingly interested in cutting perceived waste and in balancing budgets.

Within the academy itself, faculty are also becoming more activist. Faculty unions exist in many states and they have been successful in gaining a significant voice in decision making. Faculty senates are demanding a greater say in the scope of campus administrative operations through the exercise of veto power when they oppose changes in their status and in the general affairs of the campus, especially in regard to any issue that threatens to alter the protections of tenure.

Governing boards are taking their roles much more seriously as they assume the ultimate responsibility for the activities, successes, and failures of a college or university (Gardner, 1995). Until now, "business as usual" has meant hiring a president or chancellor and letting that person run the campus while reporting back to the board only periodically, often with routine agenda items that do not require much effort or analysis. Today, the business of a board is to take responsibility for the strategic aspects of what transpires on campus (Honan, 1995). Today's board members, therefore, do more homework and are more likely to take the heat for controversial decisions.

All of these circumstances are exacerbated by the declining base of financial resources. States are increasingly placing limits on revenue increases in campus budgets, and increments do not cover the fixed and mandated costs that continue to rise unabated. Some states have reduced allocations, forcing colleges and universities to go through major cost-cutting measures. Consequently, the demand for dollars from other sources has gone up, putting a squeeze on grants, contracts, and contributions.

On the one hand, colleges and universities are being told to do more with less while, on the other hand, demands for innovation persist. The call for access and universal education also remains. The desire grows for the development and delivery of new intellectual properties and products. While all of these demands have increased, resources have shrunk, demonstrating dramatically that new ways for doing business are needed. Many colleges and universities have not yet adapted to these new conditions, and some have had to close.

Among others, Nutt and Backoff (1992) suggest that the solution to these challenges may lie in the premises of strategic planning. Strategic planning is a respected method for purposeful change developed in the private sector. But as Roessner (1977) suggests, when practitioners attempted to bring it into the confines of higher education and the public sector in the late 1970s and 1980s, demonstrated results were uneven. This is unfortunate because, as Brandt (1991) tells us, nonbusiness organizations that engage in strategic planning benefit over those that do not.

## The Advent of Strategic Planning

The central purpose of this book is to examine the issues facing colleges and universities as they become aware of the need to change strategically. The book is also intended to present a method of planning that focuses on the peculiarities and special needs of American colleges and universities (though applications beyond the United States are entirely feasible). It attempts to outline the transition that is needed to enable strategic change in the academy—a shift from short-term thinking and strictly operational decision making to strategic thinking.

Strategic thinking requires commitments to concentrate the use of resources and to focus on priorities in their use (Dodd, 1992). These commitments lead to strategic decision making, in which those who make key decisions about resources are governed by a carefully defined sense of priorities, and in which the process itself can increase the effectiveness of the outcomes of decisions (Dean and Sharfman, 1996).

Unfortunately, inertia favors the old ways of doing things. Traditionally a provider-driven enterprise (Tremblay, 1992), university decision-making is grounded internally and decisions about academics reside primarily with the faculty. The faculty are the primary providers. They design the curriculum, offer the courses, and certify competency as prerequisite to a degree. If the faculty oppose change, it often must be born through the breach. By relating what happens in the classroom or laboratory to the needs and expectations of external constituencies that have a stake in the institution, colleges and universities make an essential connection between the external environment and the internal academy. Without this connection, key constituents cannot help to shape the future of an institution, and strategic planning fails because it requires an understanding of external expectations and their context in order to shape the college's or university's successful response to the pressures for strategic change.

## Strategic Change

Based on their strategic planning at California State University at Los Angeles, Rosser and Penrod (1991) tell us that change in higher education results primarily from three conditions: a major crisis, outside pressure, or a vigorous and farsighted leader. Whatever the cause, strategic change requires creative thinking. Roach (1988) tells us that strategic planning was regarded as a way of thinking at West Texas State University. Creativity challenges and rearranges the way we see things. By seeing the present differently, one can diffract the future much as a prism turns light into component parts. This kind of insight involves more than deductive reasoning. It spawns free-ranging inquiry that probes and encourages scenarios of possibility.

As an example, a faculty member and coarchitect of the information technology initiative at a small private college in the northeastern United States responded to the dean by saying, "Ignoring technology will not reduce its impact or cause it to fail or cause it to go away. Ignoring technology will only prove to our prospective students, our funding agencies, our partner schools that we are obsolete and disconnected from their reality. The scenario of rejecting technology results in our demise."

Strategic change is unstructured rather than tightly organized. It is less grounded in fact than in footnote. It welcomes the discontinuities that jar logic and dismantle the ready answers of both great and ordinary minds. Ackoff (1970) has suggested that strategic planning is change that is purposefully induced to shape the diffracted elements of an unknown future into a sequence of elements that lead to a preferred future. Our view of strategic planning matches this view.

However, the creative thinking required to do this does not just happen. It is nurtured by learning. Unfortunately, the premises of present educational practices can actually undermine this creative effort and diminish it as unfitting to the accepted rules of the campus community. Formal education is bound by paradigms, which are models of how we see and explain things (Kuhn, 1962). The explanations that underpin present knowledge are an accumulation of those past definitions and abstractions that we believe adequately explain the world around us, and these undergird what passes for accepted knowledge.

## Key Strategic Questions Facing Higher Education

As each institution begins the assessment of campus conditions, it must wrestle with several key questions. Some of these questions are fundamental and lead to a redefinition of the institution's management perspective, while others are emergent and reflect the growing demands of the external environment. The answers to these questions form the basis on which each institution makes its own decision about whether or not it will engage in a significant strategic planning process designed to create constructive change in response to the changing world of which it is a part:

1. Who will our students be?
2. What should we teach?
3. How should we teach it?
4. How will students learn?
5. What are society's needs?
6. How does society expect us to meet its needs?
7. What role will learning play?
8. How will we pay for it?

If these questions are directly and easily answered, it is likely that some form of strategic management, by this or another name, already exists within the college or university. If, however, these questions cannot be directly or easily answered, then the college or university is probably lagging and needs to consider some form of major planning activity, such as strategic planning, that will better prepare the campus to fit into its environment.

1.   *Who will our students be?* This question leads to identification of the consumer mix a college or university will serve over the next ten to twenty years. For nearly every campus, the nature and makeup of the student body will change over the next several years. For example, it is likely that many future students will be older and more diverse. They are also likely to be more globally oriented as well as reflective of potential employer needs than most of today's "traditional" students.

2.   *What should we teach?* If the new student body will be older, more diverse, and demanding, it will also be more sophisticated in some ways and richer in the experience it brings to the classroom. It is also possible that such students will prefer to concentrate on their major and give less time to

the general courses most colleges and universities now require. As disciplines change in response to changing knowledge, so must the core of the academy. For example, the sciences, including biology, chemistry, physics, psychology, and sociology, have become more specialized, which raises the question of whether an institution can or should keep breadth in its offerings or focus its resources on certain niches and specialties.

3.   *How should we teach it?* Studies continue to show that lecturing is not always the best way to transfer knowledge (Guskin, 1994; Chickering and Gamson, 1991). With improvements in technology, the classroom of the future should be significantly different from the classroom of today. Technologically advanced students preparing for a technological world will expect methods of instruction and learning that reflect the world they are about to enter.

4.   *How will students learn?* The answer, again, is technology. Publishers are talking about individualized textbooks and putting textbooks on-line. One of the authors has recently reviewed an entire textbook, with movie vignettes and a comprehensive learning module, all on a single CD-ROM disk. Experiential learning should expand through techniques that allow students to learn in a community, regional, national, international, and even interstellar environment. Learning through group techniques will be more prevalent, and professors will need to be trained to become more capable of guiding learning in these environments. Assessment and reward structures will also change as new standards emerge to measure learning.

5.   *What are society's needs?* This question begins the process of defining the context for higher education in the twenty-first century. Clearly the information age will require a closer and lifelong connection to learning facilitators. Facilitators cannot anticipate or provide everything the learner needs throughout life, but they can serve as a gateway.

6.   *How does society expect us to meet its needs?* This question tests the link between the knowledge base found within the institution and external expectations. The historical autonomy from societal controls of colleges and universities, and the

role of universities as the repositories of knowledge, have made it possible for the university as provider to take the lead in defining and shaping what shall be offered, and therefore what may be consumed. But society's accommodation to this relationship has lessened, especially as student-consumers are paying more of the cost of their education. An adequate response cannot arise if the institution has not conducted a critical analysis of the needs and wants of society and the capability of the institution to meet those needs and wants. Since the central thrust of strategic planning is to align the institution with its environment, it is important that colleges and universities come to understand that environment.

7.   *What role will learning play?* Learning will be the primary means by which individuals succeed in society. Those who learn will flourish. Those who do not will possibly sink.

8.   *How will we pay for it?* The costs of higher education continue to rise. The salaries of faculty, staff, and administration have historically risen in national trends, especially in the professional disciplines (Tully, 1995). To compete with other institutions for the services and expertise of faculty, colleges and universities must match national salary norms or settle for less than the best candidates for open positions. Further, cost containment confounds this need along with pressures for efficiency and accountability. As educational demands shift, institutions of higher education are challenged to find resources to fund these changes.

## A Time to Choose

The eight questions just posed suggest several reasons for using a strategic planning exercise. But there are other forces at play as well. In the face of all of this, effective adaptation involves realigning the college or university with its emergent environment. Words such as "restructuring," "reengineering," and "reform" begin to make sense as higher education grapples with the realities of change. However, regardless of the rhetoric of change, what the institution does and how it does it can no longer be left to tradition or chance. What is essential is to refocus what a college or university does best and match that focus with opportunities and challenges emanating from the greater society. As colleges and universities change strategically, they gain a better self-understanding and chart a self-defined course that is more likely to succeed. They partner internal and external constituents and emphasize disciplines and expertise that best use their unique strengths and capabilities.

## Some Definitions

Jargon exists in most disciplines, and the general study of strategic planning and strategic management is no exception. Unfortunately, even in the strategic planning and strategic management literature, many of these terms are used differently among various writers in the field. Before we begin a more substantive discussion regarding strategic planning and how it is developed within colleges and universities, we develop here some specific definitions for several of the terms we use throughout the rest of this book.

> *Aligning:* recognizing and exploiting knowledge about an institution's strengths, weaknesses, opportunities, and threats to achieve congruity between the institution and the environment, a dynamic equilibrium of the ecosphere of an institution and its environment.
>
> *Environment:* the political, social, economic, technological, and educational ecosystem, both internal and external to the organization, within which the college or university resides.
>
> *Strategic:* that which relates to the relationship between the institution and its environment.
>
> *Strategic decision making:* making the optimal choice or the choice that best fits the needs of the institution's strategic plan or strategic management.

*Strategic learning:* the institutional process of learning from successes and failures for the purpose of informing the institution during the next stages of the strategic planning or strategic management process.

*Strategic management:* the assurance that the institution's attention and focus are applied to maintain an optimal alignment with the environment.

*Strategic planning:* a formal process designed to help an organization identify and maintain an optimal alignment with the most important elements of its environment.

*Strategic thinking:* arraying options through a process of opening up institutional thinking to a range of alternatives and decisions that identify the best fit between the institution, its resources, and the environment.

*Strategy:* an agreed-upon course of action and direction that changes the relationship or maintains an alignment that helps to assure a more optimal relationship between the institution and its environment.

# CHAPTER 2

# Why the Academy Needs Strategic Planning

Most of the areas within higher education that are currently under fire function according to traditions and values that have developed over several centuries. This chapter discusses the stages that higher education has gone through during these years of development. This general overview should help strategic planners to understand many of the tenets that govern how colleges and universities perceive themselves, and to understand how these institutions become positioned relative to a changing society.

## Understanding Where We Came from Helps Us Know Where We Are

The tendency of the academy to turn within and to function independently from the external environment is a problem with several origins. First, higher education in the United States is rooted in private, primarily religious or church-related endeavors. Harvard and the other private pioneers exemplify this origin. Public universities emerged primarily under the Morrill Act of 1862, landmark national legislation that gave federal land to states to establish public universities to promote liberal and practical education (Eddy, 1963). These institutions emulated private ones, inculcating and codifying their rules and practices (Pulliam, 1988; French, 1964). Clinchy (1994) also suggests that because the academy is embedded in these origins, it is insulated from the secular state. Add to this a traditional medieval structure with an overlay of First Amendment protection of free speech, a principle unique to the United States, and the tendency toward insularity is both logical and obvious.

One area that is among the most sensitive is the existence and use of tenure within the academy. For most academics, tenure is the mantle of First Amendment protection. Once secularism took hold and freed academics from the control of religious dogma, there was a need for protection within the academy so that the free expression of ideas could occur without fear of retribution (Sowell, 1993). As secular political pressures replaced religious ones, the academy argued successfully that academic freedom required the protection afforded by a lifetime job, to assure that dissenters would not be punished by losing their jobs for expressing ideas that might be controversial.

The combination of sectarian origins, medieval traditions, dedication to free speech, and job security derived from tenure have preserved the academy from unwanted and injurious intrusion. At the same time, these important protections have also helped to insulate the academy from external forces. The autonomy that grows out of tenure was allowed to flourish as long as the public was satisfied with the role and contribution of higher education, especially public higher education, but changed when the United States appeared to be losing its national competitive edge and when various states began to feel the pinch of economic downturns (Daly, 1994).

This bond of trust has now been challenged in the midst of restructuring of the economy and growing public resistance to additional taxes for the support of higher education (Marshall and Palca, 1992). While the breaking of this public trust has led to reduced appropriations and challenges to tenure, the academy has largely remained protected within the framework of its traditional practices. Insulated from these external forces, many faculty have resisted change, steadfast in the belief that they hold a secure position and are obligated to pursue quality as the expert providers of knowledge, no matter how these beliefs may clash with public expectations.

## The Environment in Transition

The world of higher education today is not the world of its origin. While this may seem trite, it is true in a real and important way. Today, change is not a choice for a college or university; it is a necessity. Students have changed, their needs have changed, society has changed, business has changed, government has changed, as has the fabric of international life. During the decade from 1983 to 1993, students over thirty-five years of age increased by 83 percent (Hussar, 1995, p. 4). During the same period, the number of women attending college increased by 27 percent. While majority student enrollments declined or were stable in the early 1990s, they have increased since then (Carter and Wilson, 1995, p. 3). Throughout the 1990s, U.S. business has been restructuring to improve its competitiveness in the global marketplace. We can get to Pretoria as easily as we can get to Peoria. Consequently, colleges and universities are being challenged, if not forced, into realigning their roles to fit this new age. They are increasingly turning to strategic planning to help them make this realignment, because they are finding that traditional resources and traditional planning methods are no longer effective.

It is also worth remembering that external agricultural and rural social needs led to the land grant initiative that spawned the public university in the nineteenth century (Veysey, 1965). World War II and the GI Bill, along with Sputnik, gave rise to big science in the twentieth century, stimulating the growth of today's major research universities. Current demands for change appear to have comparable force for shaping higher education in the beginning of the twenty-first century. These forces include cutting the cost of education, shortening the time required to complete a degree, and shaping curricula to educate for global competition in the coming decades.

## Change and the Academy

New ideas and a new vocabulary come with change. *Account-ability, efficiency,* and *planning* are among the trigger words creeping steadily from the outside world into the mainstream of discussions about today's colleges and universities. The academy must adapt to what is taking place in a world where global competition holds the key to success. If college and university graduates are not able to converse in the languages and cultures of that marketplace or if they lack the skills to trade effectively in it, the U.S. economy and society will find other sources for this talent.

In addition, the traditional support for higher education may continue to erode. Because the academy is the storehouse of past erudition and the creator of new knowledge, how it adapts to these forces is important. Too much undirected change could further weaken what is arguably the world's best system of higher education. After all, more of the best minds of other countries come to study here than we send abroad, especially at the graduate level (Pickert, 1992). A lack of thoughtful change could lead to inept adaptation and undermine the quality of our universities.

Present world leadership by U.S. higher education in research science, medicine, and other professions and fields came from adapting old knowledge to new fields of inquiry. A substantive and focused process of change built on the excellence of the past and the present would seem a sensible way to refashion universities into a freshly defined and harmonious relationship with a changing world.

### Entering the Information Age

The paradigms presently in use in higher education are models of thinking derived for earlier societies, societies that produced goods. They fall short in the emerging society, which primarily produces information and ideas. For example, business graduates trained in traditional business practices useful for manufacturing goods will not likely be skilled in using technology that can provide them with the knowledge they will need to interact with the information age (Luft and Noll, 1993), nor will they be skilled properly in other languages and cultures (Philpott, 1994). In a global economy, they may not be competitive.

The present educational system is rooted in the socioeconomic fabric of U.S. society, for while education serves the mind, it also trains the person to function in society. We therefore should not be surprised that the paradigms that guide education come from an earlier age. After all, Horace Mann sired public education through the *common schools,* as they were called, over a century ago (Hinsdale, 1898). John Dewey's reform of Mann's approach to education came in the early twentieth century (French, 1964). Higher education evolved in comparable intervals from the founding of Harvard to the rise of the research university. These models for discovery and learning evolved in the industrial age when the emphasis was on the production of goods. Today the emphasis is changing to the production of ideas and information, aided by rapidly changing technology.

As an illustration, Kember and Gow (1994) conducted a study that suggested that the old model of knowledge transmission is not as effective in the modern classroom as are learning facilitation models in which students interact with the knowledge with which they are presented. We are all familiar with this scenario. The use of computers across the campus is multiplying faster than the proverbial hare.

In general, however, the academy has struggled to adjust, and true leadership in communication technology is coming from outside academic walls. For example, a recent issue of *Business Week* (Byrne, 1995) featured an article on "Virtual B-Schools." The story featured twenty institutions around the world that bring executive education to client businesses through use of information technology. Their revenues range from $4 million to more than $30 million. Also featured were nine business schools that offer education via satellite, recognizing the need to position themselves globally.

This is just one example of the growing gap between what the public wants and what education provides, a gap that further disconnects the public from public education. As this century draws to a close, many believe that U.S. public education is in decline.

## Responding to External Change

The decline of higher education is popularized in the widely held view that college graduates cannot write well or think critically (Candy and Crebert, 1991). These and other criticisms tend to be anecdotal. Yet their cumulative effect is the perception of diminished quality among college graduates or that graduates are increasingly unable to jump directly into the workplace. It is more likely that this apprehension results from the lag between change in higher education and public expectations, and is confounded by the fact that corporations are downsizing and much of middle management (a fertile ground for the employment of many of our graduates) is disappearing. The graduates of the last five to six classes are competing with each other and often with their own parents for the same jobs.

Unfortunately, modern higher education is discipline-based and increasingly oriented toward even more specialization. Where there used to be just biologists, there are now microbiologists, molecular biotechnologists, wildlife biologists, biochemists, and biophysicists. These growing specialties change traditional practices and redefine the models for thinking and learning with which we are familiar and which we accept. As knowledge becomes more complex, specialization increases until there comes a point when the public sees this proliferation as serving the needs of the academy but largely meaningless in their own lives. To the extent that graduates still come out of disciplines embedded in traditional ways of thinking (some of which are perceived as esoteric or narrow) and go into jobs that change more quickly than their preparation for those jobs, the impression of lessened quality is reified.

Lovett (1996) tells us that many aspects of the current system of higher education are artifacts of the industrial age. In the industrial age, universities produced the business elites that built the U.S. economy on the backs of the less educated who worked the production lines. As the economy now changes from the production of goods to the processing of information, the common schools and higher education produce traditionally trained workers who do not routinely think critically or write well in the languages required by a new and globally-competitive economy (Kenny, 1993). In addition, when the American economy buckled in the 1980s, so did the broader support for education in the general public (Marshall and Palca, 1992). Since more of the public has graduated from college than ever before in our history, many of the growing body of critics are the graduates of the very colleges and universities they criticize.

## External Change Models

The resurgence of the American economy has left in its wake tools that the business world believes account for their new successes. These include concepts such as "downsizing," "restructuring," "reengineering," "flatter organizations," or "focused companies" with "market niches" (Ehrlich, 1995). At the core of this kind of thinking is the idea that an organization can reorganize and redeploy itself quickly, while its market is changing. It can do this if it strategically inventories the nature of the changes that are under way, assesses its own strengths and unique competencies, and matches the latter to the opportunities offered by the former.

Some people believe that these business strategies are transferrable to higher education. After all, they argue, isn't education a service industry? Yet this view runs counter to a view held by many inside the academy. Here education is seen as a matter of quality—and why should colleges or universities change their way of doing things? After all, it was higher education that made the United States first in the world of things and ideas, and is it not better to stay with the practices that created that quality and status in the first place? Besides, many see the academy as the storehouse of established knowledge and the preserver of the wisdom of the ages. Further, many contend that colleges and universities have an obligation to preserve the accretions of the human mind for the sake of humankind. While these views have their merits, they have proved to be not particularly useful in facing the growing criticism of education.

A fundamental change has occurred. The vast amounts of knowledge are rapidly becoming available to anyone connected to the extensive digital interlinkages of the Internet and the World Wide Web. Colleges and universities are no longer the gatekeepers—they no longer hold the only way of creating and disseminating information, let alone learning from it.

## Dispelling the Obvious

Much of education deals with the abstract and the complex. Answers, therefore, do not come easily, if they come at all. In the information age, knowledge and discovery have changed in an important and novel way. Rather than one "Eureka!" event, discovery often now results from accumulating bits of information over many experiments, involving the contributions of many minds. In some instances, discovery may occur without observation of the discovered entity.

In physics, for example, it took two decades and 420 scientists to unravel the discovery and comprehension of quarks, which are subatomic particles that give rise to the essence of matter (Broad, 1994). No one scientist could have lived long enough to have accomplished this alone. More important, this discovery and the knowledge it created was accomplished through making a case without the smoking gun. Traditionally, proof has required the unique defining event.

To extend this example, take the case of top quarks, which were believed to have vanished after existing less than a billionth of a second during the "big bang" that created the universe (Broad, 1994). They have never been seen. All that has been observed is the debris left by their presence. In science, where hard evidence underpins discovery and the subsequent definition of truth, truth is becoming a matter of uncovering the preponderance of evidence rather than discovering the unique defining event. This presents a new standard of proof, for it is proof without the proven thing. This means that in some cases the acquisition of knowledge has changed from observation of the demonstrable and visible event to determination of the persuasive weight of evidence gathered over many events. Here proof is less what we observe and more what we agree on. Hence, knowledge by negotiation is becoming a post–Copernican basis for proof and human understanding. Combine this "new scholarship" with ubiquitous networks for sharing the evidence and conducting the debate, and the very nature of the academy as a community of scholars changes. This condition must be kept in mind as one begins to develop the ability to think strategically about academic programming and the direction in which higher education is headed.

All of this is to say that the obvious is no longer the reality. Knowledge is less a matter of dependence on personal brilliance and more a matter of the collective talent of minds and disciplines pursuing problems and sorting out intersubjective understandings. In this world, traditional disciplines are confining. The wisdom of the many is as significant as the brilliance of the few. Teachers are becoming less the expert fonts of wisdom and are more the guides and coaches who stimulate rather than dominate learning. As one arts and sciences dean put it, the teacher is less the "sage on the stage" and more the "guide on the side."

## The Need for a Different Kind of Higher Education

If this is so, students are no longer passive receptacles of the wisdom of their teachers (Kember and Gow, 1994). They must increasingly behave as partners in the dialogue that intersubjectivity requires. Technology facilitates that requisite dialogue. Higher education is in the transition from a "time-out" model to a perpetual learning model (Dolence and Norris, 1994).

Already we are capable of placing the text for a class, along with a diskette of the course lectures, in the typical university bookstore or even on the campus network. With personal computers, the student's room or the dormitory computer lounge can become the "first classroom" where basic information is transmitted. Where this occurs, the regular classroom can move more easily from being a site for the initial transfer of information to being a place where problems are solved and ideas challenged. As is already the case in graduate education, research can drive learning earlier in the process, as faculty share inquiry and discovery with students through joint projects. These experiences encourage learning through active means such as simulation, experiments, internships, or software illustrations. They can extend understanding such that inquiry can lead students to "push the envelope" of their own talents and comprehension.

As Kember and Gow (1994) further suggest, in this classroom, teaching that conveys secondhand knowledge through lectures will not likely suffice. Once more, tradition and habit can inhibit change. We must not ignore the econometrics of today's higher education—the model that is limited to class, course, credit hour, and required seat time is a huge barrier.

## Unleashing the Possible

Clark Kerr (1982) once observed that the major test of a modern U.S. university is how wisely and how quickly it is able to adjust to important new possibilities. It is risk, not replication, that drives this active stance. Such learning, however, can easily conflict with the mores of the practicing academic. While the scholar is urged, as an intellectual activity, to challenge the paradigms in use, the practicing scholar is also tied to tradition and the paradigms in use (Kuhn, 1962).

This umbilical link to the past is found in the literature, the canon, or the methodology of the academy. While the urge of the mind is to inquire, the tendency of the profession is to discipline. Thus, the tie to a practicing orthodoxy weakens the tie to challenging it.

## Tenets of Academic Change

Adam Urbanski better poses the issue: "If you always do what you always have done, you'll always get what you always got" (Chaffee and Sherr, 1992). Einstein is also purported to have put this more elegantly—that the significant problems we have cannot be solved at the same level of thinking with which we created them. Replication is useful, but risk and experimentation are imperative in the house of learning. Every college and university has its own traditions, environs, and character. But in changing and challenging times, those institutions that adjust by means anchored in their strengths and their character are more likely to progress than those that do not.

Being anchored is important for strategic change. As character anchors a person, so does a sense of purpose. Uniqueness anchors institutions in their response to external expectations. In higher education, however, the triumph of science after World War II led many universities to abandon their character and emulate the research university. The number of doctorate-granting institutions grew, many colleges changed their name to "The University of . . .", and the strive for sameness prevailed. In the hurry to be like some other place, identity, mission, and uniqueness were diluted or ignored, if not orphaned. Even in athletics, the ambition to play in Division I with the "name" schools took precedence over the capacity to sustain a lesser-division program and to control the effect that change would have on the academic life of the institution.

Now, as resources shrink, sameness does not sell, particularly to resource-granting constituencies. So as colleges and universities prune themselves, they need to do so with a purpose in mind beyond mere survival. The key for many is to find a niche, an anchoring point that reflects the college's or university's unique character and particular excellence. The trick, of course, is to identify how character and excellence in that niche can make an institution stand out in the academic crowd.

George Keller (1983) makes an important point in this regard by suggesting that the management of a college or university is distinguished from a business, military, or religious organization in that it is a republic of sorts. Republics are tied together by compromises and coalitions that have some stability, even as times change. Thus, any effort to bring about change within this social context and its structure of norms must involve participation and bargaining. If change is not negotiated, it will not likely persist. What applies to change generally applies even better to strategic change.

## Finding the Distinguishing Characteristic

Colleges and universities are about quality and creating value. Changing and redefining quality is not easy to do. It means changing the agenda of groups served by present levels of quality and dealing with their short-term interests. This is especially true when resource allocation shifts as a consequence of new internal directions and priorities designed to respond to external needs. The dilemma is that the bulk of the academy is engaged in a political battle for control of present allocation patterns (Lee, 1991). Departments and schools or colleges are composites of disciplines and professions, and these vested interests tend to focus on perpetuating familiar and comfortable practices (Munitz, 1995). By contrast, governing boards, trustees, presidents, chancellors, and other administrators are, by role and habit, prone to focus on long-range and strategic organizational responsibilities, and to consider how they can meet their constituency's expectations.

So when people argue over whether planning should be top-down or bottom-up, this debate, while interesting, is largely irrelevant. The issue is how negotiation can be encouraged by those with leadership responsibilities at all levels. Chaffee and Sherr (1992) make a salient point that as the orientation toward quality matures, leaders will delegate considerably more authority for operational and tactical matters than before.

The challenge is to get the debate over quality to mature beyond present practice. Starting by articulating the mission seems an obvious first step; but as we discuss at greater length in the next chapter, it will not always work, because mission statements, at worst, are mired in the past and, at best, serve as summaries of agreements reached, not as instruments with which to strike new agreements. As Keller (1994–1995) observes, in higher education, mission statements are often nothing more than a "bland stew of platitudes, beliefs, and vague goals" (p. 8). A campus seminar or discussions by blue chip academics may help, but these mechanisms usually become ways to extend the present pattern of monopoly within an organization. The real clue lies in the campus culture.

Chaffee and Sherr (1992) also have observed that campus cultures that already exhibit many of the values and behaviors targeted in quality improvement efforts are more likely than others to be hospitable to improvement in quality. Where thinking is short term—for example, about this or next year's budget—management turns over frequently, efforts at influencing quality are inconsistent, competition precludes cooperation or collaboration, and gross data supplant qualitative ideas as the basis for resource allocation. Here the culture is not hospitable and the resistance will be endemic and deep. In such environments, campus leadership must be politically sensitive about how far and how fast to push change. If governing boards are not supportive, the effort will abort.

## Shaping Change

Happily, change does not occur in a vacuum. The present disconnection between public higher education institutions and the taxpaying public has made it clear that "business as usual" will not suffice. Thus, the choice for a college or university is either to shape change or have it dictated by external forces, particularly trustees, state governors, legislators, or significant donors. This dilemma can provide the wedge for dealing with recalcitrant cultures by forcing the issue onto the table and providing an opening for strategically addressing issues related to quality. These include such elements as the strengths of the institution, its pathfinding programs, its areas of excellence, its programs of opportunity, its role, and how resources should be allocated to enhance redefined quality. By considering these questions, the debate will move from the trite nostrums of quality embedded in mission statements and catalogues to talking about quality in realistic and useful terms, including discussing specific programs with identifiable resource requirements. It will also shift thinking from close-minded beliefs about preservation of the way things are to more strategic arguments about the way things can become.

This discussion shows that strategic change and the strategic planning that defines it are driven by thinking that begins with a political assessment of the campus culture. This assessment must identify the capacity of that culture to deal with the kinds of analyses and discussions that can move an institution from defense of the status quo to defining quality in a forward-looking manner. This view of quality can then lead to discussing the benchmarks and indicators that will serve as evidence that change has been observed and progress has been noted, and a maturing skill to shape change can replace reaction to crisis.

# CHAPTER 3

# Creating a Unique Model of Strategic Planning for Higher Education

While there is general acceptance of the concept and value of strategic planning in both business and nonbusiness organizations, there is also a fair amount of discussion and confusion concerning the term *strategic planning.* This may be because, as Mintzberg (1994b) has suggested, there is a major difference between what many call strategic planning and what strategic planning really is. Or as Leontiades (1982) has suggested, much of the strategic planning language has been reduced to sheer jargon and is as confusing as it is uninformative.

In this chapter we examine the problems associated with understanding more precisely just what strategic planning is in higher education and the problems associated with the model of strategic planning that comes from the business world. We will also focus on the objectives of strategic planning as well as on the general environment of higher education within which strategic planning is developed.

## Everyone Knows What Planning Is

What we refer to here as traditional planning, by which we mean conventional organizational planning and long-term planning, has been around for a long time. Long-range planning was trivialized by the general sentiment of campus leaders that "we can't see the future." The default planning system was in fact the annual budgeting process. This habit of relying on the annual budget cycle was enshrined in phrases such as "How do we plan if we don't know how much money we have?"

Planning therefore became a euphemism for "How are we going to spend (allocate) our resources (money), time, attention, focus," and so on. In this way, higher education has feigned accountability by substituting an accounting audit trail for meeting the needs of society—a catch-22 that became very comfortable. "Tell me what we have to spend for five years, then I'll allocate resources against a plan for five years."

Another form of planning prevalent in higher education is related to accreditation. In this context, good basic planning has always been an essential part of helping to assure that the balance between available resources and the provision of critical academic programs is maintained as efficiently and effectively as possible. For the most part, accreditation planning looks backward and becomes a tool or mechanism for articulating the impact of a situation that often assumed unlimited or at least abundant resources. It considers and directs the appropriate management of students, programs, faculty, administrators, staffs, facilities, and budgets. In performing these important activities, institutional planners evaluate the current state of the campus, describe trends that will require attention, and develop goals and plans for the institution to follow, most often over a one-year time frame.

The central value of planning, as we have come to know it, is the guidance it provides an organization. Traditional planning allows the organization to examine itself and make decisions related to its needs and values. By delineating what is needed to fulfill the institution's purpose and role, planning allows the institution to set short-term priorities and establish operational objectives that it believes will lead to desired achievements on a year-to-year basis.

## When Conventional Planning Just Does Not Do It

Though conventional planning is part of the normal operations of a college or university (as it also is in traditional business, not-for-profit, and governmental organizations), when things start to get a bit offtrack, or when dramatic changes occur that might affect the campus, it is not unusual for campus leaders to call for a different type of planning exercise (Chiarelott, Reed, and Russell, 1991; Jones, 1990). They look for a planning event that will recognize the change or the challenge, reorient the campus in some way, and then allow it to get back to "business as usual." Increasingly this exercise is referred to as developing a strategic plan for the campus. However, what many call strategic planning and what strategic planning actually is are not the same.

## An Example

Both faculty and administrators at the University of Northern Colorado (UNC) used a major occasion—a presidential transition—as an opportunity to undertake a planning exercise to try to better align the campus with several major changes in its environment. They did this under the banner of strategic planning. These groups felt that the time had come for the university to reorient itself and they began what they called "strategic planning" to help identify, for themselves and the new president, the directions and priorities that reflected the tradition, culture, and assets of the institution.

Once the new president was on board, the process of strategic planning was also embraced by the university's governing board, and a strategic planner was appointed. The process had begun, with the apparent support of major university constituencies. However, when the process did not go forward in the traditional way and did not result in expected traditional planning outcomes (for example, a short-term problem-solving venture), with a document containing specific goals and objectives and the steps needed to achieve them precisely spelled out, support from midlevel administrators and faculty leaders began to evaporate. Many of those who had initially called for a strategic planning exercise disavowed it, and ownership of the process devolved to the office of the president and to the board of trustees, both of whom had gone on record as fully supporting the process and both of whom strongly believed in the benefits of a purer form of strategic planning.

What happened at UNC was that those who had called for strategic planning had really wanted traditional planning but had been caught up in the trendy talk of this new planning technique called strategic planning, as Leontiades (1982) had suggested might occur when any organization first adopts a strategic planning process. They ended up with something they did not want. However, those directly involved with the strategic planning process appeared to have a stronger sense of what strategic planning is and were eager to apply it to a campus that was troubled, drifting, and in need of a newly defined direction.

Further, it also became apparent that the ambiguity posed by a strategically guided process focusing on the changing external environment was highly threatening to the more traditional constituencies on the campus. Worse, no single campus group or coalition of groups outside of the president's office would be in a position to control it. Interestingly, this example is not too far from the experiences that many other colleges and universities have had as they have begun their processes of strategic planning (Chiarelott, Reed, and Russell, 1991; Cline and Meringolo, 1991; Eaton and Adams, 1991; Dooris and Lozier, 1990; Cyert, 1988; Foote, 1988; Roach, 1988; Swain, 1988; Aggarwal, 1987).

## Oranges and Apples

Traditional planning and strategic planning in higher education are simply different animals. As Smith (1994) has suggested, education generally is disorganized and disorderly, unplanned, and dysfunctional. As one looks at the current state of a college or university, it is important to understand that the current state of the campus is the result of neither comprehensive planning nor rational decision making. Worse, in the academy not only is strategic planning different from traditional planning, it is also different from the model of strategic planning found in the business literature, as we further describe in the next section of this chapter.

The good old-fashioned deductive process of deriving objectives from internal goals keeps the emphasis internal to the institution, giving campus constituencies a basis for shaping, if not controlling, the results of such planning. So, as many campuses begin a planning exercise, as long as planning begins with a statement of purpose, looks traditional, and speaks to internal traditions, it is permissible. This is the case in part because such a plan can always be redefined, shelved, or superseded by the events of the day. That is, after all, what happens to many planning exercises in higher education.

Again, the critical difference between traditional planning (operations-driven planning) and strategic planning (opportunity-seeking planning) had not been considered by the original instigators of the process at UNC, nor had it been very well communicated by those who then worked to develop the strategic plan. After nearly one full year of work, the difference became apparent and one college dean formally confronted the president and the strategic planner, expressing grave concern that this was *not* the process that he and the other deans, as well as the faculty senate, had believed they were supporting during the presidential transition. He also stated that he did not believe in the planning process that was under way. To him, it was diffuse, it was not guided by a clear sense of mission, and no one could tell where it was headed.

The desire for predictability and a stable planning target was clear. Strategic planning with a dynamic focus on a shifting environment and its constant adjustments to changing conditions brought no comfort and engendered little support.

## "Traditional Planning" vs. "Strategic Planning": The Confusion of Terms

In the past, when business had been taken with a new management term or concept, that term or concept tended to become trendy. Currently, the term *strategic planning* is trendy, and is being used widely to describe planning exercises in many institutions (Thompson and Strickland, 1996), both business and nonbusiness. By becoming involved in a strategic planning exercise, an organization exhibits a strong hope that this revolutionary new form of planning will lead to solutions for the organization's major directional, financial, and structural problems, while at the same time bringing it both growth and financial stability (Hunger and Wheelen, 1996; Nutt, 1992). Unfortunately, in many cases, the practice of what is called *strategic planning* is really nothing more than *traditional planning*. In practice, many organizations are simply doing good old-fashioned planning under a new name.

When the desired outcomes do not occur, or occur more slowly than anticipated, many organizations simply conclude that strategic planning does not work and is a failure. As Mintzberg (1994b) laments, there is a general misconception of what strategic planning is and what it is not. The result is a growing view in some circles that the processes labeled *strategic planning* generally do not work well, and this view leads to doubting the value of the actual practice of strategic planning. Rosser and Penrod (1991) tell us that the planners at California State University at Los Angeles recognized these differences. In 1986 they decided to design their strategic planning process so that it would be (1) evolutionary, (2) a change process that developed through the usual decision-making process, (3) focused not on documents but instead on actions and decisions, (4) flexible, (5) tied to operational work plans, and (6) linked to the resource allocation process.

### The Major Differences

Conventional planning tends to be oriented toward looking at problems based on current understanding or an inside-out mind-set. Strategic planning, however, requires an understanding of the nature of the issue and then the finding of an appropriate response, or an outside-in mind-set.

*Alignment.* The major difference between traditional planning and strategic planning is that the former permits the setting of goals, either short-term or long-term, and then the development of steps to achieve those goals, while the latter aligns an organization with its environment (Steiner, Miner, and Gray, 1982). There are several major and critical differences between these two processes, the most important of which is the issue of time frame. Most conventional planning is done on either a yearly, cyclical basis, or for the accomplishment of a particular desired outcome at a certain time. Strategic planning, however, is long-term and tends to define major outcomes several years in advance.

*Specificity Versus Direction.* Another major difference between the two planning methods is the substance that each targets. Conventional planning identifies specific items, such as budget lines, that planners expect the organization to hit within a specific time frame. Strategic planning identifies directions and states of being that generally lack specificity (Quinn, 1980). Though some strategic planning targets do consist of actual numbers or events, planners generally avoid too much specificity because it is impossible to predict specific outcomes that lie five, ten, or twenty years in the future. For example, within UNC's strategic plan, we developed a ten-year goal that 18.6 percent of the graduation class of 2000 would be Colorado minority students. This is a specific number, yet it is understood that this number is pegged to the graduation rate of Colorado high school seniors and can change from year to year between the initial goal-setting event in 1992 and the year 2000. Also, the number 18.6 is a state mandate, and UNC planners were aware that there was pressure on the Colorado Commission on Higher Education from state colleges and universities to reduce the number because the trend of high school minority graduates had showed signs of declining since the 1992 start date. The point here is that strategic planners at UNC set a target, the specificity of which would most likely change over time, but one that established a clear direction for recruiting and retention activities of the university.

*Focus.* Another major difference between the two methods is the area of focus. Because it tends to be specific, conventional planning can be very parochial in its orientation. Colleges, schools, departments, and even individual professors might have specific operational targets for their activities (two publications a year, for example) and will devise plans on how these targets will be achieved. In such a setting, the organization within which these targets exist is generally ignored. In strategic planning, the opposite is true. Strategic planning seeks to align the organization with the environment *in order to help assure long-term stability and survival* (Gilbert, 1993; Porter, 1980, 1985; Steiner, Miner, and Gray, 1982). According to Doerle (1991), strategic planning allows organizations to *focus,* because it is a process of dynamic, continuous activities of self-analysis.

Further, the first and major concern in strategic planning on college and university campuses *is* the organization. While strategic planning does not overlook the importance of operational goals, it seeks to establish the context for these.

*Time-Relatedness.* Several colleges and universities that have developed successful strategic plans have recognized early that strategic planning is an ongoing process rather than an event tied to a single completion date. Cline and Meringolo (1991) state that at Penn State University planners recognized that in order to be viable strategic planning must be ongoing. Cyert (1988) calls continual strategic planning one of the key elements of the process he oversaw at Carnegie Mellon University. And Roach (1988) tells us that West Texas State University has developed a series of five-year rolling plans to keep the central tenets of the plan consistent with the constantly changing environment of the university. At the University of San Francisco, not only is the university's strategic plan updated each year by adding new goals and strategies and deleting old ones as the university accomplishes them, but division and college plans are also updated in the same fashion (University of San Francisco, 1995).

## The Nature and Time Frame of Strategic Institutional Change

In further analyzing the criticisms we received at UNC, we discovered a paradox. On the one hand, a great number of people throughout the administration, faculty, staff, and student body opposed the process because they were fearful of the changes the process might engender. On the other hand, several people, including deans and vice presidents, were critical because the changes that strategic planning began would not be fully realized in the immediate future—and therefore would not directly solve problems in the short term. Some people were so heavily preoccupied with today's problems that they could not disengage long enough to deal with tomorrow's challenges, even though the latter were far more important to the future of the institution.

This situation further underscores the confusion that exists over the difference between traditional planning and strategic planning. In traditional planning, a goal is established. In order to be considered an appropriate goal, the goal must fulfill certain criteria (Warner, 1967; Etzioni, 1964). A key criterion is that the goal should be measurable, time-specific, achievable, and acceptable. The plan to accomplish the goal must reasonably explain how this can be done. The process is rational, and one that managers can easily understand and with which they can comply. Lockstep progress over a specified time is the touchstone. Benchmarks are deductively established and finality can be achieved when there is no next task to perform.

In strategic planning, this touchstone is absent. In charting a direction, time is not of the essence. Instead, the strategic plan will indicate how the institution's purpose and direction might change *over time* or adapt to changes in the environment (Harrison and St. John, 1994; Chorn, 1991). Dramatic change events that alter the nature or position of the college's or university's structure in the short-term might receive attention, but the plan will only deal with such potentialities within the larger frame of a longer-term strategic perspective.

As one of the authors likes to say in his training sessions, managing the strategic plan is analogous to steering a ship. Rather than changing course with a hard-right rudder, where everyone on board feels the shift, in strategic planning the process gently changes course a few degrees at a time in response to internal (fuel) and external (weather) elements. The result is that people on board may not notice the change at all. Yet, over time the ship reaches the desired port—a different port than the one for which it was originally headed. This lack of *dramatic short-term results* is another characteristic that distinguishes strategic planning from traditional planning. Strategic planning always sees present action as part of a longer-term strategy. The central chosen direction is always to get to port rather than to change direction simply to avoid the squall line.

The long-term perspective of strategic planning and the short-term adaptiveness of traditional planning can be brought together. However, it is more important for strategic planning to develop the strategic context *first* before short-term planning can address short-term needs. To continue the metaphor, the choice of port is critical to the tack required by a sudden storm if the course is to be generally maintained. By creating the context first, priorities can be established, resources can be identified or pledged, and short-term plans can address immediate needs as part of the scheme for long-term progress. This is the wisdom that strategic planning can give to the short-term management of a college or university familiar with traditional planning techniques.

## Different Functions, Operational Harmony

Effective overall organizational planning is actually a *comprehensive activity* that incorporates *both* processes and recognizes that one form of planning complements the other. As we point out throughout this book, however, we firmly believe that strategic planning does, in fact, supersede the other forms of planning. In this way, the ongoing operational activities and objectives of an organization that are most often identified as the results of traditional planning are accomplished within the defined guidelines of an organization's responses to its environment. These issues emanate from a well-constructed strategic plan. By pursuing long-term goals that are consistent with an organization's relationship with its environment, strategic planning sets a context within which operational planning makes more sense, and which helps organizational constituencies understand specific strategic priorities of the organization and the short-term needs to support them.

## Differences Between the "Business Model" and the "Higher Educational Model"

The most popular model found today for developing a strategic plan in any organization comes from the business literature. As far back as the 1960s and 1970s, business recognized the importance of strategic management (Harrison and St. John, 1994). As strategic management techniques have grown in reputation and popularity, several examples of their success have been documented (Herold, 1973; Ansoff and others, 1970). These successful techniques have more recently begun to appeal to organizations beyond the business sector such as not-for-profit, governmental, and other public sector institutions, including colleges and universities (Steeples, 1990; Skok, 1989). Yet in general terms nonbusiness institutions, particularly colleges and universities, have not had particularly positive results from their experimentation with strategic planning. In many instances, the process has not yielded the outcomes desired for institutions of higher education in ways comparable to business applications. We believe there are some fundamental reasons for these lackluster outcomes.

### Different Types of Organizations

The first reason is that there are fundamental differences between the nature of a business and the nature of a college or university, particularly in the United States. Many successful businesses are begun by entrepreneurs who find a way of applying their unique talents or products to a demonstrated need in the marketplace. As these businesses grow, the entrepreneurs take the responsibility of monitoring changes in market need and attempt to move ahead, or move proactively, to make sure that they continue to develop their uniqueness while maintaining or expanding their market niche. Within a chosen segment of business activity, such businesses thrive when they make changes ahead of the market and, more importantly, ahead of their competition. Innovation and entrepreneurship epitomize success in business. Competitors who follow the lead of such businesses can also achieve certain levels of success through carefully calculated competition, "niching," and low-cost leadership, but they seldom achieve the successful innovator's level of success.

## The Range of Choices

What distinguishes the successful business from the unsuccessful business is, first, the recognition of available choices, and then, the strategic activities of matching the unique qualifications of the firm with the available niches in the marketplace. Having choices and being innovative allow the successful business to move from product line to product line, service to service, or even domain to domain as changes in critical environments occur.

It becomes increasingly clear, however, that the general approach to strategic planning taken by business poses a significant dilemma to institutions of higher education. The fundamental issue here is locus of control. Starting with a mission that is to be used as the central guideline for planning and subsequent management basically implies that the organization can control its own destiny and manipulate its environment. Public colleges and universities, however, do not control their niche in the market or manipulate their environment as readily as private businesses do. For example, at West Texas State University, strategic planning was begun when there were growing pressures brought by the state of Texas for greater differentiation among the publicly supported colleges and universities (Roach, 1988). Public colleges and universities sometimes have to serve a constituency by legislative mandate, regardless of economic consequences or their own areas of strength and excellence.

Private colleges and universities are often constrained by a tradition of service or a religious obligation that limits their ability to take advantage of shifts in the demand for higher education among the general population. For example, sectarian schools cannot easily adapt to a growing demand for secular education.

## Mission-Driven Planning: Another Area of Difference

Several writers in the field, including Allen (1993), portray the statement of mission as a key ingredient in successful strategic planning and strategic management. Interestingly enough, however, there is no uniform agreement in the literature as to specifically when or how the mission statement should enter into the development of the strategic plan. Nonetheless, the basic role of a mission statement is clear in literature that suggests the primacy of mission. *Mission statements lead both the strategic planning and strategic management processes* (Thompson and Strickland, 1996; Matthes, 1993; Byars, 1991; David, 1991). A real danger exists, however, when, as Klimoski (1991) suggests, mission statements become like grandmother's fine china—taken out for convenience to be admired by others, but hardly useful for day-to-day operations.

### Mission Statements and Business

Clearly many business organizations can successfully use mission-driven planning (Lammers, 1992). For example, highly entrepreneurial enterprises, large companies that have a major controlling presence in their market, and companies that are easily capable of changing their niche or their domain, can all develop a strong statement of mission and use it as their basis for planning. These types of organization have a significantly high internal locus of control and are able not only to chart their own direction but also to change their direction if it does not meet the requirements for survival of the organization. Besides, top-level management usually has great discretion and can make strategic decisions about mission more quickly and opportunistically.

Yet not everyone associated with the business literature is supportive of mission. For example, McSherry (1994) finds them practically useless, and Newman (1992) not only echoes that sentiment but suggests that in many cases they can be downright harmful.

## Mission-Driven Planning in Different Settings

As these two authors have suggested, other organizations simply cannot use mission-driven planning. In these organizations, external forces have established an appreciably high locus of control that takes from internal managers the freedom required to change direction. For example, businesses that are not market trend leaders, companies that have a significant capital stake in technological modes of a given industry, and organizations that are chartered by other entities for specific purposes (such as governments and most not-for-profits) all have very little freedom of choice over their central direction or domain of activity. For example, Dominick (1990) has observed that often mission statements found in higher education are merely boilerplate material, restating the basics of teaching, research, and service—nothing more.

For colleges and universities, especially those in the public sector, the basic first choice of purpose and of which domain to be a part of is determined by others; often state legislatures, university system managers, and governing boards make these decisions. An additional reality in most colleges and universities is the presence of shared governance, and the fact that strategic decisions about slightly or significantly changing the direction of the institution cannot be easily made without broad internal consensus. Further, depending on the enormity of the issue, even internal consensus may require external approvals as well.

In such a setting, the college's or university's statement of mission may be of little direct value as a beginning. Yet, as McSherry (1994) has suggested, most current college and university mission statements generally state that the institution provides education, conducts research, and conveys service to the community. This type of statement is far too simplistic and general to give substance or direction to planning. Such broad mission statements better describe a domain of activity rather than a single institution's direction and purpose. For example, in developing their strategic plan, the Ohio Board of Regents (1993) concluded that for colleges and universities "mission statements are often very similar, making it difficult or impossible to distinguish one institution from another. . . . For purposes of providing a strategic focus and a foundation upon which to base planning activities, most mission statements are less than effective." Foote (1988) notes that at the University of Miami, the strategic planners discovered early on that developing a mission was an "empty exercise" and instead forced themselves to think about actual obligations of the campus as the basis for planning. We support this approach.

Ireland and Hitt (1992) tell us that *a good mission statement* is one that describes the institution's fundamental and unique purpose, and *how* the organization is unique in its scope of operations and the services it offers. The mission statement therefore needs to indicate what the institution intends to accomplish, how it identifies its markets, and how it reflects the philosophical premises it uses to guide actions.

It is still problematic, however, to begin a "better planning exercise" by simply attempting to develop a "better statement of mission" without doing the work that is needed to understand what Ireland and Hitt suggest. The reason for this is found in how colleges and universities are legitimized and supported.

## The Locus of Control in Colleges and Universities

The formal legitimacy of a college or university is largely external. Most institutions have a founding charter or statute that is often more than one hundred years old. Accreditation serves as a mantle of recognition, and this power resides in an external regional organization. Professionals who receive their basic training within the academy are also externally licensed, and their education must reflect these external standards. For public institutions, a state legislature is typically the final authority, and banker, and the trustees carry out the fiduciary responsibility for the state. State legislatures, state constitutions, and state regulating boards basically determine which public institutions will exist and how they will receive public funds. Some even set levels for tuition and service fees. Alumni, donors, grantors and contractors, development and athletics boards, and other financial partners also exercise some measure of control over both public and private institutions.

Unlike businesses, whose market choice constraints are nowhere as restrictive and who can use profits to build increasingly stronger internal resource and power bases, many colleges and universities produce few surplus resources and are heavily dependent upon outside revenue stakeholders to keep them both active and solvent. This dependence gives stakeholders formidable influence over the affairs, activities, and outcomes of the institution. It also limits options and requires that the preferences of these external partners be considered when trying to plan strategically.

The existence of a strong external locus of control suggests that organizations and firms in this category have less capability than those with an internal locus of control to establish a guiding mission for themselves based on their own wishes and desires, or to respond to changes in their industrial setting without the significant interplay with and approval of external constituents. For such organizations, an internally developed mission statement may be completely meaningless, particularly as a base on which to build a strategic plan.

Clearly, because public as well as many private colleges and universities fit into the category of institutions that have high levels of external control, they generally face established and concise limits to their ability to develop independent organizational strategic planning. Institutions of higher education in the public sector are creatures of the states, and they serve the purposes that have been outlined either implicitly or explicitly by legal state authorities. This is a significant limit to internal locus of control, and implies that these institutions must frame their strategic planning within the context set for them by external legal entities. The underlying mission of the institution is determined by the state, and not by the institution.

This is not as bad as it may seem. These descriptions of some of the severe limitations under which college and university strategic planning takes place could suggest to the reader that it is futile to develop an internal strategic planning effort in institutions of higher education. If institutions of higher education have so little maneuvering room, then it may well be that *any* strategic planning process will be ineffectual. Yet the opposite is true.

Were we to assume that the possibilities for growth and innovation in higher education were severely limited or in permanent decline, or that somehow they no longer fit with worldwide or regional socioeconomic changes, such a conclusion would make sense. But this is simply not the case. The continued growth of the nation's (and the world's) population, the continued improvement in the general standard of living, the continuous improvements in technology, and the dawn of the information age all call for more, not less, education for a broader segment of the population. Further, nothing on the horizon suggests that these trends will alter significantly in the foreseeable future. Future opportunities for growth in higher education are substantial, and some of these opportunities for growth may also be lucrative. So while the purposes and directions of colleges and universities may be defined and limited by external sources, the possibilities for a focused niche are profound.

## The Challenge of "Niching"

Cyert (1988) states that "the objective of strategic planning is to establish a plan by which a department, college, or university can achieve a position that gives it a special place among other departments, colleges or universities" (p. 92). He used this premise in developing the strategic plan at Carnegie Mellon University. Brown (1988) says that within the strategic planning process at the University of North Carolina at Asheville each college is challenged to identify and nourish its "marketable difference." Determining which niche makes the best sense for a given college or university to develop and exploit could well provide focus for planning. But making this determination is not necessarily straightforward. The current mix of institutions in higher education does not provide a profile of much that can be called unique. The basic structure of higher education, especially at the undergraduate level, seems to be duplicated across the country. While specializations, especially at the graduate level, offer some differentiation, a medical school in one university may be quite similar to that of another university.

By and large, most college graduates have relatively the same level of expertise and preparation for the world they are about to enter. Accrediting bodies, while maintaining high standards, generally discourage highly innovative program development, thus helping to perpetuate a sameness across college and university offerings. Other factors, including the preparation of new doctoral students, publishing house policy and marketing efforts, and pressures from within professional organizations and disciplines, all reward mainstream methods of teaching and management. The burden of proof for change is always on the innovator introducing completely new methods or directions in teaching, research, and management.

## The Benefits of Delineation

While these constraints exist, there is little doubt that change must occur. Through calls for better skill competency and creativity among college graduates, and through the growing call for accountability, the sameness that exists from institution to institution is being called into question.

The real threat of wholesale duplication is irrelevancy. If it ultimately makes no difference where one goes to obtain a higher education, then consolidation will become a viable option for legislatures and state systems to reduce costs and concentrate resources.

If, however, individual colleges and universities can begin to distinguish themselves along academic and research lines, duplication of effort will be reduced and resources will be better channeled to support the growth of excellence within particular campus program mixes. The strategic planning process can be very useful in helping to determine this distinguishing and focusing process within higher education. By developing a thorough self-examination, by discovering the opportunities that exist and may be exploited by the institution's primary constituencies, and by determining the relevant niches that are available and that fit its unique capabilities, a college or university can begin to shape its own destiny. This is a major reason why colleges and universities should engage in substantive strategic planning.

# CHAPTER 4

# Planning to Fit the Institution's Environments

When a college or university makes a commitment to do strategic planning, its strategic planners need to begin the process by developing a strong understanding of the internal and external environmental forces that will set the guidelines by which they must build the plan. This chapter examines many of the issues related to both of these sets of environmental influences, and describes how these influences play a major role in the development of a college's or university's strategic plan.

## The Critical Environments of Higher Education

As Keller (1983) argues, the context within which higher education has existed for centuries is changing dramatically. The speed of this change is also picking up, which means that today colleges and universities are not simply looking at a different set of external demands than they saw in the past. It also means that the time required to respond to these changes is increasingly shorter. Moreover, higher education cannot ignore these changes. State governments, students, alumni, donors, employers, voters, and others no longer seem content to allow the ivory tower to go about its business without being accountable (Steeples, 1990; Jonsen, 1986). In addition, these external constituents *have power,* power that they have not wielded in the past but which they now threaten to use. Higher education has little choice but to make certain lifestyle changes in order to respond in short order to these new demands.

While the extent of these changes for individual institutions is daunting, generically these environmental challenges come from the following strategic constituencies:

- State funding authorities
- Other financial supporters and benefactors
- Students and their families
- Faculty, administrators, and staff
- Employers
- Community residents, officials, and businesses

Each of these constituencies has had some claim on the institutions of higher education for a long time. In the past, however, these groups allowed the academy to conduct its affairs without interference, because there was general acceptance that the academy was a special place where the intellectual pursuits of a respected faculty produced high-quality and needed research, a place that provided the world's best education for its students and served as a beacon for the improvement of universal knowledge, technology, and the general American dream. These functions were self-justifying and no one seriously questioned what colleges or universities did, or how they did it.

The internal result of this general acceptance was that some faculties and administrations took academic freedom as a shield for increasing autonomy and disconnection from the publics they served. The campus became a kind of holy place where others came to be enlightened. While this is an oversimplified caricature, it is clear that some faculties and administrations began to see themselves as special in the general scheme of things, and that what they developed was good for others or good for its own sake. This ivory-tower-like perception further distanced scholarship and its good consequences from an increasingly disconnected public.

The turbulent sixties rocked the academy, as Lipset (1993) describes the times, in one of the early tremors of this disconnection. The social revolution associated with the war in Vietnam called for more relevancy. This wake-up call was short-lived, however, as the affluence of the seventies and eighties muted social consciousness. In the nineties, the wake-up call of economic restructuring and global competition has became loud and persistent, this time coming from a much wider range of external constituents, including the benefactors of both public and private higher education. No tier of American higher education has been exempt from these questions, and an attendant temptation to wrest away autonomy and control from colleges and universities appears to be growing.

Each constituency listed earlier is now active at some level in questioning the activities and motivations of higher education in the United States. The response is crucial. In the final analysis, there are no guarantees for the longevity of any college or university beyond its present resource base. As these external constituencies continue to develop knowledge of their ability to shape or control resources, they will want more say in the management and in the curriculum of the particular institutions with which they are associated. The challenge, then, is clear: to what extent will the academy be willing to alter itself to meet the growing challenges from its strategic constituencies? And how will it do so? Will it respond as a misunderstood victim of the forces of change, or will it respond proactively by inviting its strategic constituencies to share at the table of change?

Though the answers to these questions should be obvious, they are not. Many in higher education reject the notion that the academy should change to meet the demands of the external world. What those external to the academy view as arrogance is more likely the academy protecting its culture and reflective posture.

Unfortunately, very few of these critical external changes have been widely recognized by most colleges and universities. Strengthening signals from the outside have not yet convinced the internal campus constituencies, especially the faculty, that change is necessary or inevitable. Many administrators have actually worked hard to insulate faculty from these forces, while many other administrators and faculty members simply do not believe in them. Many faculty seek refuge in tenure and academic freedom. The consequence is a serious challenge to the development of strategic thinking, a critical factor in building long-term stability and prosperity. How do you get people to think about long-term issues of great import if they believe they are impervious to these issues?

To plan strategically, an institution must first come to terms with its changing role in the greater society. What that role should be and how quickly the institution will need to make the transition is situational, but defining that role is a strategic imperative. While strategic planning can be a tool in a number of ways for achieving this transition, its central contribution is to align the institution with the opportunities and constraints in its environment.

## Changing the Paradigm: Provider-Driven to Consumer-Driven Higher Education

Colleges and universities are grounded in expertise. This is where quality comes from. Common knowledge has it that students go to institutions of higher education to acquire information and understanding. They do this by following procedures set forth by the expert faculty. This inherent monopoly of the faculty means simply that the providers of expertise properly dominate the student-faculty relationship. Everything from the requirements for entrance to those for graduation and certification are set forth by the faculty providers. Expertise preempts any relationship other than satisfying the terms set forth by the faculty to verify the satisfactory transfer of knowledge and skills.

Also, in this provider-driven organization disciplines and professions outside the university dictate standards, and therefore curriculum content. The institution combines these in certain ways, but basically colleges and universities are conveyor belts of discipline- and profession-approved content. Because of this tradition, which dates from the Middle Ages, change is slow and adaptation to new ideas is gradual.

The present provider-driven model of higher education was fashioned for the industrial and postindustrial ages. But the transition to an information age that is now underway has resulted in a growing disconnection between the consumers of higher education and their providers.

## Strategic Planning's Basic Premise

As we have stated, the central tenet of strategic planning is to align the organization with its environment. And as Starr (1993) tells us, the strategic planning process must also redefine the college's or university's intellectual and moral identity to better meet this objective. This involves accepting the capacity of various internal and external constituents to lay claims on the college or university and its future. It rejects the perspective that internal constituents have a monopoly on the future of the university. In strategic planning, the critical need is for the institution to respond in a forward-thinking, proactive manner to shape the internal effects of external forces on the institution. Bryson (1995) tells us that the key to success for any public or nonprofit organization is the satisfaction of key stakeholders. This leads planners to identify individual stakeholders and other organizations that exercise claims on the institution and to align the activities of the college or university with the expectations and needs of the most critical stakeholders.

This is not to argue that external influences absolutely determine internal responses. It is to emphasize that institutions of higher education need to recognize the legitimacy of external expectations and respond to them through the use of the internal strengths of the institution, while taking advantage of appropriate external opportunities as strategic centerpieces for shaping the future.

It is not easy for colleges and universities to recognize the validity of the claims and expectations their publics lay on them. This problem is endemic to the foundation of the academy itself. Put simply, colleges and universities have established themselves as the primary creators of knowledge and have actively developed the role of being responsible for distilling and disseminating that knowledge largely on their own terms. This is what academic freedom and tenure imply. And while providing knowledge, understanding, and innovation is critically important, when these elements no longer address specific needs, dissonance and dissatisfaction set in among the consumers of scholarly information. Support soon wanes. For public institutions this has the added effect of undermining public trust and public funding. For private institutions, it erodes identity, mission, and the private funding sources that sustain these institutions.

We are not arguing here that colleges and universities should provide only those services that their stakeholders demand. Proprietary institutions, "free universities," continuing education programs, and community colleges generally provide such forms of education. However, these institutions typically convey knowledge that others have discovered or created. Colleges and universities are where this discovery and creative scholarship take place, and the activities and resources these efforts require cannot easily be redirected.

Put another way, universities and colleges cannot move completely away from a provider-driven model to a consumer-driven form of higher education. For one thing, the quest for new knowledge, the analysis of theories and practices, and the free exchange of ideas would suffer if colleges and universities only offered what was popular. However, if a central purpose of higher education is to advance knowledge while helping to create a better society, then colleges and universities must respond to consumer demand in ways not yet perfected by present practice (Tremblay, 1992). And as Zemsky, Massy, and Oedel (1993) put it, "Today's students expect of colleges and universities what they demand elsewhere: better service, lower costs, higher quality, and a mix of products that satisfies their own sense of what a good education ought to provide" (p. 56). Add to this the trend toward incorporating as methodologies such programs as Total Quality Management to help assure that as institutions develop their strategic plan quality concerns are high, there is a commitment to customer satisfaction, and there are ongoing efforts to improve quality (Vinzant and Vinzant, 1993)—and the entire planning scenario can easily become quite complex. The responsiveness of colleges and universities must include taking responsibility for the products that scholarship creates, and discovering and disseminating knowledge that will enrich society.

Responsiveness to consumers is therefore a matter of degree, and obviously the degree of movement toward responsiveness is critically important. Determining this degree involves adopting a strategy, which can be satisfactorily identified through strategic planning. The report of the strategic planning steering committee at Northeastern University states that "to become a truly student-centered campus we must shift our general focus from faculty as deliverers of information to students as learners" (Northeastern University Strategic Planning Steering Committee, 1994). As this statement demonstrates, some colleges and universities are beginning to get this particular message.

## Developing "Organizational Buy-In"

Developing a strategic plan that addresses the needs of the external environment is certainly an important part of the overall planning process. Yet the needs of the internal environments of higher education are just as critical. Strategic planners must develop a relationship with, and a method of planning that considers, the realities of tradition, circumstances, faculty, students, staff, resources, and administrative processes. Moreover, participative planning is absolutely critical not only for developing the plan but also for implementing it.

## The Imperative of Participatory Planning

Continuing the discussion begun in Chapter Three, there is yet another major difference between strategic planning in business and that done in the academy: the need for a participative process. On the whole, business organizations do not deal with the issue of shared governance. Though industrial democracy has given workers more and more of a say in organizational activities, and though unionization has legitimized a process of influencing management decisions, strategic decisions remain the responsibility of the chief executive officer (Steiner, Miner, and Gray, 1982). Within colleges and universities, however, the major means of production (teaching, research, and service) are regarded as the exclusive rights of the faculty, and there is a general consensus in the literature of strategic planning in higher education that top-level strategic decision making cannot be adequately accomplished without the advice and consent of the professoriate, among other constituents (Birnbaum, 1991). But while the faculty may constitute the predominant interest group on the campus, and while they may not have the capacity to govern directly, they can also exercise significant veto power over the options available to university administrative leadership. After all, as Foote (1988) reminds us, power in colleges and universities is shared among the board, president, senior administrators, faculty, and even students in some cases. To use business terminology, this power stems from their monopoly of the means of production as well as the outcomes of production.

The ultimate capacity to be innovative or reactionary to planning is embedded in the culture of the institution, especially in the culture of the faculty. If the faculty are senior, tenured, and not heavily engaged in creative activity or research, their resistance will be nearly impermeable. If the administration and the governing board are not in unison on planning, the resistance can prevail and prevent major change. Participatory planning is the only answer.

## Participative Versus Top-Down Planning

As we noted in the last chapter, most of the literature on the subject of strategic planning and strategic management comes from the discipline of business management. In this literature, one of the most critical responsibilities of the chief executive officer is to oversee the processes of strategic planning and strategic management (Farmer, 1990; Cyert, 1988, Steiner, Miner, and Gray, 1982). In his pioneering book on strategic planning and strategic management in higher education, Keller (1983) also seems to suggest that much of the strategic planning activity is the responsibility of top campus administrative and academic managers.

Though we will not argue that top college and university management should not be significantly involved in the process, it is also apparent that institutions of higher education are different from traditional business organizations to the degree that a completely top-down strategic planning process, followed by strategic management, will be highly problematic and may not work at all if it is not participatory in nature. As Bryson and Bromiley (1993) point out, the behavioral side of the process helps explain the success or failure of a strategic planning exercise.

The principle of shared governance is alive and well on most U.S. campuses. Professional groups such as the American Association of University Professors have helped establish guidelines for operational power distribution across the campus, and have also helped to establish significant faculty input in the general activities and directions of the college or university.

In addition, academics—the primary product and service of the campus—are the purview of the faculty (Birnbaum, 1991). Top level administration is for all intents and purposes prohibited from interfering with or directing the development of curricula and the establishment of research agendas, and from attempting to influence the direction that various disciplines are taking. Academic freedom is treated as a sacred right by faculty, and when administrative actions begin to threaten it, there are many local and national resources that can be mustered to "keep the administration in its place."

## Exercising Shared Governance

To effectively operate the academic and administrative function of a college or university, the principle of shared governance has evolved (Gilmour, 1991). One result has been the establishment of a clear distinction between administrative activities and academic activities. In reality, however, both are dependent upon each other. Administrations rely on the academic side of the house to develop and deliver the academic products of the college or university, and academics rely on the several administrative functions of the campus to handle the business, logistics, and support services the campus needs.

Since strategic planning, strategic decision making, and strategic thinking are all activities that affect the operations of the entire campus, the entire campus needs to be involved in their development and implementation. In fact, according to Cline and Meringolo (1991), the strategic planners at Penn State University felt so strongly about this issue that they placed major emphasis in their process on developing strategic thinking and acting.

It is a mistake to attempt to develop or implement any strategic planning or strategic management activities using a top-down model, even though this is the model found in the business literature. Instead, the campus needs to approach the process of strategic planning using a participative model.

## The Search for Models

There is, unfortunately, no major literature base backing this approach to strategic planning, though several published case studies confirm the wisdom of it (Chiarelott, Reed, and Russell, 1991; Cline and Meringolo, 1991; Eaton and Adams, 1991;

Dooris and Lozier, 1990; Cyert, 1988; Foote, 1988; Roach, 1988; Swain, 1988: Aggarwal, 1987). It is important to understand that the general field of strategic planning and strategic management has not been around all that long, even in the business sector (Harrison and St. John, 1994). Substantive research in the field began in the late 1950s and early 1960s and became a popular management tool in business in the late 1970s and early 1980s (Harrison and St. John, 1994). It is a modicum of theory and practice that is still under development and refinement. Mintzberg's recent book *The Rise and Fall of Strategic Planning* (1994b) mirrors these efforts.

The literature base on strategic planning in nonbusiness organizations is still in formation. In specific regard to strategic planning in higher education, Keller's 1983 book, which identifies *the need* for strategic planning in colleges and universities (rather than providing a schema for conducting it), is one of the few major works that have been published to date.

Models that apply to higher education have been developed by Shirley (1988) and by Morrison, Renfro, and Boucher (1984), and Bryson has developed a model for strategic planning in public and nonprofit organizations (1989, 1995). These models represent the first specifically nonbusiness models that many colleges and universities have adopted to guide their strategic planning processes. Shirley's model presents a method of planning that is sensitive to many of the issues that colleges and universities face, but it is based on developing the mission first. Morrison, Renfro, and Boucher, as well as Morrison and Brock (1991), present an important discussion regarding the need to base strategic management in higher education on the various forces of the environment, which we agree is central to the beginning stages of the strategic planning process. Unfortunately, these contributions do not go into much detail about the other aspects of the process. Finally, Bryson's method of strategic planning comprehensively looks at the issues faced by those organizations outside the business community, but it does not deal specifically with the parochial issues of higher education (and it calls for a planning scheme based on mission).

All of these methods have given tremendous insight into the process, and many colleges and universities have benefited from using them, though we feel that none of these models is complete. However, through the ongoing work of other researchers, such as that of Dolence and Norris (1994), the literature base has been extended.

Nonetheless, there plainly is not the substantive research activity and resulting literature that tests all areas of the identified strategic planning process. So it may well be that further research and practice will reveal the importance of altering the top-down model in certain settings, such as in higher education, and instead adapt the participative model of planning more broadly. In the absence of such a research and literature base, experience remains the best guide to developing principles for subsequent practice. Our own experience has demonstrated, as has the published case experience referred to earlier, that at least in the settings of higher education where we have conducted strategic planning, top-down planning, like mission-driven planning, has not been successful, and participative planning has proven to be much more effective.

## Making Participative Planning Work

Looking ahead to the imposing challenges of implementing the plan, it is imperative to begin the process as a truly participatory and responsive one. Yet, one imposing challenge in the participative model of planning in colleges and universities is the potential problem of getting academics and administrators to work together (Schmidtlein, 1990). On some campuses this is not much of a problem. On others, however, this may be more difficult. On these campuses it is normal that the central figures and decision makers from both the faculty and the administration will engage in some preplanning discussions regarding the formation of a common working relationship. Techniques such as contracting, open forums, give-and-take group discussions, and in extreme cases sensitivity training may be useful in getting all critical members of the planning team into a common frame of operation and may help to develop a higher degree of trust. Certainly this may add to the time frames set forth to go through the planning exercise, but it may be necessary to face up front some of the issues that have prevented the development of high levels of trust or interaction between campus factions in order to help prevent the process from later being bogged down by these sensitive issues.

Once achieved, this participative mode of planning should be extended throughout the campus by improving communication on how the college's or university's central strategic planning committee (SPC) is developing the plan. Particularly on those campuses where initial trust is low or there is a history of poor cooperation and coordination, having the major participants in the process regularly and religiously communicate what the SPC is doing is an essential part of overall campus buy-in. Trust is a difficult commodity to attempt to create, but it is a critical element of the strategic planning process.

## Implementation and Integration of Constituencies

How to implement the strategic plan, or perhaps more properly the process that the strategic plan will set in motion, is something campus strategic planners need to think about from the very beginning. Many different segments of the campus will be involved to a variety of degrees. Failure to take these constituencies into account early on could lead to major problems down the road.

### Internal Constituents

When the process has successfully developed the basic plan and is ready to move into the implementation phase (Phase One), or the strategic management phase (Phase Two), the institution must have already forged a new relationship with the internal community. Most likely, many of the committees that were formed to develop the basic plan will be reduced, combined, or eliminated altogether. This will cut down on the number of people directly involved in monitoring and updating the strategic plan, and could also falsely signal to many the end of strategic planning. Yet the institution must continue to monitor its progress, as well as its environment, and be in a position to update and upgrade the central planning tenets as the experience of the institution moves forward.

Therefore, the institution's SPC most likely needs to become a permanent committee—again, with strong people representing the major segments of the campus community as active and participating members. The work of this group will change from planning to monitoring and controlling, but its work must continue to be viewed by the campus community as necessary and important.

## External Dialogue

The dialogue that the institution began with its critical external constituents needs to be continued. For example, as part of the assessment program, the institution can stay connected with alumni, critical donors, and significant community contingencies by asking focused questions that help the committee better understand how the strategies of the planning process are actually affecting outcomes. Also, ongoing focus groups with major external constituencies can continue to provide important information to the institution, as well as to provide a mechanism for crucial external constituents to have a voice in the strategic decision-making process of the college or university.

Because this is a long-term process, and because the intent of strategic planning is to align the institution with its most critical environments, it is important to keep these external connections active and to remain willing to listen to what they say. Change will always be a reality, and it is important for the college or university to continuously nurture its external linkages in order to help the institution better identify changes that will affect it and be in a position to be as proactive as possible, as early as possible, when changes are going to be made.

## Planning in a New Mind-Set

Throughout this chapter we have talked about the fact that strategic planning in an institution of higher education is different from strategic planning in business settings. The challenge to the planner in an institution of higher education is to think and plan with an open mind—to be ready to use the already-identified tools that fit and are useful, but also to be open to the use of a new set of tools that intuition or experimentation suggests may be of some use.

### A Formidable Challenge

The college or university strategic planning process is faced with circumstances and challenges that require a more collaborative, externally oriented, and long-term approach than most business organizations use. Resistance to this extensive validation through broad participation is natural. It is hard to plan with many players. But by being participative, the well-being of the institution is more accurately defined and understood, and the improved communication required among participants helps break down the barriers of culture and habit that undermine trust, both within and outside of the institution. This should result in a better alignment of the institution with its most critical environment.

### The Commitment to Do Substantive Strategic Planning

One last word regarding the decision to do strategic planning. While nearly every institution of higher education we are familiar with says it is doing strategic planning, the evidence suggests that only a few are doing the kind of substantive planning we describe in this book. Most are doing traditional planning— they just call it strategic planning.

Further, we firmly believe that every college or university could benefit from developing a substantive strategic plan at some point in its effort to deal with the changes that all of higher education faces. But the decision to do substantive strategic planning should not be made casually. As we have tried to indicate in this chapter, genuine strategic planning in a college or university is risky for leadership and it involves a lot of hard work. It also is not inexpensive. At UNC, we worked for more than three years to develop a dynamic preliminary plan, and added one full-time high-level staff member to oversee the process.

Worth repeating is the critical importance of support for planning from the board of trustees and the president, as evidenced in our experience at UNC. This support helped the planners deal with challenges from those who viewed strategic planning as a threat to their stability and as a ploy by top administrators to alter the institution's structure. This top-level commitment was strong and consistent as we moved through our initial process. We were also fortunate in having the involvement of nearly two hundred members of the university community working in nineteen different campus- and unit-level committees to steer the process forward. Faculty, staff, campus administrators, and students all contributed to the effort. Together, there was a strong-enough base of commitment to proceed in spite of organized opposition from the faculty senate and most of the deans, and the wavering of two vice presidents.

Despite the difficulties, a working strategic enrollment management system is in place at UNC. Strategic enrollment management is shaping how the university recruits and retains its student mix, as well as providing the ability to maximize tuition caps set by the state of Colorado. Technology planning for the campus is integrated, and building a communications and information system that connects the campus with the world and improves the quality of education. Information technology planning has resulted in the establishment of a distributed information environment and the building of a campuswide management information structure, all the results of the strategic planning process. Resource planning is providing a fiscal analysis of any proposed planning change or program shift and beginning to develop the foundations on which a larger resource base for the university can be built. The resource planning committee has been expanded to serve as the campus budget advising committee, and academic program planning has produced several general policies and priorities for trustee approval as the important initial step toward establishing program priorities. These priorities are essential for budget development in the face of impending reductions and the need to reinvest resources in essential programs rather than rely on a legislative bailout. In the 1996–1997 budget request, planning priorities guided both the expenditures of new dollars and the redistribution of 3.14 percent of the base budget.

It is important to note that as these planning segments evolved, the planning overlay of committees and the existing governance structure merged after the initial phases of planning. The strategic enrollment management subcommittee took over enrollment management, the technology planning subcommittee merged with the technology management committee, and the resource subcommittee dissolved into the campus budget advisory committee. This kind of shifting and merging is a natural and necessary consequence of putting planning into practice.

Without this willingness to "stick to the knitting" and to integrate functions into routine organization, the process we describe in this book would be only a theory. This need for persistence will most likely be true on any campus that attempts to do strategic planning in the face of apprehension or opposition, or where planning is in response to external pressures.

## Where All This Strategic Planning Is Headed

A central theme of this book is that developing a strategic plan is essential to the future of a college or university. However, once the activities of planning are developed and successful, planning should be *replaced* by something else. In order for the process to be effective, *strategic planning* must be replaced by *strategic management* and by *strategic thinking* and *strategic decision making*.

This replacement occurs when the planning superstructure blends into, or displaces, the routine governance and management organization on a given campus.

This is not to suggest that strategic management and strategic thinking and decision making begin only *after* planning has ceased. An effective planning process includes transitions from conventional and traditional thinking and decision-making models to strategic ones *as the plan develops.* In fact, it is unlikely that the plan will speak effectively to change without transitions occurring during the planning phase.

Strategic thinking is required to develop plans that better match the capabilities of the institution with its most critical environment, and as those elements change, so does the plan. Because strategic planning is dynamic, such transitions become commonplace and reflect the ability of the plan to relate to or resolve real issues of importance as they arise. As described in Chapter One, most colleges and universities are not used to making ongoing plans and decisions based on their linkage to the external environment. The activities of strategic planning require that planners begin to think strategically, beginning as early in the process as possible, in order to formulate a plan that embraces these relationships and takes steps to address them.

## What to Expect in the Transformation

In our own experiences on several campuses, we have seen major breakthroughs occur in planning groups when this transition within the process has begun. People soon understand that they need to develop key performance indicators, goals, policies, and operational strategies and tactics that address the long-term survival of the institution as it interacts with its external environments. This understanding matures as they see cause and effect relationships between their planning decisions and their ability to understand and respond to or affect their environment.

When these transformations occur, they forge the planning group together and move planning activities substantively toward a useful plan. By the time an institution is in a position to move out of Phase One (the initial planning phase) into Phase Two (the management and decision-making phase), people are already thinking and acting differently as they deal with both short-term operational goals and long-term strategic goals and accomplishments.

When looking at the time required to develop a strategic plan, it is important to consider the transformations that must occur in the form of internal policies and strategies that emerge to cope with the environment in response to a real issue posed by that environment. This leads us to the view that in the early phases of planning, *the process is more important than the plan itself.* The end product of strategic planning is not so much to write a "plan" as it is to change thinking and introduce a model in which ongoing decisions are made *strategically.* This is the essential outcome if strategic planning is to be effective.

# CHAPTER 5

# Negotiating
# Campus Politics

Throughout this book we talk about the need for participation and communication, and we also discuss the role of campus constituencies that have a stake in the college or university. In any organizational setting, a variety of groups will inevitably compete for resources, and in doing so will engage in power struggles (Pfeffer, 1992). This is certainly true in colleges and universities (Dooris and Lozier, 1990). Competition over who controls resources and the allocation of goods and values is at the core of campus politics, and consequently it is an important consideration in the strategic planning process of a college or university. Plus, as Richards (1990) has demonstrated, many decisions made in a political environment can be chaotic, which makes the process less predictable and the outcomes problematic.

In order to be successful, Flack (1994) tells us, the strategic planning process must have three elements: (1) a good technology for evaluating the internal and external environment, (2) a process that is collaborative, and (3) a positive political environment of acceptance and implementation. This chapter examines the campus political environment, assesses the potential impact it will have as well as the constraints it will impose, and suggests some appropriate strategies for dealing with campus politics.

## The Nature of Politics

Politics are neither good nor bad. Rather, as Kanter, Stein, and Jick (1992) define the phenomenon, "politics is the jockeying for position that goes on as groups of individuals advance their own interests and make their own claim on the organization's resources" (p. 46). When campus groups have a vested interest in the overall success of the college or university, politics can serve as a positive force by helping to clarify issues and identify remedies (Birnbaum, 1991). These are good and necessary outcomes in the life of an institution because they help outline the courses of action that can lead to the resolution of issues.

There is, however, another side to campus politics. Birnbaum also tells us that if campus politics are not taken into consideration when decisions regarding campus issues are being made, they can derail decisions and sometimes veto efforts, regardless of the merit or contribution of those decisions and efforts to the good of the order. Campus politics often lead to conflict (Hardy, 1991), and thus become a negative force posing obstacles to meaningful change. In extreme circumstances, negative politics can induce destructive behaviors that undermine the essential collegiality of the academic community (Lee, 1991). Putting it in even stronger terms, Frank (1996) observed that the strategic planning process and implementation at Rutgers University were "a test as to whether we are one university" (p. 2).

### The Dangers of Negative Politics

The words *college* and *university* imply collegiality and a shared or broadly unified set of values. Yet on some campuses politics resembles feudal times and rationality is nonexistent (Hardy, 1990). When collegiality and the respect it engenders diminish, negative politics and the conflict of special interests that such politics generate displace community as one element gains at the expense of another. This zero-sum aspect of negative politics corrupts the rational dialogue that is required in an intellectual community and the willingness to trade and compromise that retains community in the face of diversity and pluralism.

Negative politics are rooted in the ability to nay-say, obstruct, and veto processes for change. While lacking the power to create change, negative politics are based on coalescing enough support to object in ways that impede change. For this reason, negative politics can be thought of as veto politics.

## Politics at Work in Strategic Planning

In strategic planning, politics come into play partially because strategic planning involves significant change and issues of control of resources (Knights and Morgan, 1991). This change occurs because strategic planning is usually invoked when the routines of a campus cannot resolve an issue or deal effectively with constraints or challenges posed by external sources or authorities. Change usually means a rearrangement of influence, authority, and the prerogatives that govern the allocation of goods and values. Change of this kind leads to uncertain results, and the uncertainty of unpredictable outcomes is especially threatening to most people.

Since strategic planning is dynamic, inductive, and open-ended, it is particularly vulnerable to fear of uncertainty. Moreover, different groups on a campus are generally not equal in position or resources; the campus community is stratified. Academics believe that they have the traditional primary status, while other groups lack the legitimacy to challenge this position (Newton, 1992). As a consequence, the entitlement to resources is highest for the faculty and academic affairs. This is best exemplified in the long tradition of cutting student affairs or the physical plant and its operations whenever there is a bump in the steady flow of funding for higher education. Strategic planning promises to realign the organization with the environment, and to many constituents realignment means taking resources from one group and giving it to another. For these reasons, among others, it is a serious mistake to begin campuswide strategic planning without developing a realistic understanding of campus politics and some strategies for dealing with them.

## Campus Politics in Action

Different groups find different reasons to either support or oppose change. For example, Cline and Meringolo (1991) tell us that at Penn State, in order to move ahead in their successful strategic planning process, they had to overcome some major skepticism—those who had been involved in previous planning exercises in which the results had been only partially implemented were not supportive of going through another such exercise. As the process proceeded, the nature of the politics changed as different parts of the campus began to realize that they were suddenly competing for enhancement status and funds as a result of the academic portion of the strategic planning exercise. Unfortunately, these and more potential issues exist.

### Issues Worth Fighting Over

Based on the preceding discussion, one can argue that procedure is the shield that protects campus groups from facing the forces of change proactively rather than defensively. Traditionally, campuses have handbooks, manuals, codes, or in the case of unionized campuses, negotiated contracts that define the processes for governance, oversight of the curriculum, and other items, including workload and productivity. By habit, however, these processes are seen as protective devices for mitigating against any change in existing policies and rules.

The consequent focus on rules and procedures forces planning into Byzantine paths. New ideas, policies, programs, and strategies most typically must be blessed, approved, or reviewed, or undergo some other local tradition in order to pass the muster of processes peculiar to the individual campus.

*Veto Power Through Legislation.* Because process is the gateway to veto power, that power will be used in strategic planning the moment that change with an uncertain outcome is implied. At UNC, the issue worth fighting over became two faces of the same issue. Since planning had involved both the council of deans and the faculty senate, both groups argued that they had the prerogative to review and approve the results of strategic planning, that is, the strategic plan. Since the plan would be evolving, there was a basic question as to which version should be reviewed.

This concern over the right to review was part of a larger overlay of concerns. At UNC, strategic planning was being undertaken partially at the behest of the board of trustees, and according to the coded policies adopted by the board, approval by either the deans or the senate was not authorized. Neither group had power directly derived from the board to exercise such a prerogative. The senate in particular, however, could review and offer its advice on anything it chose. After discussion, the senate passed a resolution calling for a review of the plan by the senate before it was adopted by the board of trustees. Approval was finessed, but review persisted.

The underlying political idea was obvious. If the senate disapproved of the plan, and did so in a loud political manner, it would have a chance to veto implementation by the board. Consequently, negative politics surfaced early in the senate action to review the plan, an action that on its surface appeared benign and respectful of the traditional role of the faculty yet was available for political use to oppose the plan by challenging its legitimacy.

*Veto Power Through Applying the Rules.* By asserting the right to review, an opening was provided for opposition to be grounded in good traditional practice; the faculty exercise of review powers was traditionally acceptable. This also meant that the likelihood grew of vetoing the plan if it did not satisfy the senate, a common political technique identified by Lee (1991).

Therein lies the second element of negative politics.

Through its committees the strategic planning process was by definition getting into areas where the standing committees of the senate and other committees to which faculty had access claimed exclusive jurisdiction (such as enrollment). Matters of jurisdiction were ordinarily clarified in Codification, which was the repository of rules and regulations (not all of which were approved by the president or the board of trustees). This mix of policies approved by the board and regulations inserted by the senate became a hedgerow behind which opponents could hide and block planning results. The specific grounds were that planning should appropriately be linked to existing governance processes. What could not be vetoed by a straw vote of faculty opinion through the senate could be smothered by the traditional practices of the labyrinth of standing committees—practices that contributed to the very problems that planning was supposed to resolve. Under these circumstances, moves to veto were inevitable, and process was its harbinger.

*Veto Power Through Tradition.* Finally, there are always idiosyncratic local practices that become traditions over time. At UNC, such a practice was the salary model. The model had been negotiated in 1987–88 to meet concerns of parity, originally in relation to administrative salaries. The model was designed to keep faculty salaries at the same percentage of parity that characterized administrative salaries. If administrative salaries at UNC were at 98 percent of administrative salaries at peer universities, then faculty salaries at UNC should be at 98 percent of faculty salaries at the same peers. This model did not permit merit increases, although it did allow for market adjustments in highly competitive disciplines and professions. Over time, the model had moved salaries by rank, with the top rank of full professors gaining most, in a calculated effort to catch up with higher paying administrative salaries. This situation created important inequities by discipline or profession and by race and gender, especially as affirmative action resulted in growing numbers of women and minorities in the entry ranks. Salaries lagged in the humanities and in other fields in which there were no market adjustments, and these were often the fields in which women and minorities were hired at entry-level wages. The model benefitted the senior rank while keeping overall salaries low, because of the cost of rewarding at the highest rank coupled with low to modest legislative appropriations. If the institution does not have significant new appropriations for salaries and it places what it gets among the highest-paid ranks first, the result is a widening gap within faculty ranks that penalizes the lower and entry ranks.

As the strategic planning process unfolded, the lag between administrative and faculty salaries became the object of a lawsuit. Initially, fifty-five senior faculty filed suit as planning got fully under way, charging the university with permanently damaging their present salaries and subsequent retirements through a decade of inadequate compensation (*Meilahn and others* v. *the Board of Trustees of the University of Northern Colorado,* Weld County District Court Case 93CV616, Dec. 28, 1993).

Ironically, the rank that benefitted most by the salary model was grieving about the inadequacy of that model. This local tradition of the salary model provided a fertile political base for gathering opposition to the university by challenging its fairness to faculty. This issue of fairness in the process of compensation was available to be linked to the idea of fairness in planning. Was planning just a subterfuge for further administrative unfairness? To the extent that planning was developing its own processes independent of existing governance procedures and challenging present practices, it would not take much to turn apprehension into paranoia.

## A Campus Full of Political Groups

While the example just presented demonstrates the politics that can occur between administrative groups and faculty senates, these are not the only groups that engage in political activities. Certainly other faculty groups, such as departments or campuswide academic communities, can do so as well. Political activism on the part of students is a phenomenon that every college and university has had to deal with since the activist sixties and seventies. Students have governance councils and their own administrative boards, and they are active in many parts of campus life. With the growing concern for escalating costs, more and more students are speaking up and beginning to exercise their power to have a greater say in the decisions of the institution. Here, too, politics can be either positive or negative. Administrative groups, including the core of vice presidents or vice chancellors, also control a fair amount of campus power and use it from time to time to advance their causes and positions. And finally, classified or unionized staff also form governance structures and can wield considerable political power when resource reallocations appear imminent.

## Structural Moves to Reduce Negative Politics

While requiring a stretch of sorts, at UNC all of this politicking could be boiled down to the view that planning was an illegitimate Trojan horse until it was approved by the deans, faculty, students, and professional administrative and classified governance structures, or until it was made consistent with the shield of protection embedded in codification. The lesson is worth noting. Strategic planning has three options: (1) finesse the process issue by gradually absorbing existing committee functions into newly designated committees, (2) transfer the strategic methodology to existing committees, or (3) follow a mixed strategy depending on local idiosyncrasies. Any latent issues related to the changing functions should then be resolved. After the issues have been resolved, planning should, under option one, merge by absorbing the previous structure's role, or under option two, end by being folded into existing structures. In the third option, one can pick and choose depending on what will be successful in a given function or situation. The choice should be dictated by which action is easier and seen as more legitimate given local norms and circumstances. The cue for change should be when practical success has occurred in the planning committee, so that merging shifts the burden of concern from argument over process to results that benefit and can breed their own processes.

## Co-Opting Processes

Legitimized in this way, planning can now include all elements of various campus political groups, regardless of their posture on planning. This can be accomplished by requiring involvement, such as having the trustees call for it as an expectation of the board. By being included, those from the opposition have some responsibility for, if not shared ownership in, the results that accrue from the planning effort. This makes it less likely that the opposition can act as free critics without any responsibility to help resolve differences or improve the planning result. Such strategies require incrementalism and the early avoidance of directly challenging local hot button traditions and the sacred procedures that are inculcated in campus governance practices.

## Why Strategic Planning Threatens Campus Political Groups

We argued earlier that strategic planning is an open, dynamic, and adaptive process that is always unfolding. Because of this nature, it lacks certainty and relies on thoughtful analyses about what approach best fits an institution's needs given the strengths, weaknesses, opportunities, and threats that define the external environment and the internal capacity to cope with change. This inductive attribute conflicts with the deductive preferences of those who like closed systems, in which goals define objectives that in turn define action. As McCloskey (1991) points out, an "invisible college" exists on many campuses, populated by those who are specialized in narrow disciplines (not particularly market relevant) and who perpetuate themselves and the state of their narrow disciplines through co-optation of faculty in other disciplines.

Mission statements and other artifacts of tradition-based

rituals and procedures clash with this "let's learn as we go" perspective. The lack of imperatives bothers those who like certainty and the clarity that such certainty gives about what needs to be changed. Besides, the rationality of deductive thinking fits nicely with the rational tradition of the academy.

## The Vulnerability of the Process

The lack of deductive rationality makes strategic planning vulnerable. Without the legitimacy of tradition, strategic planning is weak at the outset. Because planning results from process, this initial weakness makes the procedures of strategic planning ripe for challenge by practices and processes already in place. Since the present distribution of resources and values is embedded in existing structure, the threat to change a process is a threat to reconfigure the pattern of resource allocation already in place. When the threat against the existing distribution of resources and values is coupled with the threat of uncertainty, which is inherent in strategic planning, there is occasion for a formidable call to arms among campus groups.

In addition, the hierarchy of campus groups is not random or unique. The pecking order is fairly common from campus to campus. Faculty have the highest status and staff have the lowest. Thus, existing processes allocate resources, prerogatives, values, and expectations unevenly. As those processes distribute privilege and prerogative over time, the processes become substantive. The result is an imperative that is not merely "if it ain't broke don't fix it," but rather "even if it is broke, it's better than what a fix might bring"—the constraint you know is better than the opportunity you do not know.

## The Acceptability of Doing Nothing

As a consequence, some campus leaders prefer doing nothing as an acceptable alternative to change of any kind. If campus groups can make the campus stick to present circumstances, they thwart change they cannot control. Isolation from external pressures makes this possible by diminishing the sense of urgency about change that those who are better connected may feel. Usually, those who are better connected to the external pressures are administrators, governing board members, and others who deal regularly with everything from legislators to donors.

Moreover, faculty are, by role and ability, experts. Experts do not heed others well. Expertise, a bias for tradition, protection offered by existing process, and insulation from external pressures all engrain themselves in faculty instincts. This condition is reinforced by the basic skepticism that is endemic to scholarship and its derived instinct for careful consideration and deliberation before making a judgment. Instincts buttressed by scholarly methods lead to an inertia that is not easily reversed.

Besides, U.S. higher education ranks among the best in the world. So it is quite natural to ask, If present practice has produced such excellence, why should we change anything? This is a reasonable question that mists the ability of the academy to see external signs of discontent. It is not uncommon to find faculty groups unimpressed by public attitudes such as the obvious and growing view that the public is not willing to support higher education at its present level of cost, or the growing attitude that students with bachelor's degrees are not a ready resource for a restructuring economy because many lack the new skills demanded by the changing global marketplace. The price of higher education is rising and the product is less satisfying. In economics, the result is obvious: prices rise in relation to the quality of the product. As dissatisfaction with graduates increases, the willingness of state legislatures, students, and even employers to pay higher prices for higher education declines.

In colleges and universities, this condition is often ignored or downplayed. In some ways, this response of higher education seems a replay of the problem that U.S. automobile manufacturers faced in the 1980s; they continued to produce larger cars of poorer quality and at higher prices for global consumers with smaller wallets and crowded streets. The result for the manufacturers was loss of market primacy.

## How Political Groups Can Band Together

Groups generally need a battle cry to band together. If the organizing theme can be tied to hallowed processes, the call is strong. An example can be found in the response of the UNC faculty senate to the instruction by the board of trustees that codification—as noted earlier, the campus collection of policies, rules, regulations—and other actions taken in the name of the campus be revised and reduced only to those policy documents previously approved by the board. This instruction was related to the strategic planning process because planning posed a threat to the existing code once the planning committee structure began to displace standing committees mentioned in the code. The faculty response to the threat posed by the board's directive is exemplified in this action taken on April 17, 1995 (*Faculty Senate Forum,* 1995, p. 3):

> The UNC Faculty Senate and its committees, as well as other UNC faculty units and committees, have worked diligently with current and past administrations and Boards of Trustees towards ensuring that the codified policies, rules and regulations for the University are internally consistent, fair, equitable and workable. We have endeavored to make these consistent with the laws of the State of Colorado and the United States, where applicable. We believe that the Codification helps to protect the faculty staff, administration and the Board of Trustees from capricious, unfair or unwise actions which could endanger each individual involved as well as the University itself. . . .
>
> It has been stated that the Board might consider "sunsetting" the current rules and regulations on or about January 1, 1996 and substituting new rules, if changes in Codification are not forthcoming. The needed changes have not been specified. The faculty believes that such a radical removal of Codification would be extremely inadvisable. This would imperil our continued accreditation, since accrediting boards look for consistent and sustained following of the

goals and rules of the University. If suddenly imposed new rules involved the process by which curriculum was determined and approved, that would require "advice and consent" of the faculty and would involve a long, time-consuming process. If the suddenly imposed new rules involved modifications to working conditions for the faculty members, that would lay the University open to lawsuits by those faculty members on continuing contracts who believed that the University's contractual obligations were not being upheld. A similar situation could occur for some student or staff members. Finally, as an American institution, we need to provide an example of good governance. Evolutionary change rather than revolutionary overthrow is the example of governance which we in the United States should and normally do support when possible.

The hot buttons that sound the rallying cry are several and worth noting. They include phrases such as "radical removal," "imperil accreditation," "following rules," "curriculum approval," "advice and consent," "process," "lawsuit," "students and staff," "American institution," and "revolutionary overthrow." The symbolic content is obvious and stirring. The sequence is instructive. Yet such remarks can be designed to subvert or derail an important campus process.

First, attention is obtained by labeling the effort a radical removal or action. It is careless radicalism because it threatens accreditation (the North Central Accreditation site visit had just been completed). It is not only careless and threatening, but it is also illegitimate because it does not follow the rules. It could touch on the curriculum, and that is faculty domain; so not only does it threaten the institution, it transgresses faculty territory. Advice and consent is a time-honored U.S. tradition and surely it should be sought. If sought, a long and time-consuming process is expected and proper. If none of this transpires, then a lawsuit would follow, and the threats could well extend to students and staff. Beyond students and staff, a U.S. institution is in peril of revolutionary overthrow.

Chiarelott, Reed, and Russell (1991) tell us that the strategic planning process at Bowling Green State University was also marked by several politically related incidents. One regarded the use of language, where faculty reacted negatively to the use of business-oriented language in the initial plan more so than to its content. A second incident was a more traditional conflict about shared governance, in which major concern was raised over who would formulate the plan, and then who would review and approve it. A third incident was a general discussion among faculty and administrators as to whether or not strategic planning was worth anything.

This kind of sweeping reasoning allows a case to be made for linking the defense of faculty prerogatives to the preservation of the flag and democracy itself, all within two paragraphs. The threat is broad, encompassing the institution's certification, students and staff, and U.S. tradition itself. The message could also be interpreted that trustee directives (and by easy extension, strategic planning) are threats to the American Way. The clarion call gives a basis for groups to band together and resist.

## Recognizing When Politics Is Becoming Negative

We have argued that the power of negative politics rests in the ability to obstruct and veto. The natural tendency for groups is to use procedures as the pry bar of opposition and to avoid the substance of the issue. Finding defense behind the process is predictable: the process contradicts code; it does not follow rules and custom; or it is illegal. If these formalistic conditions do not work, the groups then move to innuendo and discredit. They argue that the process is illogical, expensive, cumbersome, illegitimate, flies in the face of time-honored tradition, undermines quality, hurts the institution or does not fit its character, or is un–American. In the quicksand of innuendo, there is no standard for proof or refutation. Accusation is its own confirmation. When the rhetoric evidences these objections or others like them, negative politics are already at work.

## The Great Silent Majority

One of the realities of campus politics is that when it heats up it is generally the result of a relatively few people. Most campuses provide inviting and open opportunities for politically oriented individuals to gain power in a faculty senate, academic committee, administrative governing board, student council, or support staff governing group. With persistence comes power, and with this power these people begin to put their particular political agenda on the map. Again, much of this is good, and the political process can be beneficial in bringing new ideas and operational methods to the campus. But since most faculty choose the teaching profession not to deal in campus politics but to engage their disciplines in the classroom, the lab, or the external environment, most really do not seek involvement in these political groups. Many actively seek ways of not being involved with them. The notion of serving on the faculty senate, for example, may be seen by several such faculty members as "a necessary evil," something they might have to do because it is their turn, because no one else would run, or for some other reason—an activity they would just as soon forego if they could. This leaves the road clear for those other faculty members who want to engage in the politics of the campus, and who perhaps have a particular ax to grind. Whether true or not, such people tend to be associated with the "old guard" or with some of the tenured full professors who have, presumably, nothing better to do with their time. These are generally the ones who engage in the politics of the campus, and who also may be involved in the negative side of the equation.

The great question is, then, do such people represent the bulk of their constituencies? Maybe, maybe not. At any level, the answer is not straightforward. Further, when great political debates arise the presumption is that those on governing boards speak for their constituents, when in fact they may not. If they do not, why do the greater number of constituents remain silent, even in the face of great controversy often generated by their own representatives on such councils?

The answer is an unhappy one for many campus political face-offs: most campus constituents are so comfortable in what they are doing, and honestly do not believe that the political debate will lead to any meaningful result that will affect them in any way, that the course of least resistance and comfort is that of no involvement at all at any level. Most faculty, students, professional administrators, and support staff feel protected from the heat of political debate, which makes it easy for them to ignore it. At UNC, when the council of deans and the faculty senate publicly denounced strategic planning as a failure, those of us who were engaged not only in creating a plan but also in successfully implementing it hoped that the faculty at large, the student body, and rest of the UNC staff and administrators would know better and support the process. Such support was never forthcoming. Perhaps this lack of concern and feeling of being secure in their own jobs helps explain why.

## Working with the Politics of Resistance

Resistance to change is common. Political resistance to change can be a severe challenge, particularly when strategic planners find little rational reasoning driving the forces to prevent change. There are, however, several things that planners can do to help manage the strategic plan through the negative political environment, when they encounter it, and to help turn negative political sentiments into positive support.

### Parsing Negative Politics

Negative politics are negative in two senses. They are based in fear, specifically the fear of change, and they act as an obstruction to that change. So, dealing with negative politics involves their dissection. What are the fears that drive negative politics on a given campus, and what tools of process are available for obstructive use? This is the key question, and its answer requires a careful analysis of the source and nature of negative politics on a campus.

## Naming the Beast

Looking negative politics in the eye requires certain talent. The analysis should involve a group effort. Included in such a group should be a respected faculty member with instinctive understanding of the campus and its hot spots; a representative dean; someone in tune with student interests and empathetic to their needs; a veteran administrator with a good sense of institutional history; the designated strategic planning person; a staff representative with ties to staff cliques; and a bright graduate student, as the committee staffer. Naturally, it is better for a group like this to come together before planning gets under way. Otherwise, it must come together when the cues of opposition described earlier initially become evident.

The challenges this group should consider include the following questions:

1. What are the hot buttons that the planning exercise may trigger?
2. Whose oxen will be gored?
3. What procedures are likely to be invoked?
4. Can planning be linked to the concerns, interests, and procedures identified by the first three questions?
5. Which groups are available as allies?
6. How can the connecting points identified by the fourth question and available allies be combined as the basis for dealing with resistance?

In the analysis that ensues, several things are worth remembering. The first is that entrenched campus groups are prone to overestimate their capacity to obstruct and to rally others to their side. For example, as long holders of privilege and status, faculty may make the mistake made by many aristocrats, namely, judging that others are lesser and not of their stature or sophistication. It is not the arrogance of "Let them eat cake" but rather the faculty's view that "they can only get their cake through us." As a result, faculty resistance will begin with a kind of disdain for strategic planning and much discussion about its weaknesses, its origin in the private sector (and therefore its lack of fit), and its lack of logic, coherence, or certainty. This is a view that many other campus groups may adopt as well. Typically this resistance will be followed by an effort to legitimize planning by trying to absorb it into existing governance or by requiring its connection to faculty governance at some point. This is largely a strategy of foxes and hen houses; if the faculty can co-opt planning into governance bodies they control, they can veto anything they do not like. Finally, there will be a call for faculty review before "the plan" can go forward, which sets the stage for exercising veto power if all else fails.

## Identifying the Elements of Fear

Since fear underlies the urge to control, it is important that the operative fears be isolated. Each campus has its own set of fears, but some fears are fairly common. In many universities, planning precedes cuts, so many faculty and staff fear that strategic planning is the midwife of layoffs.

Those employed in student affairs fear that technology will not only eliminate jobs but will also depersonalize services. In administrative services and auxiliaries, the fear is that efficiency through planning will result in privatizing. After all, the trend in campus food services has been to replace campus-owned services with large external contractors. Among the faculty, the fear is related to the issue of aligning workload with productivity measures, the increasingly sensitive issue of tenure, and the concern over what academic program prioritization really means.

All of these fears are reasonable; each is given meaning by some history of local events that vivify the threat. Moreover, such fears lead regularly to simplistic solutions, and the simplest of them is the view that if we do not plan for change, change will not come.

## An Ounce of Prevention

The antidote is a careful and clear crafting of the rationale for planning before any process is designed. This rationale and the basic themes it engenders must be clearly, simply, and consistently used to preface discussions about planning. Serendipitously "winging it" as you go will open strategic planning to charges of being confusing, having ulterior motives, being overly complicated, or involving overkill, among other characterizations. But the significant point is that lack of a clear rationale will launch strategic planning as a defensive war, a kind of bureaucratic Vietnam in which the ordinary people suffer while the planners use key performance indicators to shape strategy like the army used body counts. Then logic is quickly displaced by the effort to undermine. When the resisters become the defenders of what is good and virtuous, strategic planning is lost.

## Seeking Allies

The rationale, once enunciated, should be a general guide for the kind of process that is designed. It is easier to seek allies than to convert resisters. Accordingly, opportunities to bring in those who are neutral or available for support should be designed into the process.

Further, the process must be incremental. And to be truly demand driven, it should begin with development of the strategic enrollment management portion of the plan. This is especially true given the present emphasis on revenue and the increasing role that tuition plays as a revenue source. Since money makes believers out of people, effective enrollment management will provide a practical base for building support.

For example, every campus employs people who manage enrollment. Their fears must be isolated and considered as the approach to enrollment management is outlined. It is important, however, to reach outside of this core of technicals to faculty, particularly those who understand markets, those in the graduate school, and people from the pockets of excellence in the university. Ready allies are the deans and chairs from departments in which enrollments are rising and faculty entitlements are not following, because tenure has them housed elsewhere. In short, look for those who can have a stake in enrollment management and include them in the enrollment management planning process.

## Governing Boards

Certain allies are essential to the strategic planning process. Trustees, regents, or governing board members are foremost among them. It is important that these people be aware and supportive of the process early in planning. They can also be helpful, especially in the development of the analysis of the institution's strengths, weaknesses, opportunities, and threats. They are important sources of ideas about strengths and weaknesses, and their views can help sort out the more important external concerns. Once they are involved, governing board members should be kept abreast of the evolving strategic process. Each year at its annual retreat, when the board's agenda of key issues for the coming year is set, an update accompanied by debate about the essential processes, expectations, and outcomes of strategic planning is very important.

In describing how the plan is unfolding, it is critical that governing boards be initiated into and get used to the fact that academic processes take time. Impatience will be typical among those from the private sector who sit on boards and sense the urgency for change. But faculty governance tends to move slowly and this must be accommodated in some reasonable way. In addition, because planning in business is top-down, there will be impatience about the participatory nature of planning in the university. As Skoldberg (1991) points out, the danger that the board or other outside group will force change on the institution is real and may well blur or distort the issues that the strategic plan addresses. Understanding by lay and private sector board members of the emphasis on process and participation in the academy is very important.

## The Role of Communication

In developing effective lines of communication, not only should the process be set forth and reiterated but as soon as results begin to appear they should be communicated broadly and regularly (especially to essential allies) with their implications spelled out. Using enrollment management as an example, it is important to inform relevant constituencies about how the enrollment management strategy is resulting in enrollments and in a particular enrollment mix. Then it is important to relate these outcomes to revenue and to isolate strategic management enrollment activities that were essential to enrollment success (or shortfall). Further, it is important to relate these results to budget lines as soon as possible, so that, for example, enrollment-generating activities can be given precedence in building the next proximate budget request. When the results of planning are tied to budgets in this manner, people will take planning more seriously. Finally, it is also important to tie results to the overall theme mentioned earlier. When trustees or governing boards feel that the decision-making infrastructure is adapting to the consequences of planning, they will support planning even in the face of faculty or other objection.

At UNC, in spite of a slow start and significant administrative, faculty, and staff criticisms, a key theme was consistently raised—that strategic planning was essential to shaping the future of UNC. Effective enrollment management would generate new revenues by getting the most out of its enrollment and related tuition opportunities. Since UNC had traditionally underenrolled, any means of maximizing authorized enrollments would be an improvement; doing so with the right mix of students (resident and nonresident as well as undergraduate and graduate) would result in maximizing the tuition dollars possible under the enrollment authorization set by its legislative funding.

Shortly after strategic planning began, Colorado passed a

constitutional amendment, Amendment I, in 1992, which restricted the way the state funded institutions. With the passage of this constitutional amendment, higher education could no longer depend on general revenue funds to provide the lion's share of its operating budget. Instead, while a portion of those funds would continue, students would need to bear larger amounts of the costs through tuition increases. But even here, there was a catch. Universities were authorized to raise revenues from tuition up to a designated ceiling that was built into the total revenue appropriated and authorized by the state for a given institution. The failure to reach that ceiling would result in a reduction of the base and a shortfall in current available revenue. In other words, failure to meet the cap meant a *voluntary reduction* of the college's or university's budget. By emphasizing the value of strategically managing enrollments in order to maximize tuition revenues allowed under the cap, strategic planning at UNC began to receive cautious support and growing legitimacy.

## Negotiating to Head Off Problems

As planning unfolds, the focus should be placed on building support by keeping the effort centered on resolving real issues. As real issues are resolved, the web of supporters can increase through deliberate efforts to negotiate differences and seize opportunities to tie those who gain more permanently to planning.

One place where negotiation can work is on committee membership. Turnover usually occurs on volunteer committees. Sometimes that turnover comes from resisters who simply stop coming. As vacancies arise, the opportunity presents itself to fill them in a calculated pattern, by restaffing with those who can help the institution build shared ownership in what is unfolding through the developing strategic planning process.

At UNC, the deans were initially excluded from university-wide planning because a new vice president of academic affairs wanted to use the process to dilute the strong hand the deans had developed by linking them to planning only through the vice president. As university-level planning advanced and unit-level planning began (where the deans initially did not have a role), it became increasingly clear that the *deans should have been included from the very beginning* in academic program planning. As it was, the deans were in a strong position to disavow what emerged, giving those who were generally resisting the process influential allies.

Finally, a year into the process, the deans were appointed to the academic program planning subcommittee. This appointment coincided with the beginning of the process of taking academic policies to the board of trustees for their approval, an action that caused a fair amount of concern for the deans. Initially the deans used their membership to try to control the committee, but as yet another new provost began to move the university's academic program planning from traditional operational tactics to dealing with strategic management issues, the deans were slowly led away from their overt opposition.

In the strategic planning process at Carnegie Mellon University, Cyert (1988) tells us, winning support for the strategic plan was a time-consuming challenge. He reports that it took about five years to develop a university-wide acceptance of the plan, from the president to the deans, department chairs, and finally senior faculty members.

Calculated opportunism is essential in seeking allies. Since academic program planning should come after enrollment management and planning related to a campus-specific need (in UNC's case, technology), the key to seeking allies in academic planning lies in the academic proclivity for approving curriculum and other academic program changes. While trustees or governing board members will desire program priorities driven by the new enrollment mix and their curricular demands, deans will fight hard for control over academic program changes. Yet if governing board members direct that policies governing program changes should be forthcoming by some given date in the planning process, deans and faculty will be hard pressed to ignore or oppose this. To do so would be to forfeit their role as guardians of the curriculum. In this opportunistic way, groups can accede to the deans' desire to control while constraining that desire by a clear directive from the trustees or governing boards. In systems of higher education, the chief executive officer can act as an important source of such directives.

## Dealing with Destructive Factions

Dealing with factions requires a dual strategy. The first element of that strategy is to deny factions a reason to unite. The second element is to play them against each other or wean some of them to your side.

***Denying Opponents a Reason to Unite.*** The importance of not giving opposing factions a reason to unite is easy to overlook. In the UNC case, by excluding the deans initially, the deans were given a reason to listen to and ally with those faculty who opposed planning. The excluded and the opposed are natural partners, so long as they can share fear bred by exclusion, whether or not that exclusion is self-imposed. As strategic planning persisted in the face of opposition via strong support from the president's office and the board of trustees, the coalescing of opposition began to focus on the president—especially once the vice president who had initially excluded the deans had left the campus. By circumstance this focus occurred when the president was up for contract renewal. The coalition of deans, disaffected faculty, and disgruntled staff knew that if the students could also be brought into the growing fervor, destructive factions from the major campus constituencies could unite for a preemptive strike and use of veto power to get rid of the president and "his" planning scheme all at the same time.

The move to unite came a few months later, when students were upset over a ruling by the president regarding compensation for student government employees. The students interpreted their constitution one way and the president interpreted it another way. The issue was who should interpret the student constitution. A hot button was touched when the president used the clear and authoritative prerogative defined in university codification to overrule the student interpretation. A no-confidence-in-the-president vote by the student representative council ensued and was followed by a faculty senate vote of no confidence in the trustees (who were supporting the president). Soon thereafter, five of the seven deans demanded the president's resignation in writing. Reasons to unite had evolved and they were seized.

*Dividing and Weaning Factions.* Playing one faction off against another may not be as easy as it sounds. At UNC, faculty opposition would have crippled academic program planning unless someone who was open-minded and respected by the faculty resisters could lead the process. The perfect choice was a former senate chair who was also a former faculty trustee, a professor of biology, and an individual widely respected and liked on the campus. He was asked and agreed to chair the academic planning process. Since the interest of the deans on the committee was not necessarily identical on every issue with that of the senate representatives, from the point of view of the faculty factions and the deans a respected and neutral chair would moderate conflict and keep some balance among contending points of view in the progress of the committee.

Also, because the trustees had asked for academic program policies as the first step toward identifying academic program priorities, the option of stalemate was ruled out. The academic program planning subcommittee began to work directly with the standing faculty committees, and took to writing academic policies that dealt with such things as the curriculum and expectations of graduates. It was important to form a different alliance with standing faculty governance groups because the faculty had come to feel that if they were not involved in authoring these policies, they would become subject to policies imposed on them by the trustees. The deans were also resistant but could not veto the activity. Seeing how the process was going, however, some deans began actively to help shape the policies. The result was the emergence of twelve academic program policies by the trustee-set deadline.

Weaning resisters to one's side is complicated. Circumstances control the opportunity. At UNC, two ongoing enrollment management committees were threatened by the complexity of the emerging strategic enrollment management system, and by the worry that the new strategic enrollment management subcommittee (SEM) would displace them. So as much as possible the committees charged with the day-to-day activities of enrollment management were included in the SEM committee. Reluctant at first, they were weaned when SEM turned a projected enrollment shortfall around during the second year of planning. Made believers by success, they turned into supporters. The former committees willingly disbanded to be replaced by the SEM.

In another example, the resources subcommittee of the university's strategic planning committee was headed by an assistant vice president who was skeptical about strategic planning. The connection between strategic planning policies and key performance indicators (measures of crucial outcomes of campus activities) on the one hand and budget management on the other was not straightforward. Yet the need for academic program planning to guide academic program priorities that were *essential to budgeting* seemed a desirable place to develop a link and set the tone for strategic resource planning. The trick was to bring this about. When a new assistant vice president was named (during a major restructuring of the president's staff), she came up with the idea that the resource planning committee should function much as a legislative budget committee had been doing over the years, providing analyses and fiscal notes to proposals coming forward from the other strategic planning committees. Almost immediately, the cautious committee was weaned away from skepticism to participation, and it began developing cost scenarios for various kinds of academic programs in advance of the development of priorities by the academic program planning subcommittee. The desire was to be ready to attach cost estimates to academic priorities when those became available.

## Orchestrating Change

Eaton and Adams (1991) tell us that at Iowa State University, while their efforts to develop a viable strategic planning process were successful, for the first two years the faculty found the process painful and sometimes highly divisive. It seriously strained morale. They call their long-range strategic planning committee "politically courageous," and commend the work it did to overcome this adversity and move forward on an exciting new course of action. We mention this to point out that even though the politics of strategic planning can raise obstacles, solutions can be found.

### It Cannot Happen All at Once

If one reads the literature on strategic planning, one is quickly struck by the urge to be neat, holistic, and structured. Things like developing an articulated annual process or a mechanism for accomplishing some purpose are not infrequently invoked (Society for College and University Planning, 1994–1995). Neatness seems instinctive. If, however, there is a lesson from the UNC experience, and to some extent from planning problems elsewhere, success requires foregoing rigid structure and design with creativity and common sense, while staying the course. To survive, planning must be *incremental and opportunistic rather than comprehensive and neat,* as we describe in the next several chapters of this book. In short, planning can be very political, and as in all political situations, success requires sufficient support of coalitions to withstand resisters and those who veto change.

### Focusing on the People Aspect of Planning

Opportunism requires *embedding planning in people,* not just in process. The best-designed process, no matter how elegantly put together, will crumble in the face of opposition unless the key players are respected and skillful. In some instances, outside consultants can be useful in helping inside planners address and deal with these issues. But even in those cases, the ultimate delivery depends on internal talent being appropriately placed.

At UNC, control and goal achievement in strategic enrollment management occurred because the chair was an openminded, respected problem solver. An associate dean of the College of Health and Human Sciences, she managed enrollments for the college and understood them well. A quick study, she grasped what the consultant described as the essentials and helped build rapport with the old enrollment committees and the new SEM committee. In addition, she worked with the vice president for student affairs, who was initially skeptical and could have blocked a smooth beginning. But both people turned their energies to the problem at hand and brought about success.

The subcommittee chairs for technology, resources, and academic program planning each helped planning mature in the face of skepticism and opposition. The dean of the College of Business, well known on campus for his technological prowess, defused student opposition and desire to dictate how their technology fees (which were essential for change) could be used, and turned students into supportive players. The chair of the academic program planning subcommittee kept faculty within the committee on board, in spite of overt and serious pressure from the faculty senate to abort the process as flawed. And the assistant vice president for university administration and management offered leadership at an opportune moment, when academic program planning was stalling and the utility of the committee was being called into question.

If there is a lesson to be learned from all of this it is that talented people who can be flexible and opportunistic while staying the course are the centerpiece of successful planning. They can make bad processes do good things. Good process cannot turn bad leaders into doers of good things.

## Containment

Besides incremental, opportunistic planning and good leadership, the capacity to contain negative politics is also a important element of strategic planning. It is essential not to let resisters set the agenda by turning planning into a defensive exercise. Since resisters can more easily veto than shape change, they cannot make good things happen. Thus planning must be turned into a process that brings good results. At UNC, SEM brought revenue increases, and when resisters resorted to calling it beginner's luck, they stretched their believability beyond acceptable bounds.

When reduced to labeling or name-calling, resisters become carpers for special interests. When this strategy becomes obvious, they undermine themselves and corrupt their message. So the lesson is, it is important to stay on the task, to adapt the task to changing circumstances, but to adjust and deliver good planning results.

Ordinarily, it is best *not* to stop the inevitable. At UNC, when it became obvious that the faculty senate would require a vote of approval by the faculty, before the plan could go to the Trustees, the wisest course was to get out of the way and let it happen. The corresponding tactic was obvious: delay the vote until a plan that was more than very preliminary was in hand. This would increase the likelihood of support. But it would also take time. Therefore, instead of waiting until "the plan" was in hand to get board involvement, individual sets of policies were taken to the board and approved in separate packages.

This allowed those subcommittees, which were well on their way toward the development of their parts of the strategic plan, the chance to forge ahead. Board approval began with the SEM policies that governed the SEM strategies. Because these policies worked the first time they were used, there could be no defensible opposition. The board approved them and strategic planning began to develop legitimacy.

Technology policies were next. Because they worked, they were also approved. Besides, the results of these policies were already apparent to many faculty who were provided with personal computers and hooked to the central campus system and to external programs and databases such as the Internet. Those who were not immediate recipients of these new technologies were now crying out, not so much against planning but for its rewards. Once again, resisters were slowly being turned into carpers.

## The Value of Patience

Not all political activity is straightforward, developing logical sides of an issue and entering into spirited debate. One of the hardest parts of strategic planning is tolerating the opposition when behaviors become irrational. Criticism, particularly unfair criticism, can turn nasty and personal. It can dominate the campus dialogue and infect or sour discourse on other issues. It may often seem like the process is headed for troubled times. The best advice is to keep above the fray of rhetorical criticism, to stay on course, and to reinforce positive themes. Because as planning builds successes, the results will offer a better defense than any contrived rhetoric or defensive counterattack.

Finally, in the throes of early planning, it is an absolute requirement that trustees, regents, system leaders, or governing board members be made aware of what is going on, have a general understanding of how strategic planning is to proceed, and be willing to intercede on behalf of those charged with planning at their behest. At UNC, the willingness of the board to approve policies and to call for academic program planning policies, when the opposition could have scuttled planning, accounted significantly for the success achieved. By staying on course, the trustees let strategic planning mature until its fledgling successes became firm signs of effectiveness.

For institutional strategic planners, perhaps an anecdote might help make the point about staying the course. In a dense fog, a ship's captain saw what looked like the lights of an oncoming ship. He blinked a message to the other ship, "Change course to ten degrees south." The answer came, "Change your course ten degrees north," to which the stubborn captain replied, "I am a captain, change your course south." The reply came, simply, "This is the lighthouse, change your course ten degrees north."

# The Practices

# CHAPTER 6

# Concepts and Principles Underlying the Planning Process

In Part One of this book we looked at some of the principles that form the foundation of strategic planning in colleges and universities. In Part Two we look at application models that planners can use to develop an effective strategic planning process. In this chapter we concentrate on the description of the overall theoretical model, called the *strategic planning engine*, which identifies several of the components that form the foundation of the planning process. With this *theory* in place we then develop the *process* of implementing strategic planning, beginning in Chapter Seven, where we discuss several key steps required to take a campus through the basic strategic planning process, as well as a few case examples. In succeeding chapters we go into more detail about the staffing and structuring of various committees, about the interplay between strategic planning and the central campus, and about several specific operational areas within which strategic planning occurs.

## The Strategic Planning Engine

The theoretical base we have used to develop our model of strategic planning is referred to as the *strategic planning engine* and was developed by Dolence and Norris (1994). Conceptually, the strategic planning engine links strategic decision making with organizational key performance indicators, or KPIs, as we call them throughout the rest of this book. The strategic planning engine is a ten-step cyclic method that helps complex organizations make strategic decisions at any level of the planning process. A model of the strategic planning engine is depicted in Figure 6.1.

The strategic planning engine provides a theoretically simple method for building the strategic planning process. It works equally well at the institutional, college, school, and departmental levels. It also provides a consistent framework that ties each of the levels together automatically. At the same time, it is effective in keeping diverse groups of decision makers focused on the most important elements of the organization's success. The strategic planning engine consists of the following ten steps:

1. Develop KPIs.
2. Perform an external environmental assessment.
3. Perform an internal environmental assessment.
4. Perform a strengths, *weaknesses*, *opportunities*, and *threats* (SWOT) analysis.
5. Conduct brainstorming.
6. Evaluate the potential impact of each idea on each strength, weakness, opportunity, and threat (cross-impact analysis).
7. Formulate strategies, mission, goals, and objectives.
8. Conduct a cross-impact analysis to determine the impact of the proposed strategies, goals, and objectives on the organization's ability to achieve its KPIs.

9. Finalize and implement strategies, goals, and objectives.

10. Monitor and evaluate actual impact of strategies, goals, and objectives on organizational KPIs.

In its graphic form in Figure 6.1, the strategic planning engine appears very linear, running from left to right and from Steps 1 through 10. In practice, however, the strategic planning engine may be used to integrate many appropriate, previously developed elements and practices that the organization has already identified and implemented. Many colleges and universities already have a set of management objectives that they can easily plug into the engine's evaluation chart. For example, a Total Quality Management undertaking or the annual budget process most likely have already identified and defined a set of KPIs that are crucial to the overall efficiency, operation, and effectiveness of the institution. Other ideas that also translate easily into KPIs may have been included in requests during the annual budgeting process or through program change proposals. It is also likely that a college or university will have conducted a partial environmental analysis during program review or accreditation self-study. All of these can be plugged into the model and run without the necessity of having to reinvent these critical components of organizational life.

The analytical side of the engine is based on organizational KPIs. This is important, because the KPIs anchor the decisions that are generated through the strategic planning engine. The method is designed to help all participating decision makers fully explore and understand the relationships among the organization, the objectives it seeks to achieve, and the general environmental forces with which the organization must deal. As such, the strategic planning engine represents an effective method for helping to keep the organization aligned with its environment. Such an alignment is guided by the results of a cross-impact analysis, a modified Delphi technique (a hybrid group-decision-making technique) that gives the strategic planning committee a clear vision of how a set of factors affects

## Figure 6.1. The Strategic Planning Engine (SPE).

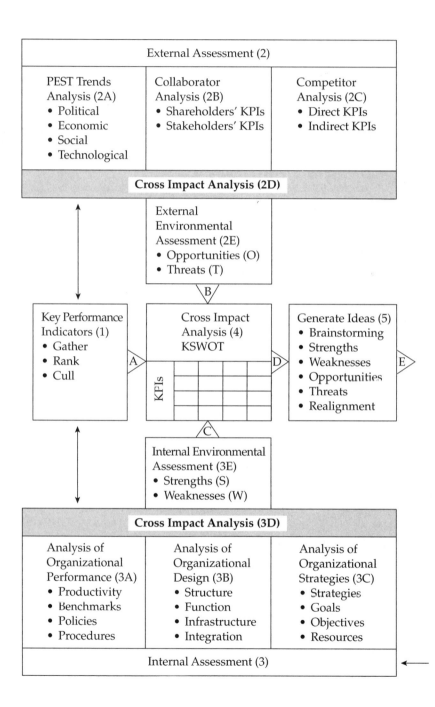

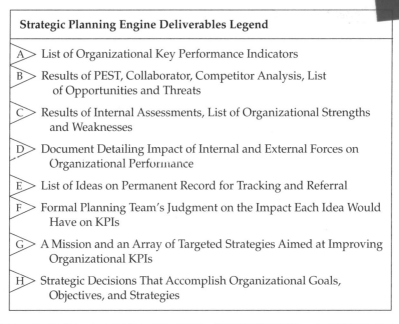

**Strategic Planning Engine Deliverables Legend**

A> List of Organizational Key Performance Indicators

B> Results of PEST, Collaborator, Competitor Analysis, List of Opportunities and Threats

C> Results of Internal Assessments, List of Organizational Strengths and Weaknesses

D> Document Detailing Impact of Internal and External Forces on Organizational Performance

E> List of Ideas on Permanent Record for Tracking and Referral

F> Formal Planning Team's Judgment on the Impact Each Idea Would Have on KPIs

G> A Mission and an Array of Targeted Strategies Aimed at Improving Organizational KPIs

H> Strategic Decisions That Accomplish Organizational Goals, Objectives, and Strategies

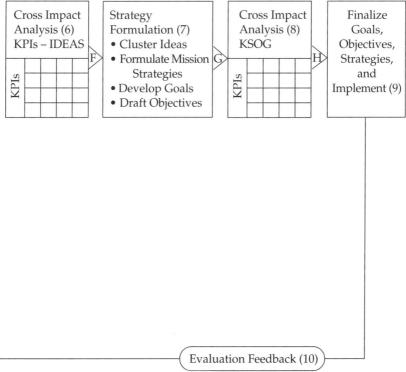

| Cross Impact Analysis (6) KPIs – IDEAS | Strategy Formulation (7) • Cluster Ideas • Formulate Mission Strategies • Develop Goals • Draft Objectives | Cross Impact Analysis (8) KSOG | Finalize Goals, Objectives, Strategies, and Implement (9) |

Evaluation Feedback (10)

*Source:* Copyright Michael G. Dolence, 1989, 1990, 1991, 1992, 1993, 1994, 1995.

the achievement of the organization's KPIs, by illuminating the impact of external and internal SWOTs on the organization's ability to achieve its KPIs. We develop the method of how to conduct a SWOT analysis more fully in Chapter Seven.

When participants understand the context of the plan and their role in its implementation, many of the ideas can be implemented immediately, because individuals and units can begin to align their focus and behavior with the needs generated throughout the strategic planning engine. Practitioners report that payback is often immediate. At each step, new insights generate new enthusiasm.

Before we begin the description of the strategic planning engine, a few additional definitions are in order. *Tactics* are the *operational methods that form the building blocks used to implement the strategy.* For example, the strategy of focusing on community college transfers to increase enrollments might be partially achieved by using a tactic of offering specific scholarships to community college students with a grade point average of 3.0. *Goals* are generally the *major milestones that have a three-to-five-year, or even longer, horizon.* An example might be reaching a retention rate of 75 percent in ten years (compared to a current retention rate of 60 percent). *Objectives* are generally *outcomes of no more than one year; they tend to be time-bound (due date assigned) and are measurable activities (meaning that their achievement can be unambiguously determined) that keep the organization or unit heading toward its strategies and goals.* An example of an objective that would support the goal in the previous example might be to increase the retention rate to 62 percent during the coming academic year. For the purposes of the present discussion, we will adhere to these more precise definitions for the terms *goals* and *strategies.* Throughout the rest of the book, however, the two words are often blurred into a single concept. We do not do this to create confusion for the reader. Rather, this blurring reflects the common usage of the terms in the general literature and in the application of management practices when discussing the overall phenomenon of goal setting or objective setting.

## The Ten Steps of the Strategic Planning Engine

Each of the ten incremental steps in the strategic planning engine that were listed earlier identifies a series of related activities that help build an overall planning and implementation approach for the campus strategic planners.

### Step 1: Gather, Rank, and Cull KPIs

To begin, it is important to develop an understanding of the core elements that determine the success or failure of the college or university. Unlike mission-driven planning, building a strategic planning process on this base ties the institution directly into those areas of planning that are most crucial to its ongoing development and long-term survival.

*The Central Role of Key Performance Indicators.* The realignment of higher education with its environments means that colleges and universities must recognize their roles and responsibilities in relation to a variety of internal and external constituencies. There really is no effective way of doing this other than to check performance against expectations (the expectations institutions have developed for themselves as well as the expectations of other constituents). Unlike mission-driven planning, planning that is based on a premise of measuring and checking performance against expectations provides a much more important and potentially highly beneficial linkage between the institution and its environments. KPIs are the linchpins that connect the most essential operations of the college or university to the strategic planning process. As Taylor, Meyerson, and Massy (1993) have suggested, the use of such indicators allows the institution to compare its performance in key strategic areas to key peers, past performance, or goals.

For the purposes of this discussion, we shall define a KPI in the following manner:

> *A key performance indicator is a measure of an essential outcome of a particular organizational performance activity, or an important indicator of a precise health condition of an organization.*

Examples of performance outcome KPIs might include academic-year-end undergraduate full-time-equivalent (FTE) enrollment and academic-year-end graduate degrees granted. Some examples of health condition KPIs might include total state allocations from year to year, public law as it reflects institutional expectations, the overall reputation of the college or university, and the percentage of scheduled maintenance performed on the campus during a given year.

The foundation of the strategic planning engine is a family of organizational KPIs. KPIs are precise numbers that have one and only one definition throughout the organization. Normally, a college or university strategic planning committee (SPC) will gather KPIs in a brainstorming session as the process becomes more formalized. The primary question for this brainstorming session is, What measures will our stakeholders and managers use to determine whether we are being successful? The strength of the KPIs is not so much in individual measures but in taking the organizational KPIs as a family of measures that compete and collaborate with each other.

*KPIs as measures of essential outcomes.* As the definition indicates, there are two different types of measures that constitute key performance indicators. The first results from the measurement of a specific outcome of an essential activity of the organization over which the institution has control. Essential activities are those that have direct bearing on the perceived well-being and success of the institution. Some of these activities may well be critical to the survival of the institution.

In preparation for determining what constitutes a list of most essential performance activities and the outcomes they generate, the institution needs to develop a profile of itself that details which of its activities are most essential to its survival and success. The research and discussion will include the financial performance of the college or university, the effectiveness of its academic program base, its academic reputation, its administrative operations, its patterns of communication, and its ability to fulfill the expectations of significant internal and external constituencies. The college's or university's central SPC should initiate this process and analyze its results.

As brainstorming sessions begin it is important to ensure that the data is as objective as possible. Unfortunately, many of the opinions that committee members give to develop the list of activities and outcomes may not be objective. It is therefore important for members accumulating this data to attempt to verify that the items that appear to receive strong support are identified and measured as accurately as possible. Further, while some KPIs are straightforward, such as meeting and balancing budgets, others are much more difficult to determine, such as the quality of the faculty.

Measurement is a substantive part of this process and it is important that planners recognize that certain KPIs, such as program quality, will raise potentially serious political issues. Nonetheless, it is important to develop a list of overall performance areas from which the most important KPIs can be selected, regardless of the political constraints of the campus.

*KPIs as health conditions.* The second part of the definition of a KPI has to do with the measurement of conditions that affect the health and well-being of the institution, conditions over which the institution may have from little or no control to a great amount of control. It may or may not be particularly useful to set goals for these conditions or to devise strategies that the institution hopes will substantially alter them. For instance, the final determination of what a state allocates to a college or university is not something an institution can set goals for, yet it is critical for the campus to know what these figures are and the trends that may be leading to their establishment or from which they emanate. On the basis of this information, the SPC can forecast anticipated allocations, based on past and current trends, and reasonably determine appropriate KPIs that will measure actual outcomes over time. Likewise, the public's opinion of a college or university is crucial, but it is usually resistant to public relations activities conducted by the institution designed to affect it one way or another. Conversely, if an institution wishes to be considered one of the top ten in the country in a particular category, this performance indicator is measurable.

These examples of external forces with which an institution must deal reflect critical environmental elements that an institution must consider but which it may not control. A reality that many public institutions face is that legal prohibitions exist that prevent or limit them from even attempting to try to influence outside constituencies. Nonetheless, since these types of external constituencies can have a significant effect on the operation of an institution, it is important to identify them and then designate them as KPIs in order to monitor their impact on the institution.

*Establishing Priorities.* The activities involved in developing a comprehensive list of KPIs will result in a set of KPIs that on the surface may not be particularly useful. The list will contain some KPIs that are quite important, as well as other KPIs that are more fuzzy or not as important, or perhaps not important at all.

In order to develop an effective working set of KPIs, the SPC needs to develop a scheme of prioritization. As the burgeoning planning process identifies overall performance and health factors, it is important to also develop a common understanding about which of the factors are most vital, and which have effects that are more long-term (as opposed to those that simply measure short-term results or conditions).

It is not unusual to have initial lists that include performance areas and health factors that do not have long-term strategic implications. For example, a heavy disruption of a college's activities due to the sudden departure of a dean is not a long-term strategic issue and should not be on any list of KPIs that the process will monitor over time. However, a long-standing history of strong differences between faculty and administration *is* a strategic issue. Such an item should most likely be on the list, even though the SPC may not initially feel that it is a top priority. The ability to distinguish between short-term and long-term issues is related to strategic thinking and strategic decision making. As the SPC becomes more familiar and comfortable with thinking strategically, the quality of the KPIs improves and the process moves forward more easily.

In developing a final list of KPIs, the aim is to create a list that is short enough to be feasible within the planning process and yet important enough to be representative of the long-term growth and survival of the institution. Since most committee members will be newcomers to this approach to planning, getting a final list can be difficult. Yet keeping focused on such a list with well-understood time lines is one of the more important activities of the SPC.

*Levels of KPIs.* As KPIs emerge from this process, some will reflect the highest level of the organization and others will be secondary subsets of them. For example, annual institutional FTE enrollment numbers reflect the aggregated enrollments of the institution at the overall level. Yet within these numbers there are most likely several composite enrollment figures, including term, college, school, department, and course enrollments. While the university's business school would have an enrollment KPI that contributes to the institution's overall KPI, within the school the departments of accounting, finance, and marketing and the MBA program would also have enrollment KPIs that contribute to the school's KPI. KPIs thus form a pyramid, with the organization-wide KPIs at the top, the division KPIs one layer underneath, and the major unit and department level KPIs forming the foundation. Annual institutional FTE enrollment represents a primary KPI while the others are considered secondary subset KPIs. Secondary should not imply and does not mean less important. To the contrary, one can see that without the component enrollments there would be no annual institutional FTE enrollment.

*Characteristics of KPIs.* As members of the SPC develop the initial list of KPIs, they need to focus on several specific KPI characteristics:

1. *Measurement:* Are the measures currently available or must they be collected?
2. *Value:* If the measure is currently available, what is the current value? It is probably important to avoid a discussion of what the value should be or of whether the KPI data is worth collecting until after the internal and external environmental assessments are conducted.
3. *Level:* Is each KPI primary (highest level) or secondary (a contributing factor to a primary)?
4. *Definition:* Precisely how is each KPI defined? The unambiguous definition of each KPI is extremely important and should be developed during the compilation process.

In this initial part of the foundation construction, it is important that the planners take care to encourage patience during the process. Often participants do not want to wade through the complexity of a definition, preferring to delegate the task to a subgroup. Yet experience suggests that delegation should only be done after consensus on basic parameters is reached.

Eventually, when the process links strategic decisions with KPIs, the result can be especially effective in aligning a college or university within its environment, prioritizing resource allocations and program initiatives, focusing attention, and setting a course of action for the organization as a whole. KPIs allow concrete specification of the milestones and indicators that mark institutional progress. In short, they guide the organization, ensuring that it becomes more effective and more competitive. Exhibit 6.1 presents fifteen examples of KPIs derived from actual planning processes.

*Beginning the Operationalization of KPIs.* Once the SPC has identified a suitable set of KPIs, adequately defined it, and appropriately categorized the list, it is time to calculate the measures for the most recent available time period. This is also

## Exhibit 6.1. Examples of KPIs with Definitions.

| KPI | Definition |
| --- | --- |
| 1. Undergraduate FTE Enrollment | Number of total units attempted divided by 15 |
| 2. Graduate FTE Enrollment | Number of total units attempted divided by 12 |
| 3. Tuition Revenue | Tuition revenue collected net of institutional financial aid |
| 4. Graduation Rate | Percentage of full-time undergraduates who graduate in four years |
| 5. Minority Enrollment | Percentage of all enrolled students who are minorities |
| 6. Placement Rate | Percentage of graduates employed or in advanced study one year after graduation |
| 7. Student-Faculty Ratio | Number of FTE students divided by number of FTE Faculty |
| 8. Recruitment Yield | Percentage of students offered admission who enroll |
| 9. Retention Rate | Percentage of students who maintain satisfactory progress |
| 10. Break-Even Major Index | Total revenue deriving from students in each major minus the attributable cost of the major department |
| 11. Average Debt Burden | Total value of loans divided by the number of loan recipients |
| 12. Student Satisfaction | Composite score from annual student needs and priorities survey |
| 13. Average SAT Score | Average SAT score of incoming freshmen |
| 14. Value of Endowment | Book value of endowment at the end of each quarter |
| 15. Deferred Maintenance | Dollar value of maintenance backlog |

a good time to add trend data, providing it is available. As they formulate this basic data set, planners should also construct a KPI update calendar to articulate each data cycle and identify when new numbers will be available, who will collect them, and who will be responsible for the calculations, reports, and distribution that result.

From this point forward, the KPIs form a basic foundation under the strategic planning process. It is therefore important that everyone involved use the same set of numbers. Any issues of multiple sources must be resolved at this point in the process.

## Step 2: External Environmental Assessment

Once the strategic planning committee has articulated the initial set of KPIs, it is ready to turn its attention to the external environment. The strategic planning engine characterizes the external environment in three domains: (1) political, economic, sociological, and technological (PEST) trends and events; (2) collaborators; and (3) competitors and the student market. The external environmental analysis focuses group attention on identifying and analyzing the impact that external environmental factors within these three domains will have on each of the organization's KPIs.

While looking at the external environment through the lens of the organization's KPIs, additional KPIs may be identified and added to the main list after appropriate discussion. In this way the analysis serves to inform the strategic planning process and *the process corrects itself* for deficiencies as the SPC works through the structured process.

*Domain Analysis.* The external environment consists of a set of domains, each of which either has or does not have the ability to affect the institution (Bedian and Zammuto, 1991). Using the cross-impact analysis tool helps identify which of these domain forces do, in fact, have a legitimate claim on the college or university. The institution's strategic planners can use the resulting information to begin to evaluate how the institution fits into those environments that have relevant claims or ties. The strategic planning engine looks at three of these domains specifically, using the following analytical methods:

*PEST trends analysis.* The first set of domain forces is defined by a PEST analysis, which evaluates *political*, *economic*, *sociological*, and *technological* trends and events. The purpose of the PEST analysis is threefold. First, it illuminates trends and events that may have a positive or negative impact on the organization's health. Second, it furnishes the SPC with an in-depth understanding of these factors and their effects. Third, and most important, the PEST analysis determines the degree to which the organization is properly aligned with the full range of significant factors in its environment. By focusing on changes in this particular environmental set, the analysis highlights where these changes can create misalignments unless the college or university takes action in anticipation of the changes.

The PEST analysis helps the SPC avoid three frequent pitfalls of the planning process. First, the analysis identifies weak environmental signals whose presence may not be widely felt or understood by the organization but that may have significant impact. Unfortunately, most organizations usually avoid this category of environmental factors. Second, the PEST analysis also recognizes that the importance and impact of each trend and event is different. This recognition allows the group to focus attention on the more important influences and to minimize time and effort devoted to less influential external forces. Finally, the PEST analysis avoids "paralysis by analysis" by focusing attention on only the trends and events that impact the KPIs.

By viewing these environmental forces through the lens of the KPIs (using cross-impact analysis), the PEST analysis is much more focused than traditional environmental scanning analyses. The focus comes from the process of centering discussion and analysis on the impact of specific environmental trends and focusing events on specific aspects of organizational performance. During the PEST analysis, the SPC is likely to discover that it has omitted an important KPI that should be monitored. That KPI is then added to the list and the analysis continues.

Once the most important PEST trends and events are identified, their potential impact on the organizational KPIs is assessed.

*Cross-impact analysis.* A cross-impact analysis is a technique for harvesting the collective judgment of the group and for focusing group discussion and supporting analysis. It is conducted using a two-dimensional matrix, as shown in the example in Table 6.1. KPIs are arrayed down the rows. The factors in this case are political, economic, sociological, and technological trends and events, which are arrayed across the columns. Each SPC member involved in the analysis assesses the impact that they believe each trend and event would have on each KPI. The appropriate impact is marked using the scale that follows the table.

Note that the scale illustrated in Table 6.1 is not the only option for scoring a cross-impact analysis. In fact, a number of alternatives can and have been used. The scale must accommodate a range of judgments regarding the impact of the PEST trend or event on a particular KPI. When conducted by an individual using the scale in the table, a cross-impact analysis might look like the example presented in Table 6.2.

Table 6.1. Generic Cross-Impact Matrix for PEST Analysis.

| KPIs | Political Trend or Event | Economic Trend or Event | Social Trend or Event | Technological Trend or Event |
|---|---|---|---|---|
| #1 | Cell 1 | Cell 6 | Cell 11 | Cell 16 |
| #2 | Cell 2 | Cell 7 | Cell 12 | Cell 17 |
| #3 | Cell 3 | Cell 8 | Cell 13 | Cell 18 |
| #4 | Cell 4 | Cell 9 | Cell 14 | Cell 19 |
| #5 | Cell 5 | Cell 10 | Cell 15 | Cell 20 |

Sample scale for rating impact in each cell:

6 = strong positive influence    2 = moderate negative influence
5 = moderate positive influence    1 = strong negative influence
4 = weak positive influence    0 = neutral, don't know, no impact, not
3 = weak negative influence        applicable

Table 6.2. Sample Individual PEST Cross-Impact Analysis.

| KPIs | (P) New governor's platform: lower tuition, lower taxes, cut state agency budgets | (E) High inflation rate and unemployment; new jobs require a college education | (S) Population increase in the region, birth rate increase, immigration increase | (T) Using technology to personalize instruction: 20 percent increase in grades |
|---|---|---|---|---|
| FTE Enrollment | 1 | 6 | 6 | 4 |
| Tuition Rate | 1 | 0 | 0 | 0 |
| Graduation Rate | 1 | 3 | 0 | 6 |
| State Appropriation | 1 | 3 | 4 | 3 |
| Financial Aid | 2 | 3 | 6 | 2 |

*Analysis of Collaborators.* The second domain of the external analysis is an analytical look at the organization's collaborators, including shareholders and stakeholders. Shareholders who own stock in a company, such as lawmakers, policy makers, and so on, have a derived responsibility for the organization. Stakeholders, on the other hand, are individuals and organizations who have a vested interest in the institution's success. Examples include employers, parents, students, suppliers, lenders, employee unions, special interest groups, government agencies, and professional associations. For public institutions, the state legislature and the executive branch of state government are especially important stakeholders.

This particular analysis first requires that these stakeholders be identified by name, then that the KPIs they use to measure their own success be articulated, as well as those by which they would measure the success of the institution with which they collaborate. A cross-impact analysis of these stakeholder KPIs with the institution's own KPIs allows the SPC to identify win-win scenarios, to pinpoint potential collaborations, and to recognize possible opportunities and threats to the institution. The cross-impact analysis for collaborators would be done along the same lines as the PEST analysis (see Tables 6.1 and 6.2).

The responses that are reflected in the results of each cross-impact analysis are the beliefs of one person. They may or may not be accurate or correct. At this point, however, this is not a critical factor in making decisions since it is the aggregated data that is used to inform decision makers.

*Analysis of Competitors.* The third domain of the external analysis is an analytical look at the organization's competitors. Competitors seek attention and resources from the same customers, suppliers, and providers. They are organizations that may have a "negative interest" in the focal institution. In the higher education context, competitors include other colleges or universities, usually those in the same geographic area. For state institutions, however, competitors also include other entities vying for state funding, such as K-12 education, law enforcement, prisons, health care, and economic development, to name a few. Again, identification of these competitors is the first step in the analytic process, followed by specification of their impact on the focal institution's KPIs.

These activities can take the form of competitive market and peer group analyses. In such a study it is important to understand the programs and services offered at other campuses within the same area served by the focal institution. By gaining such an understanding, planners discover areas of duplication as well as areas of underserved needs. By looking at the student market, such as high school graduation trends and the preferences being expressed by this emergent student group, planners can also begin to determine the needs of the future college or university student bodies and match these needs against the institution's capacity to serve them.

In addition to identifying important competitors, this analysis helps to illuminate their strategies and tactics and to develop a clearer understanding of how these practices affect the organization's own success as expressed through the KPIs identified in Step 1. Once again, the cross-impact analysis for competitors would be done along the same lines as that for the PEST analysis, shown in Tables 6.1 and 6.2.

*Step 2D: The Combined External Environmental Cross-Impact Analysis.* Step 2D in Figure 6.1 represents a series of cross-impact analyses that the SPC should go through. Each individual cross-impact analysis earlier harvests the collective judgment of the group, focuses group discussion, and identifies necessary supporting analysis. The external environmental factors that affect the institution's KPIs include PEST trends and events, collaborators' KPIs, and competitors' KPIs. Tables 6.1 and 6.2 each illustrate a component of the more complete matrix referred to as Step 2D.

Examining the scores in individual participant's cell can provoke interesting and provocative questions and discussions about what reasoning was applied to arrive at the assigned values. Why, for example, did the individual believe that the election of a new governor with a platform of low taxes, low tuition, and a commitment to reduce the state budget by cutting all agencies would result in a strong positive influence on the institution's graduation rate?

Open discussion of the perceived impact of factors on organizational KPIs is an extremely important step in preparing the SPC for effective decision making, although to overcome undue pressure on individual members, it is often much better to analyze only *group aggregate scores.* Group scores show the central tendencies of the group and avoid putting individuals on the spot by expecting them to justify responses. In either event, the analysis of the results of the cross-impact analysis provides a useful tool toward this end. Table 6.3 provides an example of the means and standard deviations for aggregate scores of a group filling in Table 6.2.

The mean indicates the average group response and the standard deviation indicates the level of consensus. The higher the standard deviation, the more widely spread the group members' individual judgments. High standard deviations reveal that more discussion may be needed to develop greater

Table 6.3. Sample Group PEST Cross-Impact Analysis.

| KPIs | (P) New governor's platform: lower tuition, lower taxes, cut state agency budgets | (E) High inflation rate and unemployment; new jobs require a college education | (S) Population increase in the region, birth rate increase, immigration increase | (T) Using technology to personalize instruction: 20 percent increase in grades |
|---|---|---|---|---|
| FTE Enrollment | Mean 1.3 STD .34 | Mean 5.55 STD .01 | Mean 5.9 STD .01 | Mean 5.8 STD .01 |
| Tuition rate | Mean 1.2 STD .46 | Mean 3.2 STD .01 | Mean 4.2 STD .01 | Mean 2.3 STD .01 |
| Graduation rate | Mean 0.9 STD 3.11 | Mean 2.1 STD 1.01 | Mean 2.6 STD 3.7 | Mean 5.1 STD 1.51 |
| State appropriation | Mean 1.4 STD .02 | Mean 1.8 STD .01 | Mean 3.7 STD 2.84 | Mean 2.8 STD .26 |
| Financial aid | Mean 2.1 STD .01 | Mean 2.1 STD .01 | Mean 3.3 STD 1.72 | Mean 3.4 STD .32 |

consensus. The cross-impact analysis group scores can also be derived by public group discussion with a facilitator seeking verbal consensus. This approach may not work well in groups composed of members of unequal status. In such cases, a variety of techniques can be used to eliminate status barriers, such as the use of a computer-based decision room or electronic voting pads that mask the identity of the individual and count everyone's vote equally.

*Step 2E: Identification of Opportunities and Threats.* The systematic evaluation of the external environment serves to identify specifically relevant opportunities that might help the institution achieve its goals, as well as to identify specific external threats to organizational success. These opportunities and threats should be carefully articulated and defined using the output from the cross-impact analyses. With the external environmental analysis complete and the threats and opportunities clearly identified, the SPC can now turn its attention to an analysis of the internal environment.

## Step 3: Internal Environmental Assessment

The purpose of the internal assessment is to evaluate the influence that organizational design, performance, strategies, goals, objectives, and resources have on achieving KPIs. Organizational units tend to use this type of review to make the case for more resources. This tendency should be avoided during this stage of the planning process. The analysis should be taken as an opportunity to describe the current state of the institution as a baseline. It includes assessments of three interrelated components: organizational performance, organizational design, and organizational strategies. These are detailed in Steps 3A, 3B, and 3C respectively on the strategic planning engine model (Figure 6.1).

*Step 3A: Analysis of Organizational Performance.* The analysis of current performance includes an evaluation of productivity, benchmarks, and organizational policies and procedures. The first step is to define productivity. The definition is then used to evaluate the extent to which the KPIs articulated in Step 1 capture productivity measures so they can be evaluated. The next step is to establish benchmarks. These can be the average performance metrics of like institutions, the performance levels of competitors, or a compilation of the "best practices" in the industry. Benchmarks help anchor the internal analysis and perspectives in performance standards set closely in line with external expectations.

Colleges and universities can only progress toward achieving the desired values for the organization's KPIs if organizational policies and procedures facilitate their realization. Ultimately, every organizational policy and procedure should be passed through a cross-impact analysis with its impact measured against the organization's KPIs. In this way the SPC can also assess the impact of each policy on benchmarks and productivity measures. A policy and procedure cross-impact analysis can be conducted immediately and provides a crisp vision of how current operations affect organizational performance.

Table 6.4. Sample Individual Cross-Impact Matrix for Policies and Procedures.

| KPIs | Academic advising is under three vice presidential jurisdictions | Information technology is under three vice presidential jurisdictions | Academic program development does not include service units | Recruitment and retention responsibility is shared by 22 different offices |
|---|---|---|---|---|
| FTE Enrollment | 2 | 1 | 2 | 2 |
| Tuition Rate | 0 | 2 | 3 | 3 |
| Graduation Rate | 4 | 0 | 0 | 0 |
| State Appropriation | 3 | 0 | 9 | 0 |
| Financial Aid | 0 | 4 | 5 | 6 |

A great deal of discussion is generated by such a review. As is evident from the example in Table 6.4, the interpretation of each cross-impact is case specific. Results pinpoint aggregate group thinking, which forces the group to carefully articulate the purpose of the policy or procedure and deal with its impact on the organization's key performance indicators. During the analysis of organizational performance, the SPC should at least review major policies and procedures in this way.

*Step 3B: Analysis of Organizational Design.* In this part of the analysis, the SPC evaluates four components of organizational design: structure, function, infrastructure, and integration. The point of this analysis is to gain insight into the impact of organizational design on KPIs.

For the purposes of this discussion, we define structure as the authority, governance, and reporting relationships that establish rules of operation within an organization. Structure is often diagramed in organizational charts and classified into organizational typologies such as hierarchical, flat, or hybrid. When structure is combined with division, unit, and individual functions and analyzed against organizational KPIs, some interesting insights begin to emerge. Once again, the group can discover these insights through the use of the cross-impact analysis, in the same manner as shown in Table 6.4. For example, it could be found that hierarchical, function-based organizational structures retard the achievement of KPI targets for enrollment and retention of students.

Also important is an analysis of the organization's infrastructure. Such an analysis should include consideration of the physical plant, telecommunication networks, administrative and academic information systems, and classroom equipment. Finally, analysis of organizational design should include assessment of how well the different divisions, units, and even individuals integrate their activity and efforts. This analysis should include judgments on the level of cross-unit integration and communication within the organization.

*Step 3C: Analysis of Current Organizational Strategies.* The SPC should next articulate the organization's present strategies, goals, objectives, tactics, and resources. This activity should be done through the lens of both the KPIs and the previously determined benchmark and productivity measures. Strategies are, or should be, long-term in nature, although they may have significant short-term impact on the organization, its collaborators, and its competitors. Resources are the fiscal, human, technological, and organizational inputs to the organization's operations. Once again, the SPC conducts a cross-impact analysis like the one illustrated in Table 6.4, evaluating the impact of current strategies, goals, objectives, and fiscal and human resources on the achievement of organizational KPIs.

*Step 3D: Internal Assessment Cross-Impact Analysis.* Step 3D in Figure 6.1 actually represents a series of cross-impact analyses for the internal environmental set, just as Step 2D did for the external environmental set. Each component cross-impact analysis harvests the collective judgment of the group, focuses group discussion, and identifies necessary supporting analysis. As in 2D, each analysis is conducted using a two-dimensional matrix in which the organization's KPIs are arrayed down the rows and the factors to be evaluated for impact on KPIs are arrayed across the columns.

The systematic evaluation of the internal environment serves to identify specific strengths and weaknesses of the organization. They should be carefully articulated and defined using the output from the cross-impact analyses. With the internal environmental analysis complete and the strengths and weaknesses clearly identified, attention is turned to an analysis of the external and internal environment on organizational KPIs.

## Step 4: KSWOT Cross-Impact Analysis

As a result of the internal and external analyses, the SPC will have uncovered many of the organization's strengths, weaknesses, opportunities, and threats. In the fourth step of the strategic planning engine, the strategic planning committee evaluates all of these planning factors against the organization's KPIs using the cross-impact analysis method described earlier. The purpose of this step is to measure the impact that each strength, weakness, opportunity, and threat has on the KPIs, as suggested in Table 6.5. The KSWOT cross-impact analysis (KSWOT stands for *K*PIs, *s*trengths, *w*eaknesses, *o*pportunities, and *t*hreats) should be a blind vote with each participant having only a single vote. This method mitigates the potential of

Table 6.5. Sample Individual Cross-Impact Matrix for KSWOT.

| KPIs | Strength 1 | Weakness 1 | Opportunity 1 | Threat 1 |
|---|---|---|---|---|
| FTE Enrollment | 6 | 0 | 3 | 4 |
| Tuition Rate | 1 | 4 | 5 | 2 |
| Graduation Rate | 3 | 1 | 0 | 5 |
| State Appropriation | 1 | 1 | 3 | 1 |
| Financial Aid | 2 | 5 | 1 | 3 |

having opinion leaders disproportionately influencing the vote. The result of this step is a ranked scoring of the external and internal factors that affect an organization's KPIs.

## Step 5: Idea Generation

With a common and focused frame of reference provided by the results of the preceding steps, the SPC is ready to generate ideas. The SPC should use another brainstorming session to solicit ideas on ways to improve the organization's performance as indicated by the KPIs. That is, the SPC members must think of ways to reduce the impacts of threats and weaknesses, and ways to seize opportunities and enhance strengths. Ideas can be contributed blindly and then listed without attribution, or simply gathered in an open meeting. One important rule applies: *participants must be free to say what they wish without negative comment by anyone else.*

Negative comments can seriously reduce the quality and quantity of the ideas. If such comments are observed, the group should move to a blind contribution process. It is also very useful to keep a permanent record of the ideas offered. This will provide a full framework for later analysis. Ideas that do not hold promise of having the desired impact on the organization's KPIs receive low scores and fall out of contention for implementation. Electronic idea organization programs, such as those found in decision support centers, offer an ideal way of generating ideas here. We have used such facilities for these purposes, and enthusiastically recommend them.

Ideas generated in this exercise give the group, and individuals within the group, the opportunity to voice opinions about things the institution can do to improve its effectiveness. This is an important step. Again, it is very useful to record ideas as completely as possible. Should ideas initially come out as broad concepts, the SPC will have the opportunity to more carefully define them later. Ideas without sufficient specificity will not make it through the KPI-idea cross-impact analysis.

Table 6.6. Sample Individual Cross-Impact Matrix
for KPI-Idea Analysis.

| KPIs | Idea 1 | Idea 2 | Idea 3 | Idea 4 |
|---|---|---|---|---|
| FTE Enrollment | 6 | 5 | 4 | 3 |
| Tuition Rate | 2 | 1 | 0 | 6 |
| Graduation Rate | 5 | 4 | 3 | 2 |
| State Appropriation | 1 | 0 | 6 | 5 |
| Financial Aid | 4 | 3 | 2 | 1 |

## Step 6: KPI-Idea Cross Impact Analysis

Once the group has generated a set of logical ideas, discussed them, and clarified them, it can evaluate them against the KPIs, again through the use of a cross-impact analysis, as shown in Table 6.6. This analysis helps to refine the ideas generated in the brainstorming session, as well as to cluster them into meaningful groups and determine their impact on the KPIs. The SPC must discuss and refine ideas that appear to be without form or specificity so that the group members can assign values from the cross-impact analysis scale. This is another example of self-information and self-correction. Again, ideas of little or negative impact will fall out of serious consideration in this analysis.

## Step 7: Strategy Formulation

The process of formulating the organization's goals, objectives, strategies, and finally the institutional mission is the culmination of the preceding six steps. Invariably a discussion arises about the definitions of these terms and it is important to take the time to be sure that all members have the same set of definitions before proceeding toward the development of strategies. Again, notice the positioning of the mission. Developing the mission at this point allows the SPC to do so based on solid information that will make the mission statement more realistic, fact-based, and niche-oriented.

Table 6.7. Sample Individual Cross-Impact Matrix
for Strategies, Goals, and Objective Analysis.

| KPIs | Strategy 1 | Goal 1.1 | Objective 1.1.1 | Objective 1.1.2 |
|---|---|---|---|---|
| FTE Enrollment | 6 | 5 | 4 | 3 |
| Tuition Rate | 2 | 1 | 0 | 1 |
| Graduation Rate | 2 | 3 | 4 | 5 |
| State Appropriation | 6 | 0 | 6 | 5 |
| Financial Aid | 4 | 3 | 2 | 1 |

With definitions secure, with the SPC comfortable with the analyses of the KSWOT and the Ideas-SWOT exercises, with a common understanding of the purpose of actions to be outlined, and with a group expectation as to the impact of these actions on organizational performance, the SPC can now begin to write meaningful long-term strategies. The SPC will now cluster ideas into strategies, develop tactics, and assign organizational goals, objectives, and responsibilities.

## Step 8: Cross-Impact Analysis of Strategies, Goals, and Objectives

Once again the SPC can use the cross-impact analysis technique to evaluate how the strategies, goals, and objectives will affect the organization's KPIs. As with all previous administrations of cross-impact analysis, group members vote anonymously and their tallies are aggregated into a composite matrix, based on the model shown in Table 6.7.

Once the group knows the final results, it should discuss the cells that contain large standard deviations to determine whether a greater consensus can be reached. Even if full consensus cannot be reached, the group should work to clarify goals, objectives, and strategies to reach a uniform understanding of their definition.

## Step 9: Finalize Strategies, Goals, and Objectives for Implementation

With the final analysis as a guide, the group can fine-tune its decisions and assign them to managers, units, and individual work plans across the campus for implementation. As part of this implementation, the SPC must give responsibility to specific operating units to maintain the information required to monitor progress according to the KPIs. Although these responsibilities may be spread throughout the organization, we recommend that a centralized support unit, such as an institutional research office, be given both a facilitating and coordinating role in assembling KPI results in a systematic fashion.

In practice, the application of the strategic planning engine must be tailored to each specific setting. The nature of individual colleges or universities, particular sets of opportunities and challenges, the history of planning on particular campuses, and the quality of campus leadership all affect the customization of the strategic planning engine. This tailoring affects the composition of the SPC, the balance among different parts of the strategic planning engine, and the nature of the KPIs, strategies, and goals that result.

## Step 10: Monitor and Evaluate Strategies, Goals, and Objectives

Perhaps the most useful tool in the strategic planning engine is the formal evaluation process of the institution's strategies, goals, and objectives. As the college or university implements its various planning components, it is usually enlightening to measure performance on a periodic basis. Annual reviews are very important, but reviews that occur more often help the campus management keep in control of activities and impact the long term results more directly. Table 6.8 presents a frequently used review form, based on quarterly reviews. Such a form enables tracking of progress toward achieving the organization's strategies, goals, and objectives. If performance falls in line with expectations, then the campus can conclude that it has

Table 6.8. Strategies, Goals, and Objectives Quarterly Evaluation Process.

| Strategies, Goals, Objectives | Q1 | Q2 | Q3 | Q4 |
|---|---|---|---|---|
| Strategy 1: (5 to 10 years) | O | D | D | O |
| Goal 1.1 (3 to 5 years) | O | D | O | O |
| Objective 1.1.1 (1 year) | O | D | O | C |
| Objective 1.1.2 (1 year) | O | O | C | C |
| Goal 1.2 (3 to 5 years) | D | D | D | O |
| Objective 1.2.1 (1 year) | O | O | O | C |
| Objective 1.2.2 (1 year) | C | C | C | C |
| Objective 1.2.3 (1 year) | D | D | D | X |
| Strategy 2: (5 to 10 years) | O | O | O | O |
| Goal 2.1 (3 to 5 years) | O | O | O | O |
| Objective 2.1.1 (1 year) | O | O | O | C |
| Objective 2.1.2 (1 year) | O | C | C | C |
| Goal 3.1 (3 to 5 years) | O | O | O | D |
| Objective 3.1.1 (1 year) | O | O | O | D |

Legend: O=On Track/D=Delayed/C=Completed/X=Abandoned

chosen appropriate strategies. If performance falls outside of expectations, then the SPC must ask hard questions about the strategies, goals, and objectives it has set in place and be willing to make adjustments that more realistically address its KPIs, SWOTs, goals, objectives, and strategies, to help guide the campus toward a successful future.

# CHAPTER 7

# The Planning Process
# in Practice

In the previous chapter we developed a theoretical model, the strategic planning engine, that provides the theoretical base for conducting a strategic planning exercise on a college or university campus and also suggests some specific activities for going through the model. In this chapter we will further examine the application issues involved in implementing the model, explore some of the foundational issues on which the planning process will be built, explain a process model for setting planning activities in motion, and take a look at the strategic planning document that is one of the usually anticipated results of the process.

## Developing an Appropriate Base on Which to Build Strategic Planning

As we discussed in Chapter Three, while a statement of mission cannot lead the process of strategic planning in colleges and universities, the results of the process can lead to a statement of mission. We will discuss this particular outcome in more detail later in this chapter. If, then, strategic planners should be discouraged from basing the planning process on a mission statement, they are nonetheless left with the question of what they should base their planning on. Beyond establishing key performance indicators (KPIs), anchoring the process in a future orientation is also important.

In the method of strategic planning we present here, the foundation of the applied process is begun when the strategic planning committee (SPC) articulates KPIs and creates a comprehensive understanding of the environments in which the organization exists, and identifies the common vision for the institution that campus leaders hold. This is done as the SPC develops its SWOT (strengths, weaknesses, opportunities, and threats) analysis, as discussed in the previous chapter, and through far-reaching and often soul-searching discussions with prominent campus and governing board leaders.

## The SWOT Analysis

As we described in Chapter Six, part of the process of developing the strategic planning model is the establishment of a clear understanding of the internal and external factors that strategic planners must take into consideration as they develop their strategic plans. The SWOT analysis is perhaps the clearest and most straightforward manner of doing this.

As we suggested in the previous chapter, it is important that the SPC conduct and develop the inventories of a SWOT analysis because these inventories help the campus better understand what it currently has in the way of internal assets and liabilities, as well as what it faces in its external environment. As Kukalis (1991) points out, "In order to be effective, a strategic planning system should be designed in such a way that the specific situational setting of the [organization] is reflected" (p. 143). Such studies often enlighten many of the members of the planning group, both by adding to the database information they were unaware of before and by developing a firmer, clearer understanding of the complexities of the campus.

This internal evaluation needs to take place early in the process (though it is most likely a good idea to set some time limits on accumulating and analyzing these studies), and members need to take these activities seriously. For example, Eaton and Adams (1991) felt that at Iowa State University the identification of key strengths and weaknesses helped their SPC determine the most important issues they needed to address through planning.

It is important that the SPC understand precisely what the institution is and can do. No college or university can be all things to all people. Planners must discover what the institution does best, and then determine how and where the college or university could use those strengths to match specific needs of the external environment. This is not particularly easy, for as Dill (1991) suggests, the postindustrial environment contains many challenges that colleges and universities have not faced before.

Strategic planning calls for the identification of a series of lists, including a list of the internal strengths and weaknesses that characterize the institution, and a list of the most critical external opportunities and constraints (threats) of those external elements that constitute the "fit" with the environment that the institution hopes to achieve. An institution must understand its own current abilities and limitations, and also have an educated feel for the expectations of present *and future* strategic constituents.

## Exhibit 7.1. Examples of Campus SWOTs.

| Internal | | External | |
|---|---|---|---|
| Strengths | Weaknesses | Opportunities | Threats |
| • Increasing applications | • High dependence on state support | • New international programs | • Increasing state scrutiny |
| • New technology building | • Generally deteriorating physical plant | • New governmental contracts | • Reduced U.S. support of grants and contracts |
| • Nationally known faculty | • Too many full professors | • New academic program areas | • Growing competition among state schools |

*Internal Analyses.* The required analysis of the internal environment, as suggested in the previous chapter, should focus on identifying the following:

1. The areas of excellence the college or university has been able to build and maintain
2. The resources it has at its disposal
3. The nature of those resources
4. Its high-demand programs and services
5. The quality of its human resources
6. Its academic tradition
7. The internal political realities of the campus
8. The quality and strength of its leadership and governance structures.

Such an analysis will lead to the development of two lists—the major *strengths* and the most prominent *weaknesses* that exist on the campus (or within a system). Examples of strengths and weaknesses can be found in Exhibit 7.1.

To be useful in the process, the analysis needs to be as factual as possible, and to carefully avoid impressions and speculation. As a result, these two lists become a simplified snapshot of what the institution is at this one point in time, and they also help to define what the campus is capable of accomplishing and what it is not. While this may not always be comforting to know, it is crucial for successful strategic planning.

*External Analyses.* The analysis of the external environment, again as suggested in the previous chapter, is usually more difficult. As Bedian and Zammuto suggest (1991), there are obstacles to identifying the crucial stakeholders of an institution, and to understanding their needs from and claims upon the institution. However difficult it may be to obtain this information, these elements must be identified as reasonably as possible. While stakeholders are numerous and differ in their claims and expectations, an inventory of stakeholders is necessary and should include at least those who maintain normal contact with the university. These groups range from legislators, media representatives, parents, lobbyists, grant coordinators, recruiters, marketing specialists, and professionals served by the university's degree programs to consultants, alumni, business leaders, governmental officials, influential community members, and the media. In addition, survey reports, assessment reports, accreditation studies, and other formal analyses can be found, and do add significantly to the database for this evaluation.

The results of collecting such data are two additional lists, of *opportunities* and *threats* (see Exhibit 7.1), which should help the SPC better understand the contexts and conditions of the institution's external stakeholder coalitions. These lists should also more directly enable the strategic planners to compare the services the college or university currently provides with the services it perhaps should or might provide. With this knowledge, strategic planners can decide how best to match what the institution does best with what the external stakeholders need or desire most. This process helps the theoretical method presented in Chapter Five to clarify how to align the institution with its most important environments. With this new level of understanding, planners are then in a better position to further strengthen the foundation for a substantive and effective planning process by ascertaining the appropriate vision for the institution and its most essential areas of performance.

## Developing Guiding Forces for the Planning Process

With a better understanding of the internal and external realities that characterize the college or university, strategic planners should then seek to determine the prevailing spirit or nature of the institution. It is important to add this information to the foundation because what the college or the university is all about heavily affects its activities. For example, a traditional engineering school has most likely developed a particular spirit, believing itself to be superior in the research and teaching of mathematics and certain engineering disciplines. People inside and outside of the institution know this, and work with the institution in ways that reflect this particular tradition and inclination. It would be unusual for the engineering school to change its nature dramatically as a result of strategic planning. Yet over time it may adjust itself to better match what it has come to believe is true of itself to what it believes it needs to become in order to preserve its particular areas of excellence and expertise.

## The Contribution of Academic Preparation

Many people who become involved with colleges and universities do so because of a deep commitment to higher education. Most of these people are committed to academic research or teaching and want to spend a significant part of their lives working in these areas. Because of the nature of the academy, many of these people have had to obtain doctoral degrees just to be considered for employment in higher education. This represents a major commitment on the part of the faculty and many administrators, and results in an enterprise whose population is highly dedicated and very able.

Yet because of the parochial nature of a doctoral degree, academics are narrow experts in specialized subject matter. They may be qualified in only one area or in a small range of subjects, but in those subject areas they attain significant levels of expertise. The doctoral training in most institutions is not simply a study of what is already known but includes where the field is headed and the research method necessary to advance knowledge. As a result of such preparation, academics are more than experts; they are also visionaries.

This preparation and shaping of the academic assures that the individual not only *conveys to others that which is known* but, through research activity, also remains active in *furthering the development of knowledge itself.* And while it is true that some people with doctoral status and tenure reduce or curtail their research, the vast majority of college and university professors remain active and visionary within their fields.

After the academic preparation of the faculty, teaching and ongoing research happen within the context of particular colleges and universities. These contexts not only provide space and opportunity within which research and teaching occur, they also have a dramatic impact on these activities. The academic environment, which persists over time in a given institution, shapes the character of the campus. Thus certain campuses are known as engineering schools or education schools or research institutions, depending on the strength of the academic departments found on those particular campuses. A combination, then, of basic academic direction found in the disciplines and the strength of certain programs can provide the database for deducing the true nature of a campus.

## The Contribution and Nature of the Campus

It is important to note that thus far this particular approach toward defining the nature of the campus is fairly simplistic and ignores the politics of vested interests on a given campus. Complex campuses, particularly large universities, tend to have ongoing political debates about dominance, which spawn factions that skew the campus in one direction or another. The competing interest groups have different understandings of the campus, and their views may not represent the overall campus. Such views must be considered even though they may not be particular helpful to strategic planners as they attempt to ascertain a more common understanding.

We suggest that substantive institutional nature derives from the long-term and fundamental character of the institution that has its roots deep in academic tradition and that characterizes the general direction in which the college or university is headed. Or as Lee (1993) suggests, if a campus does not have a clear understanding of itself to help guide the process, it will be tough to know or perhaps even care about where the campus needs to go. These *core characteristics* set the context for an understanding of why the institution exists and where it is best equipped to head.

With an understanding of these core, distinctive characteristics, the SPC is now reasonably grounded to interpret the internal and external analyses (SWOTs) in order to solidify the foundation on which the planning process should proceed. Such a foundation for strategic planning will develop discrete knowledge of how the campus is presently positioned to use its internal strengths to overcome its weaknesses while improving its interactions with its critical external environments with their complex demands, opportunities, and constraints. It is this level of preparation that needs to be in place as the SPC begins to build the strategic planning process.

## A General Process Model

With the foundation for strategic planning in place, planners can begin to concentrate on the process they will adopt for going through the theoretical model we developed in the previous chapter. In this section, we present a general process model that helps develop a framework within which the strategic planners can pursue application of the model within a given institution. We believe that the usefulness of a process model is to guide the implementation of the theoretical model. It can also help college or university strategic planners determine the levels of effort that will be needed, to schedule specific tasks, and to approximate the time required for the institution to work through each essential stage on their particular campuses. Further, this model can be used for planning at the unit level in the same way it would be used at the institutional level. The following list identifies the general stages of the process model for developing an institutional or unit strategic plan:

1. Select the initial planning committee.
2. Introduce the process.
3. Establish appropriate KPIs and organize key performance areas.
4. Survey the environment.
   a. Assess external opportunities and threats.
   b. Assess internal strengths and weaknesses.
   c. Perform a cross-impact analysis.
5. Share results with larger audience.

6. Develop definition and measurement criteria.
7. Measure current performance.
8. Establish five- and ten-year goals.
9. Determine strategies (using SWOT) in each KPI area.
10. Establish broad-based support.
    a. Develop appropriate policies for each KPI area.
    b. Begin the implementation process.
    c. Measure performance frequently.
    d. Perform one-year substantive review and modification.

## Stage 1: Select the Initial Planning Committee

The first stage involves the identification and selection of the members of the initial planning committee. In developing a comprehensive and broadly supported strategic plan, some difficult choices immediately present themselves.

This is the appropriate time to appoint the individual who will oversee the process as the institutional strategic planner. This person must be designated as the leader responsible for organizing the process and making operational decisions about how the process will proceed.

To help establish broad-based support, it may be desirable initially to have a large committee (though over time the size of this committee should shrink dramatically). Yet there are serious problems with large committees, particularly at the beginning of strategic planning. Experience has demonstrated that a relatively small proportion of an organization's population will be anxious to engage in planning. This means that a large committee may well include a fair number of people who are either not interested or apprehensive about the process. Factors of this sort complicate the planning process, particularly at the beginning. It is critical to keep committee guidelines clean, concise, defined, and in context. Nonetheless, it is important to have a broad *range* of participants in order to assure that each major element of the institution or unit is adequately represented, while at the same time keeping the size of the group manageable.

## Stage 2: Introduce the Process

Introducing the process to the group, and to the institution or unit, is the second stage in the process. Here outside assistance can be very valuable in providing substantive training for the planning group and in providing information to the general campus through activities such as open forums. Using someone from the outside who has intimate knowledge about how the process works and where it leads is an invaluable asset in getting the planning process moving. After this initial introduction is done the SPC should immediately begin developing the institutional plan and testing the knowledge gained directly against the internal and external environmental realities of its particular campus.

## Stage 3: Establish Appropriate KPIs and Organize Key Performance Areas

This stage involves establishing KPIs. Again, *key performance indicators are measures of institutional or unit outcomes or measures of institutional health that are critical to the institution's growth and long-term survival.* In developing the basis for planning it is important to answer the question, What are the most important outcomes of our performance in this institution (unit)? This question, along with What are the most critical health factors that we must be aware of and attempt to control? provide the framework for establishing campuswide or unitwide KPIs.

Procedurally, another important question is, How many KPIs should a campus or unit identify? The answer to this question is that the appropriate number of KPIs is situational. Having too many KPIs leads to a cumbersome and complicated process, which normally will create frustration and early disenchantment with the process because the scope of activities needed to build a plan with many KPIs will be far greater than anyone has time or patience to attempt. Conversely, having too few KPIs means there are not enough performance guidelines for developing and monitoring a cohesive strategy. From our experience at UNC it appears that an initial set of 12 to 20 university-wide KPIs is reasonable, providing that the group believes the items included encompass an adequate range of important organizational outcomes and related measures. Dolence and Norris (1994) give an example of a much smaller institution, Illinois Benedictine College, which had 32 KPIs, and Bottrill and Borden (1994) compiled a list of more than 250 potential performance indicators in twenty-two different categories that might apply on one campus or another. Experience has also shown that once the plan is implemented, the number of KPIs will tend to grow as the various areas of planning become more sophisticated and as related or emerging issues are identified that are considered important to measure and control.

## Stage 4: Survey the Environment

The fourth stage involves surveying the institution's or unit's internal and external environments, as described earlier in this chapter. The time involved in performing these activities can be managed, particularly if the central group already has a sense of which internal and external environmental forces are shaping the activities of the college or university. But beyond that, the *process* of inventorying these internal and external forces, calculating their effects on the direction of the institution, and identifying cause and effect relationships is a very useful exercise for the institution or unit beyond the strategic planning process. The SPC needs to refine the initial findings, both to identify and validate data and to prioritize results, in order to establish which environmental elements are most critical to the health and well-being of the institution or unit. Based on these refined lists, the planning group can then list the institution or unit's internal strengths and weaknesses and external opportunities and threats.

The next part of this stage is more fully described in Chapter Five, but it involves relating the organization's SWOTs with its KPIs. We have suggested that planners use the analytic matrix tool, cross-impact analysis, to develop a broad look at how the items developed by the SWOT analysis impact each of the KPIs. We have also suggested, in Chapter Six, the use of electronic idea organization programs, such as those found in decision support centers. Such programs can be used to develop these analyses in a modified Delphi technique. The authors have had great success both with developing the basic lists through electronic brainstorming and with developing the cross-impact analysis with the matrix program). The results provide one of the first "Eureka!" moments for a planning group as specific cause and effect relationships emerge from the exercise. At this point, both SWOTs and KPIs can be refined further and the results can be used to form the base for the basic strategic plan.

## Stage 5: Share Results with Larger Audience

In Stage 5 these initial results are shared with the broader campus community, to help assure far-reaching communication and to engender support. The internal and external analyses conducted in Stage 4 often provide important new information regarding the internal and external positioning of the campus and what is going on around it that dramatically affects it. This is important information for the entire campus community (or unit) to better understand, and since it will form most of the base of the plan itself, communicating these findings and allowing for a dialogue with various campus interest groups at this stage is important to establishing a broader understanding of what planning yields.

The concept of KPIs is usually much more difficult to communicate to a broad community than the several other elements of the strategic planning process. While the concept is information that needs to be shared and understood widely, it must be communicated carefully so that the community understands in elementary terms what KPIs are and how they form the base for planning. Several institutions have used KPIs (or KPIs by another name) within their strategic planning structures. A recent review of strategic plans found on the Internet include the Iowa State University (Iowa State University President's Office, 1995), Anglia Polytechnic University (Kitching, 1994), Northeastern University (Northeastern University Strategic

Planning Steering Committee, 1994), Kent State University (Ohio Board of Regents, 1995), the University of Queensland (Wilson, 1995), and the University of Iowa (University of Iowa Campus Communications, 1995).

## Stages 6, 7, and 8

The next three stages—6, 7, and 8—develop the initial strategic planning document. These stages help those involved in the planning process to begin to think strategically about the institution and its environment. KPIs ultimately must be measurable, means of monitoring performance over time must be identified, and the direction the college or university hopes to follow must be articulated. Exhibit 7.2 contains examples of pos-

### Exhibit 7.2. Possible College or University KPIs, Definitions, Measures, and Goals.

*FTE Graduate Enrollment:* The measure of full-time-equivalent graduate student enrollments on an annualized basis (including summer, fall, and spring enrollments) as calculated yearly by the Office of Institutional Research.

| | |
|---|---|
| Current Level (1994–1995) | 3,544 |
| Base-Year Level (1992–1993) | 3,308 |
| Five-Year Goal (1997–1998) | 3,700 |
| Ten-Year Goal (2002–2003) | 4,000 |

*Alumni Attitude Audit:* The percentage of alumni who rated their satisfaction with the general undergraduate or graduate experience as very good or excellent, as reported annually by the university's alumni office as a result of a random sampling of 1,000 alumni who graduated within the last ten years.

| | |
|---|---|
| Current Level (1995) | 76 percent |
| Base-Year Level (1993) | 75 percent |
| Five-Year Goal (1998) | 77.5 percent |
| Ten-Year Goal (2003) | 80 percent |

sible college or university KPIs, definitions, measures, and goals.

The SPC will begin implementing these concepts by taking the entire list of KPIs and dividing them into relevant activity areas (further described in Chapters Eleven and Twelve) to establish areas of concentration and analysis by subgroups that may form around them. While these areas of concentration provide some definition, each KPI must still be individually defined. The definition should include an explanation of what the KPI represents and how the group intends to measure it. KPIs related to quality present special problems of measurement. But even here, broadly accepted surrogates can be used to provide approximate but acceptable measuring devices.

A base-year performance measure is important because it provides the benchmark from which planning will proceed. Some measures, such as enrollment, may be easy to do. However, measures such as faculty productivity may require new or surrogate measures. Regardless, all KPIs must be identified with a current measure, and from these, five- and ten-year goals can be established. As the plan is implemented, current measures tell how much progress the institution has made in achieving its identified goals.

The time factor of appropriate goal setting is another very manageable activity. With large amounts of time, the planning group may wish to ask campus groups that work specifically in the areas involved to conduct feasibility studies and recommend specific five- and ten-year goals. With less time and fewer resources, it is not unacceptable for the planning group to conduct interviews and develop a "best guess" set of goals. As a function of the one-year minimum requirement, best-guess goals can be used initially and then revised at the end of the first year's activities. As the factors that affect best guesses are identified, a basis for revising five- and ten-year goals will emerge and the resulting set will be more accurate. While measurements should continue throughout the year, making the changes at the end of the year will allow decisions to be informed by ongoing analysis.

## Stage 9: Determine Strategies

After the initial goals are set, the planning group is ready to engage in Stage 9, developing first long-term and then short-term strategies that the group believes will affect the institution's or unit's performance toward its desired goals. If the analyses of the college's or university's (or unit's) internal and external environments are substantive and realistic, the group will be able to identify several viable strategies. It can do this by matching the strengths of the institution or unit to the opportunities found in the external environment in those areas that are consistent with the goals set forward in the plan. All of the elements needed to construct the planning document are now in place, and the group can proceed to the writing of a short, approximately fifteen- to twenty-page encapsulation of the plan for broad internal and external distribution. This was the size of the document at UNC, and Swain (1988) reports that in its final form the document at the University of Louisville was just sixteen pages.

At this point, a note of caution is given by Dooris and Lozier (1990), based on their experience at The Pennsylvania State University. They strongly warn that the plan must not be allowed to become a "shelf document," but it must only highlight decisions and actions that will emanate from the process of planning. This is where many strategic planning exercises have been known to experience a sudden death. As planners at The George Washington University found in developing the "Green University Strategic Plan," the processes of developing the plan are as important as the plan itself (Green University Institute for the Environment, 1996).

## Stage 10: From Planning to Implementation

In Stage 10, as implementation begins the campus or unit community should be provided with the results of the planning process. Distribution of the document, presentation of forums on and off campus, and other communication activities should be conducted to allow knowledge sharing and additional contributions and advice from across the institution's or unit's community. To assure such feedback, the document should be marked "draft" or "preliminary" and identified as a dated piece. The general community should be made to understand that the plan is emerging and that there is opportunity to contribute as the plan evolves. While some may see this approach as a severe flaw in the strategic planning process, *to be strategic and adaptive to change, the plan must remain flexible.* Since it is impossible to accurately predict the future, the plan must be allowed to change as new information becomes known. Updating the plan yearly, or more often, helps establish this central tenet of strategic planning.

It is worth repeating that the time required to go through each of these stages is a function of the size of the institution or unit, the level of cooperation and motivation among the planning participants, and the level of knowledge and organizational skills possessed by the planning coordinator. In addition, different activities and results occur at different levels of a college or university. The next several sections help identify some of these differences.

## Expanding KPIs to Develop a Basic Institutional Strategic Plan

We made a strong argument early in this chapter that establishing a practical understanding of the nature of the campus is essential for good comprehensive strategic planning. Until a base is formed by a more enlightened view of the institution's internal and external environments and the establishment of a broadly accepted institutional vision of itself, it is a mistake to move forward in any other aspect of the planning process. With this base, and now with general agreement on a set of critical KPIs, meaningful strategic planning can proceed.

KPIs play a significant role in determining how various institutional members of the planning process will proceed to build the strategic plan. A comprehensive set of KPIs, along with an understanding of the general nature of the institution, its strengths, weaknesses, opportunities, and threats, give a remarkably clear picture of where priorities rest and what elements the developing plan must consider as the institution prepares itself to interact with its most critical internal and external environments. KPIs help identify the activities of the campus that the plan must address, where management needs to focus its attention, and in what areas the faculty needs to provide direction (such as on curricular issues). Morrill (1988) relates that the strategic planning process at Centre College of Kentucky developed nearly fifty measures (while not referring to them as KPIs) that would help the college achieve its goal of becoming a national model, and he credits the process for several significant successes in its quest.

What all of this suggests is that the strategic plan will lead to different, if not new, ways of doing things in every part of the campus. Of course, this is precisely what the strategic planning process is designed to do.

By focusing on specific areas of performance and institutional health, the strategic plan can be used to develop priorities for management action and for support of academic programs. It can also provide a basis for shifting resources to where they will have the greatest beneficial effect in the long term and to where advantage can be taken of relevant opportunities.

## Definitions and Measurement Criteria

We have suggested that the people involved in the initial stages of strategic planning need to establish the proper base before going further. Once this base is in place, the next steps can be taken. One of the first steps is giving an operational definition to each KPI and developing a related scheme of measurement. Also, it is important to recognize and use the prevailing definitions of various campus data in developing the KPIs. For example, in the case of program quality, KPIs may have a significant parochial and political element associated with them, and it will be important that the definitions and measures chosen be as widely acceptable to the campus community as possible.

Getting different groups involved in developing definitions and measures is an appropriate way of establishing greater campus buy-in and furthering participation. Though it may add time to the process, soliciting comment on potentially controversial items from groups that are the most affected by them will pay off down the road with fewer arguments, and will eliminate the conjecture that important segments of the community were not involved with the development of the plan. It is evident that in establishing a definition and measure for something as potentially controversial as faculty quality, representative bodies of the faculty should be consulted. Should particular campus bodies fail to act in a timely or constructive manner, it may be acceptable to move forward without them (though not particularly wise); but in any event, it is important to have asked for comment. Our experience has proven that those who are particularly intent on stopping or hindering the process use lack of inclusion above all other reasons as the major criticism of the process as it unfolds.

## Defining Strategic Goals

With definitions and measurements completed, the next step is to develop long-range goals for each KPI. While this process should be as methodical and accurate as possible, it is important to understand that the establishment of goals should not entail inflexible benchmarks. Initial goal-setting exercises may not exhibit high levels of accuracy or quality, due to people's general unfamiliarity with this type of process and to the fact that available data may not precisely represent a given KPI. So while it is important to try to establish goals that are realistic and reasonable, in this stage of the overall strategic planning process, absolutism over goals or how they are set should be avoided.

After nearly two years of planning at UNC, there was debate in the SPC over the willingness to change our goals. After some discussion, it became clear that we needed to be flexible. As we moved through the process, we could see that several of our original goals were not as feasible as they had first appeared to be. We were willing to make alterations as more and more information became available to us. Yet there were those who found this willingness to change very disturbing. They used this as evidence that we did not know what we were doing, that if we were not willing to stick by our original goals, then we were corrupting "the process." This attitude reflects the problems some people have in distinguishing between the deductive and unyielding approach of traditional planning and the need for learning as one goes into strategic planning.

This attitude also illustrates why traditional planning often fails. The basic fact is that no one can accurately predict the future. Goals attempt to do this, but when they are held out as absolutely what will, or must, happen at some point in the future, they are almost certainly fodder for failure. Yet while initial goals, particularly those of a long-term nature, cannot precisely predict the future, predictability can at least be improved through the accumulation and refinement of data as strategic planning unfolds. This is particularly true when that data is generated by the processes the institution has employed to achieve certain goals. By being willing to alter goals based on the analysis of new data, the resulting set of goals will continuously improve over time.

In our planning efforts in several college and university settings, we used five and ten years as the appropriate time frames for measuring goals. These time frames made good sense based on the level and rate of change in higher education and the level of predictability with which we were comfortable. The fact that the ten-year time frame also coincides with the repetition of most college- and university-level accreditation visits also makes it a convenient and reasonable unit of measure. This is why planners need to take care to be sure that the accreditation process and the strategic plan are tied together.

Toward the end of the first year of living under the plan, particularly if more precise measurement methods have been identified and are in use, the strategic planning committee will have better information available to it, and this will help sharpen goals and strategies. The campus should view this process as the maturing of the plan rather than as an indication that strategic planning is not working. If planners and the people they communicate with across the campus can keep in mind that strategic planning is a long-term process, then patience should soothe the campus and help everyone recognize that the process is constantly self-improving.

## Initial Strategy Development

Once the planners have established a set of goals that have fairly widespread support, it is time to ask the question, How will we accomplish these goals? The answer requires the identification of specific operational strategies, and begins the process of identifying the specific sets of actions various responsible groups throughout the college or university will need to put into place to achieve the goals. It is not, however, the intent of the plan to identify highly discrete strategies for the accomplishment of specific KPIs. Rather, it should become apparent that KPIs cluster into sets or categories based on similarities (see, for example, Exhibit 7.3).

As we will discuss at length in Chapters Eleven and Twelve, each institution should develop planning area categories based on its own particular characteristics and operations. For example, at UNC we determined that our KPIs fit very well into four categories: enrollment management, technology, academic programs, and financial resources. At other institutions, planning groups have chosen three, four, or even more categories, and not necessarily the same ones we selected at UNC. Each campus should choose a number of categories that makes the most sense for that setting.

Once the SPC has established the type and number of planning area categories it wants to work with, it can begin to develop strategies for each category rather than for individual KPIs. This is also where the SWOT analysis, done in earlier stages of the process, comes back into play. The planning group should examine the lists of strengths, weaknesses, opportunities, and threats to determine two things: (1) the relevant opportunities that are present that would help the institution achieve its stated goals in each category, and (2) the capabilities and limitations the college or university has that will affect its ability to

## Exhibit 7.3. Examples of Possible Strategies.

*Percentage of Out-of-State Students:* FTE out-of-state students as a percentage of total FTE enrollment calculated as an average of fall and spring final registration numbers.

| | |
|---|---|
| Base Year (1992–1993): | 19.5 percent |
| Current Measure (1994–1995): | 20.2 percent |
| Five-Year Goal (1997–1998): | 22.0 percent |
| Ten-Year Goal (2002–2003): | 25.0 percent |

*Strategies:* Increase out-of-state recruiting budget by 10 percent the first two years, then by 5 percent the next three years; increase out-of-state scholarships by $30,000 the first two years, then by $15,000 for the next three years.

*Percentage of Undergraduate Students Graduating with a Second Language Proficiency:* Graduating undergraduate students who can demonstrate proficiency in a second language on standard end-of-second-college-year language exams, as a percentage of all undergraduate students graduating throughout an academic year.

| | |
|---|---|
| Base Year (1992–1993): | 27.6 percent |
| Current Measure (1994–1995): | 29.1 percent |
| Five-Year Goal (1997–1998): | 35.0 percent |
| Ten-Year Goal (2002–2003): | 45.0 percent |

*Strategies:* Make second language proficiency a general requirement for graduation as of the 1999–2000 university catalogue; increase number of foreign language instructors by 10 percent each year until adequate coverage of courses is reached; obtain local business grant to build five new language laboratories.

take advantage of particular opportunities. Threats identify potential external restraints, and this information helps the planning committee identify relevant limitations for the various categories involved.

We are not suggesting "generic strategies," such as those identified by Porter (1980, 1985) for use in the development of business strategic plans. Instead, we are suggesting that the opportunities each college and university identifies as plausible for its own particular growth and success are what form strategies. Though it needs to be refined into a sustained action plan, each appropriate opportunity should also be evaluated on its ability to positively impact a specific KPI category and the KPIs within it.

## The Strategic Planning Document

At this point, the SPC can write the initial planning document. The principle rubrics governing this document are that it be concise and that it be flexible. It is unlikely and unnecessary that the plan should ever exceed twenty pages. One of the common mistakes in the writing of a college or university strategic planning document is to include all of the analyses and results of the various processes that the committees and individuals used in its preparation. For example, the development of the external analysis can generate many pages, with details about what was studied, the analytical methods used to interpret the findings, and the formation of the opportunities and threats. The same can be said of the internal analysis, the determination of KPIs, and so on. The result can be a major volume, excessive in size and detail.

There are two real problems with planning documents of this nature. One, very few people will actually read them, and the ones that do will find it difficult to identify the tenets of the plan itself. Two, it is unlikely that this plan will change, given the amount of work that was required to create the document. Neither of these outcomes are acceptable for a process that has carefully analyzed the position of the institution and that must remain dynamic as it continuously develops a schema of future activity that will help the institution grow over the next several years.

This is why the document *must* remain concise and flexible, and as Brown (1988) tells us, successful strategic plans are "always under construction" (p. 25). Brown also states that at the University of North Carolina at Asheville there never is a "final document," because the plan always represents a sense of direction more than a detailed itinerary. In the case of most of the plans with which the authors have been associated, the physical outline of the plan has remained fairly simple, generally including the following elements:

- Title page
- Table of contents and preface
- Introduction
    Brief description of the institution
    Concise environmental analysis
- Explanation of the planning model (brief)
- Discussion of KPIs within defined planning areas (including definitions, measurement methods, current measure, initial measure, five-year goal, ten-year goal, and critical issues associated with each KPI)
- Strategies for each planning area

Explanations are kept to a minimum, and the section dealing with KPIs is done in outline form. The result is that the entire document is easily readable, and those who go through it can easily determine the major tenets of the plan. The section on strategies does require a fairly substantive discussion about how the proposed strategies will impact performance in the KPI areas, but with some careful editing the writer(s) of this section can keep it to a relatively few pages. The result is a document that a broader range of people are likely to read, and one that the strategic planning committee can easily change, particularly if the document is always kept in draft form.

Illustrative of these principles, the strategic planner at UNC updated the plan and distributed it approximately every three to four months. At UNC, the plan was not professionally printed, which allowed for quick turnaround of new plans and rapid dissemination to members of the campus community.

## The Role of an Institutional Mission Statement

In Chapter Three we attempted to explain why a statement of mission was not the appropriate first step for building an effective strategic plan in higher education. While we believe this conclusion will apply in most if not all cases, we do not want to leave the impression that a statement of institutional mission is not important and necessary, or that it has no useful place in the process. Our concern is not whether to have a mission statement but when it should be developed and how it should be blended into the strategic plan. Collins and Porras (1991) suggest that a vision, which can come from an effective mission statement, is an important if not often illusive component of organizational success. Yet as Langeler (1992) warns, such visions need to be realistic because if they become too grand or too abstract, they will not be effective.

The greatest concern about writing the mission at the beginning of the process is that until the institution has gone through a rigorous process of developing a substantive understanding of its core nature, capabilities, and limitations, and until it has also developed a clear understanding of the external forces to which it must respond, the mission statement may not be grounded in reality. Placenti (1992) advises that an organization should conduct a thorough review of its capabilities and environment prior to developing a well-focused statement of mission. It is better, then, for an organization to develop a comprehensive understanding of its actual position in a described environment and of its connections with identifiable significant internal and external stakeholders before writing a statement of its mission.

The strategic planning process we have outlined in this chapter allows the development of this substantive understanding. By gathering and analyzing critical internal and external data, and then developing a clear understanding of the expectations of the institution on the part of its most important strategic constituencies, the institution will have developed a solid sense of its purpose. At this point, the institution is in a position to write a meaningful mission statement. Few college and university mission statements could meet this criteria.

Campbell (1992) suggests that one of the major values of mission is to help align the strategic plan with the culture of the organization. And while Detomasi (1995) advocates that mission statements can lead the process (in disagreement with this book's authors), he also states that mission statements can serve as a valuable public information and marketing tool (a view with which we do agree). By developing a sense of mission, he suggests, organizations can inspire a higher sense of commitment from within the organization itself. And as McSherry (1994) and Ray (1993) strongly suggest, mission statements need to be simple expressions of clearly defined purposes if they are to have any value at all. This use of a mission statement now better fits the central definition of a mission statement and can usefully serve as a formal statement for public consumption of the purpose and direction of the organization. This is important knowledge for those who will be affected by the activities resulting from the implementation of the strategic plan. As Calfee (1993) and Nelton (1994) suggest, mission statements can be helpful in getting people to pull in the same direction in pursuing common and well-understood goals. Or as Weaver (1995) suggests, from the governing board's point of view the mission statement is the institution's most explicit statement of identity and it defines the institution's character. A good mission statement can speak clearly to the concise mission of the institution, identifying the types of programs it will offer, how it will do that, the publics it serves, and the general societal results that will accrue over the long term. Gone should be phrases such as "a leader in higher education," to be replaced with statements such as "national leader in genetic research" or "excellence in teaching to produce the most comprehensively prepared, multidisciplinary, and innovative teachers in the country." These may appear to be risky statements, but if they reflect the direction and purposes that strategic planning has sculpted, then they should appear in the statement of mission.

Properly constructed mission statements can have an important external impact as well (Stott and Walker, 1992). Harrison and St. John (1994) have suggested that mission statements should also address stakeholder interests and sometimes even the interests of remote environmental bodies that can also exert influence. As Brady (1993) suggests, mission statements can serve as a marketing call to arms, because they can express the covenant that exists between the organization and its audience. Such statements may also have important value to several external constituents, including accreditation agencies, who use the stated mission of the institution as a benchmark by which to assess the institution and its management. If the planning committee waits to construct a mission statement until after the strategic planning process has developed the central constructs of the basic plan, the resulting postanalysis mission statement will be focused, concise, and evident in the strategic choices of the institution. Compared to the generic assertions that characterize many college and university mission statements, the postanalysis statement is a refreshing difference, and a useful catalyst for strategic improvement of the institution.

Finally, a word about the planning vocabulary. We have used terms such as KPIs, SWOT analysis, PEST, and so forth. These are exemplary and not absolute terms. Each campus should use comfortable local terminology and be flexible with it. For example, at UNC, as the process has matured and a new board of trustees has inherited a commitment to continue strategic planning and tie it explicitly to budgeting, KPIs have become "performance measures" and policies have become "priorities."

# CHAPTER 8

# The People and
# Time Involved

In this chapter we examine in more detail the two issues that immediately come to the fore when an institution of higher education makes a commitment to engage in substantive strategic planning: (1) who should be involved, and (2) how much time the process will take to develop. It is naive to assume that only a few people taking no more than normal committee time over, say, a full academic year are all that is needed to come up with a substantive plan. On the contrary, to be a success and to be truly participatory, the strategic planning process must involve representation from every major area on the campus, and it will entail a considerable amount of time to go through the processes described in the previous chapter. This chapter attempts to clarify the specifics about the people and time commitments involved, to help potential strategic planners in colleges and universities better understand the extent of campus participation that is required to accomplish a meaningful and effective strategic plan.

## The Actors and Their Roles

There are two major considerations that those who initiate strategic planning need to have in mind when selecting individuals to serve in some aspect of the strategic planning process. First, the individuals selected need to be willing and motivated to go through the strategic planning process; and second, they must be able to contribute—meaning they need to have the knowledge or the structural power to help assure that the plan not only will be built on a solid foundation but also will have a good chance of being implemented.

### Willingness and Motivation

If they are to give their time and talent, everyone who is involved in the process of strategic planning needs to feel that any new committee they take on is truly important. They may also, according to Cope (1989), want a say in changes that may affect them. Unfortunately, strategic planning often represents only another set of committee meetings and assignments that fall into the category of matters not as important as publishing or teaching—the accepted primary activities of the institution. One of the first imperatives of the process is to help convince the members of the campus of the importance of strategic planning. As more and more campus constituents come to understand this, and to understand the impact it will have on their long-term association with the college or university, some gradually become willing to get involved personally. Yet as Bruton and Hildreth (1993) suggest, it is also important that the people selected to serve on the SPC possess a strong external orientation if the committees are to have a membership base that is strongly committed to planning.

Swain (1988) was specific about who should be involved with strategic planning at the University of Louisville. He encouraged the faculty senate to select faculty participants who were known to be imaginative and perceptive, and whose perspectives were known to be university-wide. As he reports, after some protracted discussions the faculty senate agreed to this approach, though reluctantly. Swain recognized the importance of having the right people on the central planning committee, even though his particular method of getting them might not work on other campuses.

## The Role of the Institutional CEO

An essential ingredient for establishing campuswide acceptance of the process is leadership. In strategic planning, it is usual that the institutional president or chancellor will play a highly visible role, and provide campuswide legitimacy, importance, and urgency to the process. This public role is very important, and keeping the issue at the forefront and as a major university-wide issue can be done best by a person in this position.

As Rothschild (1992) warns, however, it takes a certain type of leader to be effective in the development of strategy. This person will be critical not only to the development of the plan but also in the successful implementation of it (Veliyath and Shortell, 1993; Thomas, Litschert, and Ramaswamy, 1991). Also, as Das (1991) has suggested, it is important that this person be someone who has a good understanding of the institution's long-term future needs because such a person's assessment of realistic long-range objectives and goals are extremely valuable. The president or chancellor must also be active in the actual development of the plan. This can best be accomplished by being a member, but most likely not the chair, of the institution's strategic planning committee (SPC), and also by serving as the bridge between the institution and its governing board. To effectively fulfill this role, the president or chancellor must have a working knowledge of the major elements of strategic planning and be comfortable with the structure of the committee that will carry out planning activities.

Perhaps more important than *leadership by status* is the president's or chancellor's *leadership through posing issues*. For example, a president or chancellor can play a useful role by surfacing a statement of vision or making a number of speeches, both on and off campus, in which some of the significant issues before the campus are posed and probed. The contribution of these activities is not so much to offer answers as to raise questions about the character of the institution, its honored traditions, its new opportunities, the dangers to its well-being, and other challenges that the campus should address through planning. At the same time, however, it is important to reinforce that the plan itself has not yet been written and that therefore additional input would be meaningless. Such charges are common, and need to be defused as quickly as possible.

In all of this activity, the CEO must refrain from personally leading the process, especially on a recalcitrant campus. Otherwise, the plan will become the president's or chancellor's plan, and the CEO will be vulnerable to attack, and both the CEO and the plan could fail. Planning involves high stakes and CEOs should be mindful of this.

## The Role of the Other Primary Actors

Expertise is also important. The president or chancellor should not be the chief planner because of the amount of time required, because planning serves decision making by offering options and those who generate options typically should not be the ones to decide among them, and because the high visibility and status of the president or chancellor may work against making sure that the process is participatory. One alternative approach is to identify a respected faculty member who has the technical knowledge to guide planning, and have that person lead the effort. Northeastern University's SPC was chaired by a senior faculty member, a strategy that demonstrated several positive results (Northeastern University Strategic Planning Steering Committee, 1994). Before the choice is made, broad consultation should occur to assure general acceptance of the person's leadership as coordinator of planning.

Why a faculty member? One reason is that strategic planning on a college or university campus will inevitably involve the academic community because teaching and research are at the heart of higher education. Faculty can identify and weigh the developments and forces that threaten the core enterprise, so it is important that the questions and issues in strategic planning surface from, and be resolved by, the institution's faculty. Nutt and Backoff (1992) argue that the failure to identify and articulate these core issues is a prime cause of organizational decline. Identifying these issues is also an important way to bring the faculty and administration together in a collaborative manner, and collaboration is an essential ingredient for successful strategic planning in a participatory atmosphere. Swain (1988) reports that one of the clear successes at the University of Louisville was a faculty-chaired environmental assessment group that developed a comprehensive report of opportunities and dangerous pitfalls. The report was comprehensive enough to serve as a major determining factor in the university's strategic planning process.

Furthermore, administrative persons or units with traditional planning expertise should not serve as the lead. For example, offices of institutional research or other usual sources of routine institutional planning have too much at stake in their bureaucratic roles to give the appearance of openness essential for trust and acceptance of the strategic planning effort. Moreover, it is strongly argued in the literature that the range of issues that institutions consider should be broad and inclusive so that the unconventional can be considered and knee-jerk or traditional concepts do not automatically shape strategic considerations (Nutt and Backoff, 1992). As scholars, faculty are open to the unthinkable, and are one important source of new ideas. Moreover, their leadership can also bring legitimacy to the process and a sense that reason and the thoughtful criticism that attends good scholarship will guide the process and assure that planning will be relevant and useful. Staff and students can also contribute and should be active participants. But leadership by those who drive the enterprise of research and teaching is the key to success. The conventional administrative planning and research bureaucracy can best support this strategic effort by serving as planning committee staff and by providing a data-sifting resource for it.

## The Role of Committee Chairs

Committee chairs are crucial players as the planning process unfolds. They provide ongoing leadership as a campus moves from an idea to a plan and then on to strategic management. As a consequence, they should be respected for their acumen, they should appear fair-minded and evenhanded, and they should be recognized as knowledgeable about the substance of the committee's work. For example, the chair of a technology committee should not be hostile to or illiterate about computers or telecommunications. The chair of budgeting and resources must understand spreadsheets and budget reports well enough to have her or his leadership accepted by the range of expertise resident in the committee's membership.

Though the chair is critical to the process, he or she should not dominate the committee. An effective chair is one who can bring out the talents of a committee and focus them on the planning issues that are before them. Whenever possible, the chair should be a faculty member, to help broaden support of planning among faculty.

## The Choosing of Committee Members

The selection of committee members takes some careful thought. Typically, campus constituents want their own representatives, especially on those subcommittees that will deal with their program or area of the university. Turf can lead to *committee surfers*—people who have to be on every key subcommittee. Such people may or may not be helpful to the strategic planning process, and caution is the watchword when selecting people to serve.

Representativeness is important. Since an effective strategic plan will touch all parts of the campus, all sectors need to have a direct voice or be involved in some fashion. In forming the SPC, it is desirable to have at least the macro units represented (*macro* meaning faculty, administration, staff, students, and other appropriate categories). This selection process can prove to be rather delicate, as individuals from across the campus are selected and a determination is made that these individuals are truly "representative." For example, we discovered that at the University of Northern Colorado (UNC) differences among the faculty members and disciplines led to conflict when individuals from one college were selected to represent faculty from other colleges. Allowing the macro groups to select their own representatives, however, did prove to lessen the problem, or at least to move it away from being an administrative decision and toward being a selection process that was acceptable to the relevant constituency.

Membership should be driven by the ability to contribute, to keep issues broadly inclusive, and to seek the unusual rather than the comfortable alternative (Schön, 1983). Tolerance of ambiguity is also important. If people rush to closure, they will overlook the less obvious or the more creative alternative. This is not easily accomplished, because office or status often dictates the expected or automatic appointee. The best mind or the most dependable person is not always the student body president or the staff organization chair. With faculty this selection process can be especially difficult if the handbook or rules center on the prerogatives of the faculty senate. Such elected bodies often are not able to be flexible about appointments, so each campus would do well to understand the constraints of rule and practice that will affect how people accept the appointed committees and how capable these committees are for the task at hand.

Students and staff can contribute in important ways. Students see the effects of policy and practice, sometimes better than others. As the transient users of education, they have expectations, perceptions, and ideas that are useful and that can help unveil the linkages between learning and the external environment. They compete for jobs and are good sources regarding the excellence of programs or the types of courses needed. Since staff service both faculty and students, they often have very useful insights, especially regarding practices and procedures. They see students and faculty come and go; they often advise and have to fix things when practices break down;

and because they recruit and orient students, they have important perspectives about the outside world that others may overlook. Of special value are active alumni and advancement or development staff. Their interaction with key audiences off campus makes them particularly useful sources of external perceptions about successes and shortcomings.

The chairs of the planning subcommittees should help identify committee membership from among the campus constituencies. But the mix that results must include a broad pool of talent to take on the committee's planning tasks effectively. Normally, administrative staff should be used largely in support and ex officio roles, unless their expertise is particularly well known and there is both clear backing and a solid reason for their full membership. Members will tend to come and go as work leads to changes in focus or as people move on, so planners should identify a core of capable, stable members as an important backbone amidst the disruption of changing membership.

The SPC, in which central responsibility rests for developing the institutional strategic plan, should be where formal constituent representation takes place. Yet this should be done in such a way that does not create an unwieldy committee.

## Strategic Decision Making Hallmarks the Process

Henry Mintzberg (1994a) has stated that strategic planning should not be confused with strategic thinking. The first is analysis, the second is synthesis. Strategic decisions make planning strategic. Strategic decisions are those that align an organization with its changing environment. To be effective, a strategic decision must influence action at all appropriate levels within the organization. To influence action, the decision must be understood by those involved in the decision and its implementation. This understanding requires individuals to have access to information that defines the issue or problem, to be familiar with the context of the problem and its impact on the organization, and to be willing to recognize and act on an issue or problem once it is identified.

Strategic decisions occur at all levels within an organization. As the process begins and functions for a while, one challenge for strategic planning leaders is to make certain that the individuals doing the planning continue to recognize when they are making a strategic decision so that they can align their decisions and behaviors with agreed-upon organizational strategy. A second challenge is to ensure that the strategies that emerge from the process have a high probability of positioning the organization for success. A third challenge is to furnish decision makers with information that reveals whether the strategy is working, and if it is not, provides insight into the nature of the problem and its potential solution.

## The Role of the Governing Body

The role of the institution's governing board is especially sensitive, and planners must carefully consider how, when, and to what degree board members should be involved. Governing board members are especially helpful in developing the institutional SWOT analysis (see Chapter Seven), particularly in the scan of the external environment. By including them early, their understanding of planning will be enhanced and they will have better background for passing judgment on or accepting the results of planning. This shared ownership will also have the salutary effect of helping campus constituents to take planning more seriously, because the governing board members will be involved and visible.

It is probably not wise, however, to have board members as permanent members of one of the strategic planning subcommittees. Ultimately, the board will be asked to legitimize the process in one form or another, and there will be a clear conflict of interest if board members have helped create the plan that they will then also approve.

## The Role of an Outside Consultant

Outside expertise can be very useful, but it is very important that campus planners think carefully about who they want to engage and what purpose they want such people to serve. Consultants from the outside should be used only when the campus can delineate precisely what it wants a consultant to do, and the campus must be careful not to allow the consultant to dominate the process. The campus needs to develop its own capacity to continuously analyze itself and oversee the ongoing development of the strategic planning process.

Further, consultants can be expensive, but the budget for consultancy should be modest to avoid the attitude that strategic planning costs dollars that would be better used elsewhere to support campus programs. In addition, if consultants dominate the process, or are perceived as having sold a package to a campus, the natural inertia against change can be reinforced when tough issues in planning and related threats to the status quo are seen as the products of outsiders. The fragile legitimacy of the process will be undermined in the face of this kind of criticism.

However, consultants can be used effectively to help establish a better understand on the campus of the importance of planning for higher education. A general idea of what consultants can do is presented in Table 8.1. They can assist in setting the context for planning with planners and governing boards (especially to draw the difference between strategic planning in the private and public sectors). With their external perspectives, they can also support the SWOT analysis as needed, and they can often be used to help the campus strategic planners focus on certain areas of data collection (Pilon, 1991; Wergin, 1991). Finally, they can provide expertise not available on the campus in areas important to the planning subcommittees, such as technology or enrollment management.

Once the campus has developed some experience, and once subcommittees are comfortable with their roles, consultants should no longer provide visible support, but they can continue to offer valuable objective views to top decision makers regarding progress the campus is making in developing a solid strategic planning framework. They can be used as sounding boards for the president or chancellor, the strategic planning coordinator, or subcommittee chairs, and are usually just a phone call away.

Table 8.1. Different Types of Consultants.

| Type | Description | Value | Example |
|------|-------------|-------|---------|
| *Information* | Provides new information | Research | Marketing research |
| *Process* | Selects, explains, and trains in a variety of process methods | Leaves clients new processes | Accreditation consultants |
| *Production* | Conducts the process | Writes the plans for the institution | Laying out a new campus technology planning system |
| *Expert Technical* | Primarily an expert adviser | Provides advice on key technical issues | Technology improvement advice |
| *Access* | Opens up access to new resources for the campus | Increases the resource base | Head hunters |

In our planning activities at UNC, we hired two different consultants, one to do a focused study of UNC's reputation among alumni, governmental leaders, and business leaders, and a second to help us keep focused on the strategic planning process at the university, subcommittee, and unit levels. Our use of these people was monitored, and we streamlined our expectations of them so that both we and they knew exactly what we wanted and what it would cost. Despite what we felt were conservative uses of these people, one of the most damning of criticisms by faculty and students was the cost of the outside consultants. This is a sensitive issue, no matter what.

We believe that if we were to go through the process again, we would probably use the consultants again as well because we feel they did bring a series of important elements to the process that it otherwise would not have had, but perhaps we would have focused them a bit differently based on the knowledge of the process we now possess. Clearly, however, the use of consultants should be a decision made by each institution based on its needs, resources, and expectations.

As an aside, it is not the purpose of this book to endorse or discourage the use of outside consultants as an effective means of developing a successful strategic plan. However, since the type of planning we are describing in this book is not based on standard planning formulas, an institution can gain valuable assistance from an experienced and knowledgeable outside consultant who can avert false starts and miscues that inevitably add to the time involved in planning, increase frustration among those involved, and contribute to higher costs. As noted earlier, one of the more lingering and damning criticisms of the process at UNC was the cost of its outside consultants. While a campus may be able to develop a successful plan on its own, outside help can facilitate and expedite the process. Unfortunately, truly knowledgeable consultants are hard to find, and caution is clearly important in selecting someone who can help the college or university move more easily and effectively through the strategic planning process.

## Broader Participation in Developing the Plan

As we have suggested throughout, communication and broad participation are two of the essential ingredients to a successful strategic planning process. Identifying and working with those individuals and groups, both inside and outside the institution, who will have an impact on the success of the initiative is one of the major components of the experience.

### Internal Participants

There are a variety of ways of making sure that the process is broad enough to include more and more of the campus community. When the primary decision-making body is the SPC, individual members, who represent major campus constituencies, need to communicate with the groups they represent. The SPC might make such communication a requirement of members, just to be sure that communication does indeed go out. In addition, committee members should bring back to the committee comments and concerns from their constituents, and make sure that these are heard by the rest of the committee. This type of communication opens up the processes of the committee to a broader constituency. When the people in this constituency come to believe that they are being given good information, that the SPC is listening to their ideas and concerns and responding to them in an appropriate manner, they will buy into the process.

## Increasing Participation in Subcommittees and Units

Given the amount of work that goes into the development of a strategic plan, and depending on the size of the institution doing the planning, it may be advisable to develop a variety of subcommittees of the institutional SPC, and perhaps separate unit committees as well (especially in academic colleges or schools and other major program areas). The purpose of these subcommittees would be to (1) develop a more comprehensive plan, (2) include a larger number of people in the process, and (3) assure grassroot contributions to the overall planning process.

It may become apparent after the SPC has developed the initial constructs of the central institutional plan that the process will need subcommittee and unit planning to deal with large issues at different levels of the college or university. While being careful not to make the process too complex at the onset (a mistake we made at UNC), subcommittees and unit committees can begin to look at their roles within the greater institutional context, which will also add the benefit of substantively increasing internal participation. Timing and direction are critical concerns as these additional planning committees begin their work. Specific charges as to what the institution-level process needs from these groups, and the time frame within which they will be expected to work, need to be identified at the outset. Keeping the process simple and time-specific are imperatives. Further, it is important to let these committees know how their work fits into the framework of the overall strategic planning process, as well as the amount of latitude they have in deliberating their decisions.

### External Participants

A fairly common question is, Should we bring people from outside the campus into the SPC? The answer is usually no, though, as noted elsewhere, external members have proved helpful in strategic planning processes at California State University at Los Angeles and California State University at Monterey Bay, among others. The principle SPC of the college or university needs to reflect the institution's actual decision-making authorities and operational activities. While people from the outside can often bring certain insights into such a committee setting, they do not have the concise knowledge or responsibilities related to how the campus must run. The ultimate decisions about where the campus is headed need to be made by those who will be charged with the responsibility of carrying them out.

What, then, is the role of outside constituents relative to the college or university strategic planning process? One role that may emerge is that of adviser and critiquer. The internal planners need to identify the environmental realities that they must be responsive to in a critical way. The planners can then identify specific groups or individuals with whom the campus interacts within these environments. Surveys, phone interviews, focus groups, and modified Delphi-technique methods can be used to pose specific issues to such constituents and to solicit their responses and comments. Not only will this type of interaction improve the public relations activities of the college or university, but it can also produce an extremely worthwhile data set upon which to base strategic decisions.

## Committee Structuring

There may be a tendency for the designers of a campus strategic planning process to develop new committees or task forces to oversee the development of the initial plan. However, many colleges and universities are already plagued by a plethora of committees, and it is important for the success of the strategic planning initiative that the planning process not place additional committee burdens on a campus population that already believes it has too many committees. Though it seems inevitable that the SPC will become a new, additional committee, care should be taken when structuring the subcommittees charged with particular strategic planning activities to use existing committees whenever possible. Since institutionalizing strategic planning is one of the goals of the process, this use of existing committees has several benefits, including not adding to the committee burden of faculty and staff, and increasing awareness of strategic planning across the campus committee system. Also, as the process examines the structure of the campus, strategic planning may add the benefit of finding ways of reducing the number of committees campuswide as their work is coordinated and brought under the unified direction of the campus's strategic plan.

## Selecting the Institution's SPC

The most important constructs of the institution's central SPC are (1) that it be representative, (2) that its members be capable of having substantive dialogue with the groups they represent regarding the progress of the planning process, and (3) that members be positive about the potential of the strategic planning process within the college or university. Governance and leadership of the committee are secondary to these issues, although they also need to be addressed fairly early on.

Since this particular planning committee will have the greatest level of responsibility in the strategic planning process, its makeup, the training of its members, and the monitoring of its activities and progress are particularly important. Also, members of this group need to understand that of all the committees that the college or university develops to produce the initial draft of the plan, this particular group will become a permanent standing committee as the institution moves from Phase One, initial strategic planning, to Phase Two, strategic management. Based on their experience at The Pennsylvania State University,

Dooris and Lozier (1990) report that during the later phases of strategic planning, one can note a transition in how university constituents make decisions from an internally focused closed system to an externally focused open system.

Once the institution has determined who should be members of the SPC, it then needs to provide some level of substantive training for the group. This is one area in which we have found external consultants to be particularly useful. However, whether the institution is going to use internal or external resources to train committee members, this training should include instruction in team building and teamwork, the differences between traditional planning and strategic planning, communication (both within the committee and between committee members and the rest of the campus), the general format of the plan they will be expected to develop, and the time frame for planning identified by the institution.

## The Creation of Subcommittees

Again, depending on the complexity of the campus and/or the adopted planning process, the institutional SPC may form subcommittees. The advantage of these subcommittees is that they can concentrate on specific strategic areas (discussed at length in Chapters Ten and Eleven) and develop key performance indicators (KPIs), policies, strategies, and other related planning criteria. The use of subcommittees can prove to be a very efficient method of bringing focus and clarity to the process in a timely fashion. It can also extend the process to a large segment of the community by incorporating members of the campus who work directly in the areas that the planning committee's activities will affect. Cope (1989) cautions, however, that whole-system planning cannot be done in parts, which means that individual groups cannot plan independently but must work within the context of institutional planning as they develop their components.

The work of the subcommittees can either be focused and set to a particular time frame, or it can lead to standing operational committees that transcend Phase One and continue into

Phase Two. The decision about which approach is appropriate should be a part of the general planning process. It may possibly be most expedient to shift the responsibilities of several ongoing campus committees into a simplified strategic committee structure, or traditional groups can be trained to move toward strategic decision making and thinking about their areas of responsibility, in which case the strategic planning subcommittee should be phased out. In either event, it is helpful if the institution can identify up front its objectives about how the strategic plan will be integrated into its ongoing operations during Phase Two, and then communicate these decisions to the members of the committees involved.

## The Creation of Unit Committees

Unit-level planning, particularly in the academic areas, is a vital part of the overall planning process (Fountoukidis, Hahn, and Voos, 1995; Hall and Elliott, 1993). Unit committees perform activities similar to those conducted by the institutional SPC. The difference is that unit committees concentrate on the strategic planning of a specific area or program of the college or university. Just as for the institutional committee, the members selected for unit committees need to be representative of the community from which they are selected; they need to be individuals who communicate well within the unit committee and with the groups they represent; and they need to be positive about the potential outcomes of the strategic planning process.

Usually these committees need not be very large, but their size is a function of the size of the unit. For example, at UNC, the College of Business Administration had a committee of six, while the College of Education had a committee of fifteen. The size of the committees was based on the size of the units and on the level of complexity that existed in their program settings.

The time commitment and longevity of unit committees is an important issue for the institution. Whether unit committees downsize and become permanently a part of the campus landscape in Phase Two, or whether their work is transferred to standing committees that already exist within the units, is a function of the preparedness of the unit to strategically manage itself in the long run.

The work of these unit committees should parallel the general work done at the institutional level. Each needs to develop a sense of its external and internal environmental sets, establish key performance indicators, definitions, measures, goals, and strategies. Unit strategic planning documents will resemble the one written at the institutional level, described in Chapter Seven. Units also need to establish a parallel relationship between the unit plan and the institutional plan. The institutional plan will develop parameters in certain planning areas (enrollments and overall academic quality, for example) that the units will need to weave into their planning activities.

However, units may also be able to discern that certain institutional planning elements are problematic (improper or unrealistic institutional measures and goals, for example) and can then communicate these inconsistencies to the institutional planning group for reconsideration. It is therefore important that many of the people who sit on unit committees also sit on either the subcommittee that oversees their work, or on the SPC, if no subcommittees exist. An alternative approach is for an administrative structure to participate in and coordinate the separate efforts of the unit committees and the SPC. This process assures efficient two-way communication and a planning process that benefits from cross-checking to identify strengths and weaknesses of the emerging set of plans.

## Managing the Preponderance of Committees

It may well seem that we are suggesting a plethora of new committees for a campus, which will make the already complex and politically charged structures and operations of the campus even more cumbersome. At the beginning of the strategic planning process, this may seem to be the case. However, in the long run (certainly as the campus moves from the Phase One to Phase Two) the process can actually be very helpful to the campus in reducing overall committee structures and responsibilities. Moving from strategic planning to strategic management involves redefinition of how the campus is run. One possible result is that certain long-standing campus committees should take over the work done by the SPC; or the process may well indicate how work done by a multitude of committees can be simplified and combined into a much smaller number. Consolidation is the key.

For example, at UNC we were able to combine two different institutional standing committees that oversaw the various enrollment activities of the university into one strategic enrollment management committee (a subcommittee of the university's SPC). We were also able to combine three different planning groups working on the development and implementation of communications technology across the campus into a single information technology committee (again, a subcommittee of the university's SPC). In other instances, particularly those related to academics, the work of the academic planning subcommittee was substantially delegated to preexisting academic committees, which then became responsible for making the major decisions regarding emerging academic policies, KPIs, and strategies. Simplification needs to be a goal of the process, and this goal needs to be communicated to the campus from the onset.

Yet it is also important to be patient with this process. The notion that "you can't pick the fruit until it's ripe" applies to the strategic planning process and the move from Phase One to Phase Two. While some will want to get the organizing process behind them, to get on with writing the plan and putting it into place, it is important to move along as people are prepared to do so. Moving ahead too fast will cause confusion and frustration, and damage the process.

## Time-Line Considerations at the Various Levels of Planning

As we said at the beginning of this chapter, one of the first questions asked when a campus begins to consider developing a strategic plan is, How long will this take? Time is a major consideration, and planners need to carefully consider how much time they will need to produce an effective strategic plan.

Unfortunately, there is no simple answer to this question. The time required to develop a full college or university plan is primarily a function of the size of the organization, the complexity of the issues, the number of levels that will be involved in planning, and the amount of time that the critical actors are able to devote to the process. Cline and Meringolo (1991) tell us that, based on their experience at The Pennsylvania State University, college and university planners should count on an initial time requirement of from two to five years to complete its initial plan. Eaton and Adams (1991) tell us that it took planners at Iowa State University all of three years to produce an initial report. At UNC, it took four years before all portions of the planning process were finally operational. Conversely, one of the authors was able to complete the entire planning process at two different units of the University of Kansas in less than nine months each. All of these examples underscore that different situations will result in different time assessments.

## Minimum Time Requirements

One particular time requirement, however, can be established regardless of the other factors involved. Experience tells us that at least one full year is needed to develop parameters for the initial plan, to implement early strategies and related tactics, and to analyze initial outcomes. As the plan becomes more and more complex, the amount of time required grows. Also, the more complex the campus setting, the more time will be required. It is *not unusual for the planning process to take up to three years* in large, complex campus situations. On smaller, less complex campuses, the time requirement can go down significantly.

Nonetheless, the time needed to develop a substantive and useful strategic plan is an important consideration. No campus has excess resources to support an open-ended planning process that takes years to produce little. However, it does take time to allow the strategic planning process to develop. Further, if planning appears to go forward independent of the real life and crises of the campus, it will take on the aura of irrelevance or will be hampered as people go around it to "manage" the campus.

## Time-Line Considerations for Developing the Institution-Wide Plan

The *size* of the institution, and to a large degree its *nature*, will affect the time needed to conduct the planning process. Smaller and less complex institutions should require smaller time frames than larger and more complex colleges and universities. The key concern is representative involvement and the casting of strategic planning in a light that is compatible with the culture and habits of the campus.

Representativeness impacts the time line because the more people that are selected to engage in any level of the planning process, the longer the process will take. At the same time, the lower the level of representativeness, the more likely it will be that higher levels of conflict will result when the plan is presented for approval and/or implementation.

In Chapter Five we discussed the political considerations that need to be part of getting planning off to a good start. At this point, suffice it to say that assessing the culture and climate of the campus is an important consideration when attempting to identify players and develop time lines.

Perhaps the best method of setting a time line is to develop a series of benchmark stages in the process (such as those presented in Chapter Six) and then to assign them time frames that reflect what it would reasonably take to achieve them. Asking, for example, how much time it will take to adequately assess the campus's external environment, and then fixing a time frame for the analysis to occur and a report to be generated, provides those who are being asked to conduct the analysis a target for which to shoot.

## Time-Line Considerations for Developing Institutional Subcommittee Plans

In general, the process may well take more time if subcommittees are not used, because the SPC itself will need to research, analyze, and develop all of the basic material needed to form the overall strategic plan. If subcommittees are used, time may be decreased to some degree, and participation in the process can be increased. As the SPC forms subcommittees to work on the specific issue areas it develops, they can enlist the aid of a wide range of people from across the campus, including those who have day-to-day responsibility in those areas. Inclusion of these people is an important benefit to approaching the process through subcommittees, because they can be useful contributors, given their specialties and the narrower focus of subcommittees.

Another time-related benefit of subcommittees is the ability to move the subcommittee members directly from Phase One to Phase Two, since these individuals will already be involved with the operational activities of the planning areas. This will make the movement to Phase Two much smoother and decrease the amount of orientation that will be necessary to implement the plan that has come from Phase One.

In thinking about the time frame involved in working with subcommittees, it is important to consider the amount of training that will be involved in bringing new subcommittee members up to speed, the political climate of each subcommittee, and the size of the responsibility the subcommittee is undertaking. Academic planning simply takes much more time to develop than enrollment management, for example. It is advisable to set reasonable time lines for the subcommittees to help guide them toward accomplishments. It is also reasonable to anticipate that because these groups will need to go through the internal process of developing their base of activity, do research and analysis, and develop recommendations, the process will be time-consuming.

## Time-Line Considerations for Developing Unit-Level Plans

Unit-level planning, while mirroring the content of campus-level planning, will be different. The size and scope are usually much smaller, and the time involved may also be much less.

In terms of the time required to do a complete unit plan, again the factors of size, political activity, and preparedness must be taken into account. It is unlikely that a substantive plan can be produced in anything less than six months if absolutely everything goes smoothly. Since that rarely occurs, however, it is smart to plan for at least one year to produce a draft plan.

Determining *when* unit planning should occur is another issue. We believe we made a mistake at the University of Northern Colorado when we attempted to do unit planning at the same time we were developing the university-wide strategic planning process. The results were that (1) there were mixed messages about which plans would predominate—the units' or the university's; (2) communication between unit planners and university planners was often contradictory and confusing because early on neither group had much substance in their particular plans; (3) the university planner was spread far too thin, at one time overseeing the activities of sixteen different planning groups simultaneously; and (4) we found that we had presented a far more complex process to the campus than it was willing to support. Based on our experience, the lesson appears to be that the institutional plan should be formed first, with overall guidelines and expectations developed at the institutional level to help guide unit planning.

Conversely, Roach (1988) tells us that West Texas State University was much more successful in its strategic planning process by waiting to do unit planning until after the first two phases of institutional planning were completed. Swain (1988) reports that the University of Louisville purposely wanted to set a campuswide context before beginning unit planning, and also felt that such a strategy was a success.

Swain's statement may appear to fly in the face of consensual planning, but it need not. One of the reasons we began all of our planning at the same time at UNC was to encourage unit planners to help identify major trends in their disciplines and programs that would be instructive to the university-level planners dealing with the overall academic planning effort. We came to understand, however, that a university-wide plan does not need to micromanage by shaping individual program areas; this is a function that is the proper venue for the colleges, divisions, and departments. Rather, the role of the university academic planning process is to set university standards, directions, and guidelines that the units can use to decide what program priorities and processes for resource allocation make the most sense.

Once the university-wide plan has developed some substance, unit-level planning can begin. Planning can also be done harmoniously at both levels at that point, as both the university and the various units continue to refine and implement their respective plans.

## Time-Line Considerations for Implementation

Simply, once a plan, or a significant part of it, has been formulated and approved by the appropriate bodies, it can be implemented. There is no reason not to implement portions of the plan before the entire plan is complete. Brown (1988) reports that the University of North Carolina at Asheville was successful in implementing its plan incrementally, starting with those areas requiring a narrow range of expertise and fewer consultations, and that needed a narrower base of consensus to begin. An advantage of this approach is that success realized in these early implementation events may become contagious to the rest of the planning process. Since implementation is most likely incremental, the more numerically oriented areas of the planning process, such as enrollment management, may become specified more quickly than other areas, such as academic planning, that involve the more complex issues of quality, timeliness, and knowledge generation. Implementation is fundamentally the process of assigning responsibility for goal accomplishment to appropriate individuals or groups, and then beginning the process of monitoring progress toward those goals.

## Follow-Up, Control, and Revisions

Monitoring can be as time-consuming as the generation of data and the methods used to analyze it. It is important, however, for the SPC or appropriate subcommittee to monitor the other committee or subcommittee on a monthly, or at least quarterly, basis so that if problems emerge that indicate difficulties with the goals or strategies, there is plenty of time to make adjustments. The need for such adjustments cannot be determined effectively if the only time goals are reviewed is on the anniversary of the passage of the plan.

## Moving from Phase One to Phase Two

The actual time of transition from Phase One, strategic planning, to Phase Two, strategic management, is not something for which institutions can easily plan. Instead, the transition begins when the process itself begins. As the planning leaders begin to work with specific groups about specific strategic issues, it is important to begin to frame both the issue and the planning response in strategic terms. Forcing participants to view each issue in a strategic perspective will not only allow a more effective strategic planning process, but will also assure the beginning of strategic thinking. If such an approach is begun at the very beginning of the process, then with the repetition that comes from each meeting of the planning group, the pattern of strategic thinking and strategic decision making will grow stronger as the process matures. This is an important side-benefit of the process and needs to be carefully integrated into it.

## Customizing People-Needs and Time-Requirements on Individual Campuses

As indicated throughout this chapter, each campus and each institution is different. What we have tried to present here is the largest possible overview of the intricacies of planning. Yet each campus should look at its own level of complexity to determine which model of strategic planning to adopt. The authors have worked with organizations that have had very effective results with only one SPC. We have also worked with extremely large campus groups with a variety of committees at several levels that have also been effective. The key is for the person (or people) in charge of the planning process to analyze the complexity of the institution or units doing the planning, and then consider the various options available.

Though it is a challenge, it is possible to predetermine with a fair amount of accuracy the amount of time the process will need, as well as the number and types of people who need to be involved, to understand up front what is needed to take a particular college or university through a substantive strategic planning process. We have found that it is always wise to add slack time to any procedure to deal with the unexpected events that occur. And we can attest that unexpected events *do* occur.

# CHAPTER 9

# The Role and Functions of Committees

Throughout this book we have described a process of strategic planning that takes place in a unique environment, that of the university, where the issues of placement and power are significant. This chapter looks at these issues, and also addresses some of the concerns related to the creation of what many will see as another set of committees requiring more time, more involvement in complex issues, and more unnecessary bureaucracy, without any apparent tangible rewards.

To avoid problems related to these concerns, it is important to identify the committee process and define its role, both short- and long-term, in the design of the strategic planning process on college and university campuses. We will begin by looking at the options available for choosing needed committees and functions, and then at the legitimization and incorporation of the planning process into the general functioning of the campus while being careful about adding more committees and responsibilities to the work of administrators, faculty, and staff. In fact, we believe, if the process is properly designed, the end result can be a reduction of committees as the campus moves in a more focused and strategic direction.

# Hierarchy of Committees

Figure 9.1 presents a structural model of strategic planning in an academic institution. As we have stated throughout this book, the committee structure might be quite simple (only one committee) or highly complex (a variety of committees). However, the model shown in Figure 9.1 captures *the general structure of the strategic planning process itself.* Some institutions might have a specific committee for each process element found in the model, while others might combine elements or even further segment each element. This chapter discusses in detail the committee structures that each institution might want to consider, and the specific subcommittees are discussed at length in Chapters Eleven and Twelve.

## The Institutional Strategic Planning Committee

The strategic planning committee (SPC) is the nerve center of the strategic planning process. Its composition and activities are crucial to the success, or failure, of campus strategic planning.

*The Role of the SPC.* Initially, the establishment of the institution's SPC means the creation of a new, campuswide committee. However, of all the committees that the planners may develop in creating the initial plan, the SPC is intended to live past the creation of the plan and to function as a major campus committee for the long run. The institution's SPC is the group that must oversee the entire process, and it is therefore the most critical and central of all the planning committees the institution may organize within this process. The SPC becomes the institutional body of planners. With a representative membership and with leadership that can muster and maintain broad-based support, this committee must take an energetic lead in the development of the institution's strategic plan at all levels.

This group should be open-minded, have a broad perspective, and be willing to lead planning with enthusiasm for

Figure 9.1. Strategic Planning Functions, Presented in a Potential Committee Structure Format.

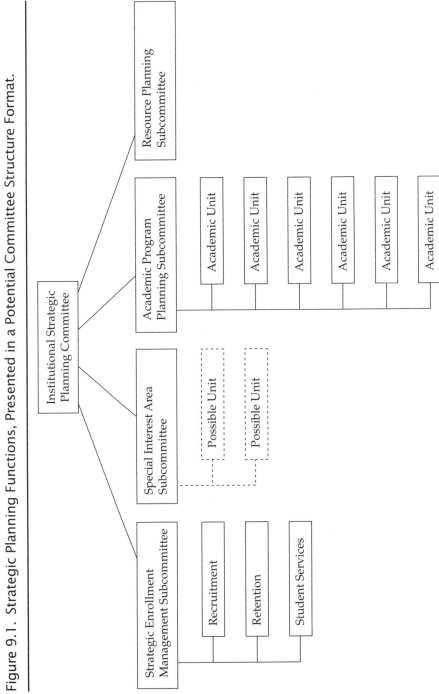

the possibilities for positive change that the process is designed to bring about. Its primary functions will be institutionally oriented, and it will speak more to the macro features of the campus rather than to the minutia of detail commonly found in the work of subcommittees and unit-level committees.

These criteria assume that the institution is large enough to support multiple levels of planning. For those institutions that will do all of their planning at a single level, developing this overall level of understanding is a particular priority before diving into the details that are necessary to fully define and describe the strategic activities of the institution.

In addition, the SPC should operate with linkages to the existing governance process and its committees. Planning committees should refer their work to the standing committees of the faculty senate or other governing body. Typically, these referrals will occur when the SPC is considering the working reports and recommendations of its subcommittees. Referral typically is to a similar committee in the governance structure. The results of such a referral should serve as advice to the SPC, which remains free to act as it sees fit in preparing material for university governance bodies to approve and forward to the regents or trustees for final action.

The SPC should develop statements of institutional purpose and direction that will guide the institutional plan. These general statements will not only give structure and direction to the groups that will be looking at the other planning areas more specifically, but will also help the broader university community gain an understanding of the workings of the SPC and the direction it is taking. Several such statements may result in additional key performance indicators (KPIs), or even policies, to guide strategic management and to be sent to the governing board for approval.

An example of a policy statement is, "The university will achieve and maintain an out-of-state to in-state student mix of 33 percent to 67 percent." This policy statement contains specific implications for strategic enrollment management (SEM) and an important choice of institutional direction with implications for resource allocations. For example, the policy dictates a two-thirds resident-student policy, which affects how the university recruits and the kind of resident/nonresident mix required at both the undergraduate and graduate levels. An institutional KPI might be the overall number of doctoral degrees awarded on a particular campus during a full academic year. This KPI will help assure the university's continuance at a particular Carnegie classification (such as a research university, a doctoral university, or a comprehensive undergraduate and masters university) or help the campus move toward a desired classification level. The academic programs planning subcommittee would work with the schools and colleges that generate the particular student enrollments and degrees on specific aspects of this KPI, such as the demand for and quality of each doctoral degree. Still another example might be a campuswide strategy to create an institutional technology network based on a single information technology platform that has easy access to external databases and information forums.

*Authorities and Integration.* To be effective, the institution's SPC must have certain powers that will allow it not only to devise the plan but also to implement it. Obviously, support by top administrators is essential to this process, since these individuals will be held accountable for the successes or failures of the plan. Support by the faculty is important, particularly to the development and implementation of the academic portion of the plan. Support by the governing board (or the system office) is also important, since most such bodies are ultimately responsible for the direction the institution takes.

But support is not enough. The SPC must be given the authority it needs to proceed. This authority can be defined by the institution's administrative council, the faculty governance council or senate, and by the institution's governing board. The governance boards of other major campus constituencies may also need to be included. This is an important issue that will help shape the success or failure of the plan itself. As we have stated before, by getting these groups involved up front in the process and by addressing this issue of authority early on, the SPC can define its appropriate decision and implementation authorities, and seek appropriate approval. *It is a major political mistake not to have developed this understanding early,* particularly for those campuses that have a political environment that will ultimately find ways of blocking the success of the process by challenging its legitimacy to make decisions or its attempts to implement changes the plan requires.

Integration of the SPC into the college or university's ongoing major campuswide committees also needs the active support of major campus groups. Because the SPC is an additional body, most standing campus committees will not be enthusiastic about its intrusion into their traditional spheres of influence. Since the SPC represents a major commitment of the institution to move strategically in the long term, this committee requires appropriate campuswide status. To that end, the chair of the SPC and the university planner, using the offices of the president and/or provost, should visit with campus staff, student, and faculty groups to spell out the SPC's role and gain support for its leadership. The result should be to place the SPC among the permanent body of campuswide committees, with defined authorities and with as much universal support as possible. This may or may not be an easy task for those promoting the strategic planning process of the institution, given the disposition of the campus toward more committees or to strategic planning in general.

At UNC, the SPC was developed with the support of the president. Initially, the president and the chair of the faculty senate cochaired the SPC, bringing legitimacy to its university-wide role. Major campus constituencies were given membership on the SPC, to assure that no group was snubbed or excluded. In addition, as policies and KPIs emerged, first from strategic enrollment management planning and then from technology and academic programs planning, they were reviewed by the SPC. Policies were also reviewed by relevant campus bodies. Academic policies were sent to the faculty senate's standing governance committees for approval and comment as part of the process of review and action at the university and trustee levels.

*Moving from Task Force to Permanent Body.* Establishing legitimacy takes time. As a consequence, the SPC should begin as a task force, with the flexibility to shape itself as it evolves. This will allow it to form itself, clarify its sense of direction, and establish its membership. This will also allow time for the SPC to develop its own sense of process and decide how it wants to conduct its business. These are important elements for success that the SPC should define prior to seeking legitimacy through codification or governing board action. Yet once the SPC has been able to define its direction and methods of operation, and once it has sought and received appropriate legitimacy, then it can begin to act more like a standing committee.

Another consideration is the nature of the planning process at the outset and what happens to that nature once the SPC has published the first-draft plan. While the SPC is busy developing the elements of the plan and getting comfortable with the processes of developing KPIs, goals, strategies, and policies, a task force mentality will prevail. This is to be expected, since it is unrealistic to assume that the work of the committee at this stage will be flawless. As we discuss later in this chapter, planning evolves through an iterative process, in which mistakes and miscalculations are allowed but serve as learning devices to help hone and shape the planning process.

Once the SPC has developed its relatively complete first draft of the strategic plan, then it will transform into a different sort of group. With its early development behind it, the SPC now faces a different role. While it must continue to maintain its centrality in the process, it now moves into the role of the thoughtful reviewer and fine-tuner of the process. It will now pattern for itself the appropriate measures and time frames for measurement that will give it the information it needs to conclude that the plan is playing itself out as expected or is in need of change at some magnitude to help assure that it achieves its goals. Clearly, at this point the SPC should perceive itself as a relatively permanent body and act appropriately to manage the long-term time frame it has set for itself.

## Institutional Subcommittees

Assuming that the campus is sufficiently large or complex enough to warrant a second level of planning, the SPC can create a series of subcommittees that focus on specific areas of planning (see Chapters Ten and Eleven) and that can expand the inclusiveness of the process by including members on the subcommittees who are more involved with the day-to-day activities in these focus areas. For those institutions that have only one committee to oversee the entire strategic planning process, this discussion represents the next set of activities that the SPC would undertake once it had established the initial campuswide planning format. Also, as Blaisdell (1993) points out, not all reforms occur at the same pace or produce desired outcomes at the same end point. This will prove to be an additional management concern of the SPC, but since this aspect of campus life is natural and expected, coordination of expectations makes sense as an integral part of the overall process. When created, these subcommittees become the expert groups that help support a more effective strategic planning process.

*The Role of SPC Subcommittees.* Focus is the key word in understanding the role of SPC subcommittees. Most likely the SPC will give a specific charge to each subcommittee it establishes, explaining the scope of the issues along with specific outcome expectations. The subcommittee will have little latitude to make decisions that affect other areas of the process. This will allow the groups to concentrate on the operationalization of the campuswide KPIs, goals, strategies, and policies.

Through this concentration, several outcomes may occur. First, subcommittees may discover problems with decisions made at the institutional level, and they can bring back to the institutional committee specific suggestions, proposals, and solutions for curing the problems. This is an important safety feature of the plan, and as long as the SPC has not taken an uncompromising position, particularly regarding its initial planning elements, this is an opportunity to help assure that the plan continues to be built on a viable and realistic basis.

Second, by bringing into the subcommittee process individuals from across the campus who deal with the issues in the focus area directly and daily, the SPC is beginning the process of implementation even before the initial plan is in place. This happens because these people will have to begin looking at their current activities and responsibilities and will become involved with the design of the changes that will most likely affect them. Theory tells us that when people are involved in change that will affect them in this manner, not only will they demonstrate less resistance, but many will become excited about the prospects and be more supportive of the overall experience (Burke, 1982; Herbert, 1981; Carroll and Tosi, 1977).

Third, the subcommittees will have the major task of operationalizing the planning tenets throughout the campus. This means that they will need to establish relevant time frames and work capabilities of the current campus human resource components. To enable them to do this, the SPC should give the subcommittees fairly extensive latitude in establishing goals in their areas of concern, and they should contribute significantly to the development of relevant strategies that will help the institution achieve those goals.

As the members of the subcommittees become more acclimated to their task, and as their recommendations become more and more authoritative, the subcommittees will take over most of the formulation of KPIs, goals, strategies, and policies. The SPC members will make the transition from the role of creators of planning elements to that of planning element reviewers, approvers, and coordinators. Particularly as a number of subcommittees begin to send their work forward, the SPC will find itself in the position of testing recommendations for consistency and possible conflict among a variety of subcommittees. This move to a more legislative role will take place toward the end of Phase One of planning, and will also allow the SPC to begin to concentrate on the formulation of the initial draft plan.

*The Issue of Permanence.* There are two different considerations in discussing the permanence of SPC subcommittees. The first is the need for such groups once the initial plan is in place; the other is the ability of the subcommittee to combine the work of other previous committees, thereby leading to their elimination. Keeping in mind the concern that this process is not meant to add another layer of burdensome committees to the college's or university's structure, if the SPC has created these subcommittees as task forces to deal with specific issues and help develop the initial plan, then there should also be time lines or a general understanding about how the subcommittees will disperse or have the work they have begun carried on by other existing or newly blended governance groups.

The value of temporary committees is that participants may be more willing to work hard for the group knowing that a specific limited amount of time is all that is required of them and that their participation has been sought because of their focused abilities to help the institution make a single, specific, direction-related move. Conversely, the members of temporary committees often lack dedication because they know they will not be involved after a certain date and that the work they begin will be carried on by others at different levels in different settings. Then which way is best? Unfortunately, there is no best answer here. It depends on whether the subcommittee is needed long-term and whether or not it adds to the overall burden of the campus committee system.

The second consideration has to do with the college's or university's ability to consolidate and simplify the existing committee structure by combining several efforts into a subcommittee as planning unfolds. At UNC, for example, we were able to do this with at least three of our subcommittees: strategic enrollment management, resources, and information technology. Through direction by the vice presidents, two initial subcommittees were folded into the three subcommittees just mentioned, eliminating at least two previously constituted campus committees. The three surviving subcommittees became permanent hubs around which long-term standing committees were developed: the SEM committee, the campus budget advisory committee, and the technology management committee.

In the case of academic program planning, that subcommittee may be disbanded once academic planning elements are firmly identified. If continued, the committee would serve to monitor progress and review the annual report of how budget dollars tied to planning priorities were used and what were the consequences of that use. Once academic program priorities are identified and approved by the trustees, implementation and monitoring will be the major remaining activities. The existing academic program structure is best suited to implementation and monitoring once the subcommittee has established the priorities and the means to assure their application. Further, the faculty and deans are much more comfortable with existing academic decision structures and would not be supportive of replacing them. Since in most cases the current academic committee structure can adequately do the required job, there is no reason to try to force the subcommittee onto the faculty or the deans in the long term.

## Unit-Level and Program-Area Strategic Planning Committees

The university-wide subcommittees can accomplish campuswide planning but they do not generally have specific expertise for dealing with campuswide issues. In some cases, such as resource planning, this level is all that is required. However, other areas need more specific attention because of their complexity or because of the general diversity in programs found on the modern campus. Academic planning is a case in point. Academic program planning requires expertise at the school or college level, since this is where degrees and curriculum reside. Moreover, there are differences among colleges and schools that require levels of expertise and understanding not typically available at the university-wide subcommittee level.

*The Role of Unit-Level and Program-Area Committees.* The SPC's academic program planning subcommittee will develop KPIs, goals, strategies, and policies for the entire institution, on institutional terms. For example, the subcommittee may develop a policy that states that the institution will be competitive with other institutions across the nation in its Carnegie classification. The school of business, however, may establish standards for itself that comply with or exceed the accreditation standards of the American Assembly of Collegiate Schools of Business, as a parallel but highly focused policy. Another example might be a campuswide KPI that establishes average class size at an initial level that will decrease to a desired standard over a specific time frame. The school of music, however, may wish to increase class sizes based on the inclusion of new technologies that allow different types of classroom experiences.

Each unit, whether an academic unit or a nonacademic program, should develop its own plan that is within the general boundaries of the institutional plan but that reflects its own unique disciplines, qualities, and activities. As was true with the development of subcommittees, unit committees have three potential benefits. First, the unit committee may discover problems with the decisions that have been made by the academic program planning subcommittee, and it can bring specific suggestions, proposals, and solutions back to the institutional committee to cure the problems. This is, again, an important safety feature of the plan, and an opportunity to help assure that the unit and institutional plans both continue to be built on a viable and realistic basis.

Second, the unit committee process will bring even more individuals from the unit into the overall strategic planning process. Further, unit committees deal more directly than other committees with issues in specific academic or program areas, and will help to bring greater definition to the outstanding areas of the academic program mix. And because these people will have to begin to look critically at their current disciplines, they should become more involved with the design of the changes that will most likely affect them.

Third, the unit committees will have the major task of extending academic or program plans to their units once those plans have been established. This means that they will need to develop relevant change and control methods that chairs and directors may use to effect change in their units. For example, in the case of the college of business and its accreditation, the unit SPC will need to establish responsibility areas, criteria, and time lines to assure that accreditation, or reaccreditation, occurs as desired. Because accreditation has unitwide implications, it is appropriate that the unit SPC be directly involved with this accreditation process.

*The Issue of Permanence.* Again, it is not the intent of this process to develop a whole new layer of committees. At the unit level, it might be wisest to identify an already established group that has unitwide responsibilities (for example, a council of chairs) and bring it into the strategic planning process. This would involve some training and the establishment of mechanisms for communicating with the institutional SPC or subcommittee, but this would avoid the creation of yet another permanent committee. Further, this method would help provide some permanence, since the ongoing group is already a permanently established committee.

The exception to this approach might be in a particular unit that does not have a group capable of taking on the responsibilities of strategic planning for the unit. In such a case the creation of a new permanent committee may be in order. The point is that the units need to do long-term strategic planning on an ongoing basis for the same reasons that the institution needs to do planning. And since planning at the unit level will help preserve the strengths and soul of the institution, it needs to be a factor in and consistent with institution-level planning. It should also contribute to adaptation as disciplines and programs evolve over time.

We strongly advocate that existing groups within units be identified and brought into the overall strategic planning process. If this is not possible, then creating such a group has more benefits attached than not doing planning at all. Further, in one form or another unit planning should be seen as a task-force event. Like institutional planning, unit planning is crucial to the long-term stability, growth, and prosperity of the program or discipline base, and must be viewed as a long-term process.

## Phasing Out the Task Forces

As we have described, some committees have a designed limited life. In other committees it becomes apparent that their work should be transferred to other permanent committees. Planners need to be aware of this possibility as they work with committees over time. For example, it is inappropriate to work with a committee throughout an academic year, adjourn for the summer, and then simply not reconvene in the fall, or to reconvene with a different group of people. It is important to remember that the people involved in committee work give time and effort to the committee, and are anxious to have some level of appropriate closure on the work they do. They need to feel that their contributions were worthwhile and an important part of the overall process. This is one of the rubrics of participative planning.

While many who will become part of the planning efforts will do so only on a limited time basis, their contributions to committees with limited life are likely to be limited as well. Yet they too need to understand when their work is complete. They need to leave the process with a positive feeling. It would seem a trite thing to add, but a simple "thank you" along with a statement of how the work of the committee will be integrated into the overall planning process is all that is necessary to assure good relations.

Again, it helps if the design of the overall process can identify those areas in which committees will be temporary, so that those who are recruited to serve know from the beginning what is expected of them. It is easy then not only to plan for the work that planners look for from such groups, but also to be prepared to close the committee down properly at the predetermined time and in a gracious way.

Where campus strategic planners might have originally thought that a committee would be permanent but later realize that the work should be transferred to other groups, it is important to be honest with those who have been recruited to serve, and to end the work of the group on a high note. This can be done, again, with a sincere thank you and communication of how the work-to-date is valued and will be integrated into the overall process. No one likes to feel pushed aside or suddenly no longer important. In putting such groups through transition, then, care must be taken to assure that people understand that their work is important and that the change is necessary for specified reasons. In this way, the process will not create more animosity when unforeseen changes are warranted.

## The Placement of Planning Committees in Institutional Governance

Some of the realities of a successful strategic planning exercise are that it changes some (or many) of the ways campuses do things, and it alters the perspective from which decision makers make decisions. These are fundamental issues, and they can raise questions about legitimacy and implementation.

### Legitimacy

Providing the strategic planning process with authority is not the only issue in institutionalizing the process within the permanent structure of the college or university. Legitimacy is also important, if not downright crucial. Legitimacy is the formal adaptation of the strategic planning/management process into the central structure of the institution. Depending on the political and administrative environment, achieving this adaptation may or may not be difficult. However, without legitimizing the process and making it part of the standard operating procedure of the college or university, it is doubtful that strategic planning will ever be more than a one-time process.

As we argued earlier in this chapter, there are several ways of achieving legitimacy, depending on the type of structure present at each college or university campus. It may be that campus codification or bylaws will need to be changed to establish and legitimize the process and its committees, or that the governing board will need to legitimize strategic planning through votes in its formal sessions. Whatever the method, it is worth repeating that the campus must establish the process and the SPC in a formal way. Failure to do so up front will guarantee problems down the road. It is also important to remember that on many campuses, faculty governance has a role in determining what committees exist, and in such cases SPCs may also need the blessing of these groups if they are to be perceived as legitimate.

## Implementation

Implementation does not take place all at one time. This is still another difference between traditional planning and strategic planning. Instead, implementation is incremental, and occurs as various parts of the plan become formalized. For example, since SEM can develop more quickly than other parts of the plan, there is no particular reason to hold it back while waiting for other elements of the plan to reach the same level of development.

This is true for a variety of reasons. First, SEM deals with hard numbers, and the strategic processes of SEM are not considerably different from the activities used to monitor enrollment. However, SEM is a different way of looking at enrollment activities and it converts current practices into those that better conform to long-range strategic methods of enrollment control. As these methods become clear, there is no reason not to go ahead and implement them and take advantage of the strategic benefits of SEM as soon as the process becomes clear. Second, it is likely that many of the people working on the SEM subcommittee will also work with enrollment management on a day-to-day basis, and will most likely be anxious to implement the new methods they have helped to develop, an outcome suggested by Hersey and Blanchard (1988). Third, since other areas of the strategic planning process will begin to key on the nature and needs of the expected populations of students, the work of this committee may well need to come first in order to provide needed information to these other committees. This will necessarily put SEM's activities on a faster pace than the other areas of planning.

In contrast, it is difficult to implement the planning tenets of academic program planning without a majority of the plan in place. This is the case because the committee working on it will need to assess the entire academic program, at least in preliminary terms, in order to develop a sense of the current program mix. Then the committee will need to develop a sense of where the program ought to go, and this cannot be done effectively without major input by major academic bodies across the campus. By the time the committee is ready to make recommendations about the future course and direction of the academic mix of the campus, a fair amount of time may have passed. Further, implementation of academic changes normally takes a great amount of time and effort, and involves a variety of departmental, college or school, and institution-wide academic committees, including faculty senates, and perhaps even a vote of the entire faculty. Add to that the need to gather information from the SEM and resources planning groups, and it is easy to see why this particular process is more time-consuming and involved than the work done in other planning groups or committees. Tying up all of the planning implementation methods until academic program planning has reached the same level of planning preparedness just does not make a lot of sense.

This means that there will be no general kickoff of the comprehensive results of planning, though information about developed decisions needs to be communicated in one form or another to the campus. The incremental approach to implementation simply means that the conversion of strategic planning to strategic decision making will happen slowly across the campus, causing very little in the way of high drama and eye-catching fallout. This is a major difference and, we think, benefit of this method of planning. Careful laying of the groundwork coupled with flexible adaptation to changing conditions assures strategic positioning and repositioning in the face of changing times. This ability to shape the future while responding to it is a major virtue, especially when change is quick or profound.

While most planning efforts have traditionally produced "a plan," many on campus will expect a plan for the campus community to scrutinize. As we discussed earlier, at UNC the faculty senate voted to have a general approval vote by the faculty prior to the final plan going to the board of trustees. This has yet to occur. What has occurred has been the review of academic planning policies by the senate and their modification by the trustees. This flexible and incremental method of planning and implementation has forestalled a single yes-or-no vote and has gradually brought some of the campus to understand that a living plan that can be shaped and reshaped is less of a threat than they perhaps fear, and more of a tool for the strategic management of the environment.

Under Colorado's Amendment 1, UNC must annually earn a ceiling of tuition dollars or face commensurate annual reductions. The ability to shift strategies as the year unfolds and thereby to maximize tuition revenues has built broader understanding of both strategic management and incremental flexibility as its tool. This understanding has in turn shaped budget thinking by the resource subcommittee (now the university budget committee) and implementation strategies by the technology management subcommittee. In each case, enrollment demands are driving strategic thinking. Dollars for recruiting and scholarships are now seen as investments in maximizing tuition revenue and not as convenience dollars better spent on academic programs, a conflict present on many campuses and usually fought in terms of the academic core versus support services. In the case of technology, serving the growing student demand for computer access is both an enrollment and technology strategy. As the pieces begin to fit, the wisdom of this approach to planning becomes gradually more apparent.

CHAPTER 10

# Educating Participants and Stakeholders About the Plan

This chapter looks at the central issue related to successful implementation—that of properly communicating to the campus the results of the decisions made during strategic planning. As we point out again and again in this book, communication is one of the central keys to successfully implementing the strategic plan. We begin by looking at the formal processes of many campuses that normally are involved in implementing a plan.

## Review and Approval

Most colleges and universities have formal governance structures that have the right, or perhaps are given the right, to oversee major changes that affect the campus. Clearly, successful implementation may not only need the proper approval of such changes but may also depend on their support to implement various components of the plan.

## Review

As we have stressed throughout, strategic planning seeks to better align the institution with its environments. It must do so by periodically checking its plan against the expectations of those environments, both internally and externally. Initially, neither internal nor external constituents may have a full understanding of their expectations of the institution. Therefore, it will be important to develop ways of checking the progress of the strategic plan and how it is defining the relationship between the institution and its critical constituency bases.

*Internal Review.* When looking at the types and levels of change that are associated with the type of strategic planning we describe in this book, and when considering the nature and climate of most U.S. colleges and universities, planners not only need to expect calls for reviews, but they should most likely build some type of review format into the overall process. Even though changes will be incremental and occur over an appreciable period of time, the emergent strategic plan will impact nearly every part of the campus. There is no doubt that the campus will naturally want to review the plan at various stages as campus strategic planners devise it, but there is also value in scheduling reviews to gather additional information and begin to build campus support as the various groups work on the plan.

Clearly, it is desirable to approach review from this second point of view. It is better to build support and gather information that will help the planning process develop better during the planning process than to try to do so once the central tenets of the plan are in place. Conversely, on some campuses the defensive posture may be unavoidable because strategic planning may have its opponents from the onset. In either case, however, reviews are necessary, and through such interactions with the greater campus community, planners can strengthen the plan, bring more of the constituency base of the campus into the process, and build support.

*Establishing and maintaining a campuswide dialogue.* The

most crucial review forum is the campus itself. This is where the greatest impact of the plan will take place, and those affected will be either the most supportive or the most vocal in their opposition. Establishing a dialogue on a campuswide basis early on in the process is important to help bolster those who are basically supportive or those who have taken a wait-and-see stance. It is also a way of immediately addressing the concerns of opponents and constructing contract-like agreement with such constituencies that should help alleviate fears or concerns.

Campus discussions will take place as a function of the prevailing culture of the campus. As such, it is important for planners to think through thoroughly how they want to establish a dialogue with the campus. Most likely, an open-forum format will work only once, if at all. People across the campus are busy and will tend to view forums on planning as an unnecessary strain on their time. Some might be willing to come once, but the majority will not. Also, it is a mistake to hold sparsely attended forums and feel comfortable that the SPC has done its job. The commitment to discuss cannot be one-time or superficial. If it is, the process will pay the price down the road.

Instead, the commitment to discuss must be sincere and as widespread as the resources of the committee will allow. Having representation from a broad sector of the campus is clearly important. But representation is not necessarily participation, and unless the representative of involved campus groups conducts an ongoing dialogue between the SPC and the group she or he represents, there can be a major problem in legitimizing the process.

Campuswide discussions certainly represent a major commitment. And it may not be as difficult to establish as we are representing it to be. On most campuses, there are key groups in which the major decision makers assemble on a scheduled basis. These groups might include a faculty senate, a classified employees representative group, a nonclassified employees representative group, a council of departmental chairs, a council of deans, an administrative council, a foundation board, an alumni board, a student council, and school or college faculty meetings. Other types of scheduled group meetings also exist. The key is to plug into appropriate groups on a timely basis and establish a dialogue using respected and influential members of those groups as the linchpins to the strategic planning process.

Timing is an issue. It is probably a mistake to have the topic of strategic planning on the agenda of each meeting of the groups with which the SPC has determined it wishes to establish a dialogue, because the process will not always produce discussable items that would be of interest or concern to the various groups on a scheduled basis. To appear at such forums with a statement such as "No report this month" is a waste of time for the committee members who made the effort to attend the meeting, and it may also take away from the impact of important items that the planners need to discuss with the focal group. At the University of Northern Colorado (UNC), strategic planning was added to the biweekly agenda of the faculty senate, and when there was nothing important to report, discussion often led to a defense of a process that did not seem to be producing anything tangible. This was an opening for those who opposed the process to ridicule it and to build cases regarding its worthlessness. When important issues did come out of the process and the SPC needed serious faculty input through the senate, otherwise-supportive senate members had been so intimidated by the nay-sayers that little positive came out of these sessions. We believe that if the strategic planners had attended the faculty senate only when we had substantive issues to present, a much more healthy dialogue would have occurred.

In contrast, representatives of the SPC met with the board of trustees only when they had a major item for discussion or approval. These focused sessions, including major segments of two annual retreats, always proved productive. Certainly, there is a difference between the forums of faculty governance and institutional governance. Nonetheless, we are suggesting that in identifying the distinction between the two approaches, we now know that we made a serious mistake with our faculty senate while doing a good job with our trustees. We needed to do a good job with both.

The nature of the discussion is also a consideration. Reports are fine, but they tend to be one-way. A dialogue, by definition, is two-way. If reports are to be the primary method of communication, the presenters need to be able to spark conversation by presenting the report in a way that invites useful responses, perhaps by presenting issues and requesting guidance from the group. The report can be the catalyst, but the conversation is the essential outcome. Clearly, some groups are better at openness than others, and often the issue is the status of the person giving the report and attempting to generate a conversation. Use of the institution's CEO to give a report to the governing board is appropriate and will generally not result in a lack of interaction. However, using a president or chancellor to give a report to the classified staff's representative group may well result in no dialogue at all. In fact, the real danger is that the group will smile and applaud, politely thank the president or chancellor for coming, and then go back to their work groups with tales of how the president or chancellor is "ramming strategic planning down our throats."

This is why it is important to make the central SPC as representative as possible, including people who are capable of interacting at a high level in both directions—with the SPC and with the groups they represent. The members of the SPC need to be encouraged to provide this interaction and to create important communication channels with the groups they represent, and perhaps to be held accountable for doing it. Ideally, status should not be a barrier to the planning process, but in reality it is. The SPC needs to be aware of this and to develop methods of interaction with campus constituencies that are comfortable for those groups and that provide the opportunity to relate what is happening in planning and implementation while gathering information from concerned constituencies about the progress of the process.

*Formal periodic reviews.* Discussions about the progress of planning tend to be ongoing, informal reviews. They serve the important purposes outlined in the previous section, but planners should not view them as conclusive or as surrogate to formal reviews. Perhaps once or at most twice a year during Phase One, the planning phase, planners need to schedule and conduct formal review opportunities. After a year's worth of work and interaction between the SPC and various groups, a cumulative meeting will hold more interest and general support. Unfortunately, on most campuses there is not one time when the entire campus comes together; nonetheless, appropriate times for such a meeting can be scheduled. At the end of the academic year, during the beginning of the fall term, or at some other strategic time, the SPC should hold an open forum and discuss progress on strategic planning. While it is still unlikely that the entire campus will attend, the level of discussion and the development of the process should heighten general interest and better inform the campus.

Once again, the key to success of these meetings is to create a sense of participation through the development of a meaningful, two-way, open discussion. Here a traditional report may be necessary, but it should be given in such a way that what is being reported is not seen as a done deal. And while it is clearly not necessary to conduct this meeting as an approval-seeking session, the presenters need to solicit input from attendees and respond substantively. They should leave this meeting feeling that the process is, indeed, inclusive. In this way the SPC can continue to build general support, as well as gather information that will help strengthen the plan within the campus.

*External Review.* As efforts to better align the organization with its environments unfold, a process of external review will help strategic planners build support and gather additional information from critical external constituencies, just as the internal dialogue and review processes helped accomplish the same thing inside the institution. However, external review and its outcomes will differ from internal dialogues and reviews. This is because the nature of the external dialogue is tied to external concerns and expectations.

Although discussions with outsiders can be very helpful, it is unlikely that any discussion about strategic planning will occur with groups off campus. It is more likely that information about the external environment's needs and wants will enter planning through internal research, or through intermittent events that require the campus to interact with some element of the external environment. Both of these methods are one-way, and neither provide either the institution or the external constituent with much substantive understanding.

Discussions between major decision makers on the campus and those associated with important external constituencies are not common among traditional administrators (Keller, 1983). Where exceptions seem to exist is in limited and focused domains. For example, a school or college of business may have a community advisory committee that it uses to review its programs, assess the job market for its graduates, and raise money for special projects. A department of psychology may have a network of professional practitioners and clinics that it works with on a regular basis to assist the professionals' practices, develop or update academic programs, and provide experience and training for the department's students. An administration may have a lobbying presence in the state legislature that keeps it up-to-date on particular legislative initiatives and attempts to influence legislation that will affect the institution. We could list other examples as well, but the point is that the usual contact with outsiders is generally parochial, narrowly issue-oriented, short-term, and seldom strategic in nature.

It is usually a new experience for many campuses to establish relationships with external constituent groups in order to gain their support and gather information that will help shape the internal strategic planning process. More importantly, the relationship must be institutional and the interchange needs to be informed and open. It is also likely that the institution can develop its end of the relationship more quickly and easily than the external constituents. For that reason, the institution must target those individuals and groups outside the campus that it believes are the influential decision makers within the critical constituencies it has identified as important to its future. Then a process must begin to bring such people into the college or university setting, orient them, and empower them to enter into a dialogue that will inform planning.

Initially, focus groups or town meetings might be useful in identifying the specific people and issues that are relevant to such a dialogue. Once institutional strategic planners identify such a group or groups, they can begin to create a more substantive relationship. After these groups are established, they should convene once or twice a year to review the institution's progress on its strategic plan, with particular emphasis on how those plans affect the constituencies of the campus.

If there is concern that the internal review of the strategic planning process not be seen as a one-way report or as resistant to input, the external reviews need to be even more careful to avoid these perceptions. It will be very helpful if someone records suggestions and concerns voiced at these meetings, and then makes certain that someone follows up in a timely fashion with the person or persons who made the suggestion or voiced the concern. Since most external people who agree to serve on such groups are likely to be business people, they will expect not only to be listened to but to be responded to as well, and soon. While the same might be true of nonbusiness people, as well as the on-campus individuals who express thoughts and concerns, careful attention to all proactive constituents will help endow planning with legitimacy in the external environment and open additional opportunities for assistance as the strategic planning process matures.

Typically, the president's or chancellor's office should arrange these meetings. Again, since it is likely that the influential decision makers will come from the top of organizations, they will interact most comfortably with top members of the institution. While selected members of the SPC should also take part in these meetings, the meeting should be chaired by the president, the chancellor, or a significantly statured person who has credibility with the audience. It is important to keep in mind that the incentive for these particular individuals to participate is probably even less than for on-campus participants. Yet because their input is potentially very valuable to the process, perhaps the extra pains required to accommodate and cater to them should not be underestimated. The plain truth is that when people outside the campus are invited to be part of the decision-making process, many feel honored and are more than pleased to participate. Further, more and more external groups believe that when a campus is engaged in a strategic planning exercise, it is a sign that that college or university is working hard to better itself and become a more powerful member of the larger community. These are very powerful side effects.

## Approval

In a sense, the mere fact that a strategic process has begun implies that approval exists at some level. Also, as we have discussed, the SPC needs to have clear authority to approve certain elements of the plan. It is a mistake, however, to assume that the SPC has a blank check to develop, implement, and approve the institutional strategic plan, even with significant input from internal and external constituents. At some point, to help establish credibility and legitimacy, a broader approval process needs to be in place that formalizes elements of the plan as it develops. Yet because the plan is developing incrementally and because different parts of the plan affect different parts of the institution, one overall, final approval does not make a lot of sense. Instead, approval should come from different constituents for different parts of the plan.

*The Administrative Role.* The implementation role of the institution's administration will be to oversee the macro areas the plan addresses, and to assess progress from a managerial point of view. Because administrators (presidents or chancellors, vice presidents or vice chancellors, operations administrative personnel, deans, and often department chairs) have this level of responsibility, they should be given a significant but not exclusive voice in the approval of the plan. Their lead role in implementation requires this at the same time that the legitimacy of planning requires the concurrence of affected constituencies. Since most top administrators will have been active in the development of the plan, other campus leaders and groups will expect that they approve of these plans prior to attempting to implement them through their individual areas of responsibility. Therefore, KPIs, goals, and strategies that have been approved by the SPC should also have the approval of the top administrators who will be responsible for them.

*The Role of the Campus Community.* Approval of the institution's strategic plan by the campus community may not be either necessary or desirable, because as various parts of the plan affect different areas of the campus, there is no reason for individuals to give approval to elements of the plan that do not affect them. Rather, campus groups affected by particular elements of the plan should be asked to participate in approving those planning outcomes. We understand that this is a volatile statement, but we point out that acceptance and implementation of the plan is going to be a lot easier if the people who will be affected by it approve of it in some way. Providing that such groups have been involved in the dialogues and reviews described earlier in this chapter, this particular action should not be too traumatic. Also, if individual items—rather than the entire segment of planning elements that affect a particular group—are brought up for approval, the likelihood increases of approval or informed discussion leading to a revision and subsequent approval.

For example, as UNC developed academic program planning we asked several of the permanent campuswide academic standing committees to look at particular policies and KPIs that the academic program planning subcommittee had developed that affected their particular areas of concern, such as undergraduate education. These standing committees studied what the subcommittee had sent to them, and approved, or revised and then approved, KPIs and policies. These approved elements went on to the SPC and, in the case of policy, the board of trustees for their approvals. The academic standing committee was thus well suited to move forward on implementation of a KPI or policy it had approved and for which it had also received institutional approval. In examples such as this, there should be no question that the proper groups were involved in the approval process or about the legitimacy of the approvals that were given. Nevertheless, the academic planning committee moved very slowly and had to be charged by the president, via the provost as its key player, to develop academic priorities by March 1996. The charge was reinforced by the board of trustees, forcing a plan. What resulted was an initial but very limited set of academic priorities that the newly established SPC of the board of trustees required, with the help of the university planner, to be tied to the 1996–97 budget.

*The Role of the Governing Board.* As we stated early on in this book, at UNC we did not ask our board of trustees to approve the strategic plan. Since the strategic plan is an iterative document (it develops and changes as it unfolds) and since the planning process constantly updates the plan, we did not want to be in a position of constantly having to go to the board when we made even minor changes in the plan. Rather, we determined that the best involvement of our governing board would be in the approval of preliminary policies that mandated the shape and direction of the strategic plan. Through the board's SPC, the full board could tie the plan's priorities to budgeting and monitor the result.

Policy is the proper area for the involvement of the institution's governing body. It is generally not desirable for governing boards to get involved with the details of the operations of the campus. Rather, they should take a position of overseeing the overall strategic direction of the institution and give this perspective to the budget through the development and approval of planning and budget policy. In the strategic planning process, policies have the effect of charting and controlling direction for the various emphasis areas of planning (SEM, academic program planning, and so on). As the subcommittees and/or SPC develops policy statements that serve this function, they ask the governing board to review and approve these policies. Once approved, these policies become part of the institution's governance authority (be that codification or other) and serve as the umbrella under which specific parts of the plan are developed and implemented by the relevant strategic planning committee. Where there is conflict, efforts are made to negotiate a solution. But in all of this, the board has the final authority.

A policy must be a clear statement about a specific direction or purpose. For example, a policy that states that "the institution will seek to maintain enrollments of minority students at a level at or above that of the high school population of the state" is a very powerful statement about a significant direction of the institution. Such a policy will then be backed up by a series of operational KPIs, goals, and strategies that the SEM committee and SPC will develop and implement. With the force of board policy, the urgency of such KPIs, goals, and strategies becomes a part of the day-to-day operations of those involved with recruiting and retaining minority students within the college or university.

## The Iterative Nature of the Planning Process

We have talked about the several subprocesses involved in the overall strategic planning process. Though these processes can range from the relatively simple to the highly complex, there is no single blueprint that helps local planners put together a perfect plan. As a result, planning is generally done by planners developing a portion of the plan, gaining approvals, implementing, analyzing results, and revising as experience unfolds. If the result is positive, planners can conclude that the planning element is performing as expected. If, however, the result is negative, then the planners know they need to make adjustments in the plan. This may mean additional development and approvals, and new implementation. Meredith (1993) suggests that this type of process works because it also provides the opportunity to engage in continuous self-improvement by examining what works and what does not.

## Institutional Learning and Strategic Planning

Any planning process, including strategic planning, attempts to shape the future. In doing so, there is an implication that the institution is trying to predict the future. This is, of course, impossible. At best, strategic planning helps develop future activity by carefully studying the forces that shape change and then making determinations about the best way to use campus resources to develop a fit between the institution and its critical environments. Unfortunately, as the planning efforts go forward, environmental elements change. For the strategic planning process to be successful in light of these new realities, elements of the process must also change.

This is disconcerting to some. At UNC we met with skepticism or opposition several times, when we discovered that a condition was different from what we had thought it would be and introduced a change. The comments we heard included, "It's obvious you don't know what you're doing"; "You can't change goals once you've set them"; and "This just proves that strategic planning doesn't work." These comments, and others like them, reflect that the ongoing confusion many have results from a lack of understanding of what strategic planning is all about.

Strategic planning is an *iterative process;* it develops and changes as it moves along. Keller calls it "slouching towards strategy" (1983, p. 72). This iterative process is a strength, not a weakness. It helps assure that the plan will continue to be as congruent as possible with its critical environments as those environments fluctuate and change. While it takes time to teach this concept to those involved in or observant of the process, this is one key area in which communication is critical and in which a dialogue can help individuals and groups understand the uneven course that planning tends to follow. Success in this area is a rich benefit of institutional learning and helps develop an institutional mentality that is more conducive to thinking strategically about the institution's position in and relationship with its critical environments.

## The Willingness to Make Mistakes, Make Corrections, and Move On

It is not easy to live with mistakes. The more campuswide and fundamental the process is within the institution, the less tolerance there is for mistakes. There appears to be a tendency in U.S. colleges and universities today to expect perfection and never to tolerate mistakes in any area of activity. This dynamic comes from the business world and is underscored by movements such as Total Quality Management (TQM). In academia, however, this intolerance is unfortunate, and a real threat to a successful strategic planning process. Even in TQM, the call is for constant improvement as well as to strive for high quality. An evolving process such as the emergence of understanding that strategic planning is a developmental process must be permitted as a basis upon which constant improvements can then be made. No one person is an expert on the exact strategic plan that makes optimal sense for any campus; this knowledge is gained only over time and through some degree of experimentation.

Strategic planning needs to be allowed to make mistakes, for all of the reasons outlined in the previous paragraphs. This means that the constituencies of the campus need to develop a willingness to allow strategic planning to evolve. Developing a certain tolerance for mistakes is essential in a learning environment, as is the willingness to make corrections. There is real benefit in allowing the process to be a self-informing and self-correcting methodology. Perhaps the best way to prepare constituencies is to describe the process up front, and to discuss the fact that changes in course will occur from time to time. Discussions of when and how the planners expect alterations to occur will go a long way in preparing people for the changes when they do come.

After all else is said, however, it gets down to a matter of people not wanting to be surprised or disappointed. Perhaps much of what we hear today about accountability results from surprises and disappointments that lowered levels of trust. Perhaps the level of tolerance will grow as the level of trust grows, if those involved in strategic planning will first outline up front which areas of planning they believe will be subject to change, and then discuss ways of keeping change from disenfranchising those affected by that change.

## The Need for Gradual, Not Dramatic, Changes

The timing of changes that accrue from planning is an important concern. So are the issues of developing an iterative planning process and establishing an acceptable tolerance level for the development of the process. In spite of all the education and dialogue that may take place, most people will be at least mildly pessimistic about the promise of strategic planning, and clearly apprehensive of the changes it may bring. No one wants the college or university where they have become comfortable and in which they lead relatively peaceful lives to go through changes that will alter forever the work they do and the environment in which they do it.

Neither is such dramatic change a necessity in the strategic planning process. With the exception of those campuses that are facing imminent catastrophe unless they change quickly and dramatically, most campuses should look forward to slow change as a result of the strategic planning process. This change is accomplished by the incremental nature of the process and the fact that most changes will take effect over the long term. The goals required by planning will trigger changes over several years, with only minor changes in place to accomplish short-term goals.

The guiding principle is planning and implementing for the long term. There are some on campus who will not like this and who would prefer immediate and dramatic changes to fix some monstrous problem they perceive. Again, unless there is some emergency that strategic planning should respond to, no change should be dramatic in any area of the planning process. So while on a year-to-year basis it may not appear that dramatic change is occurring, over a period of years that dramatic change is much more apparent. More importantly, the change is deliberate and guided.

Even when systemic reductions are required, the path is basically incremental. In Oregon, where higher education's share of the state's budget fell from 30 percent to 25 percent in four years and continues to drop toward 20 percent, adjustments were made that were serious but not disabling (Lively, 1995). When a proposal for draconian change was put forth to make the system of higher education a public corporation, the legislature and the governor resisted. It was seen as too drastic. Even when the proposal was modified and surfaced as the Higher Education Administrative Efficiency Act for the Twenty-First Century, it floundered. After extensive debate and pruning of the bill, it passed, allowing public corporation status and the autonomy it provides from state constraints only to the Oregon Health Sciences University. While Oregon institutions have cut back, the core of the system remains, and one of the most dramatic cutbacks in the history of higher education has led to little precipitous change.

After Phase One, Phase Two, or the full implementation phase, takes over to guide the implementation process and make appropriate alterations as necessary. But the real change occurs when the operational habits of the institution's internal constituents begin to change from doing business as usual to thinking strategically about how the institution's business is performed.

## Thinking Strategically, Not Linearly

We believe that the second phase of planning is characterized best by the presence of strategic thinking. To distinguish strategic thinking, it is important to identify what we believe it replaces. In standard operational thinking, a person looks at a work situation and reasons out what is needed to best address that particular issue. This is linear thinking. It is also short-term thinking. In strategic thinking, one looks at a work situation and reasons out how to adequately address that particular issue within a broader strategic context.

For example, a department chair using linear thinking

may seek to fill a sudden vacancy by doing a minimally required national search and hiring the most qualified individual in the resulting pool who is willing to accept the minimal salary the dean has authorized. Here, a person has looked at an immediate problem and solved it in a conventional short-range manner. In contrast, using strategic thinking a department chair may seek to fill a sudden vacancy by first looking at the strategic needs of the college and department. She or he may find that a priority of the college is to bring in more minority faculty to help meet a major disparity in the faculty mix of the college. A different type of search is now initiated, and top candidates are screened based on their qualifications and fit within this strategic long-term need of the department. Upon finding a highly qualified candidate, the chair then negotiates a salary from the base pool as well as monies from an additional pool that the dean has created to help the college and its departments attract high-quality minority applicants. In finally hiring this person, the chair has not only attracted a high-quality faculty member but has also helped the college achieve its strategic direction. Everyone wins and there is no major disruption to the department or the college other than that usually experienced when a faculty member leaves and another is hired.

Strategic thinking helps secure strategic decision making, as demonstrated in the example just presented. Together, strategic thinking and strategic decision making (or what we might call strategic management) begin to reshape the overall operational nature of the campus, and become infective over time. As the overall campus begins to reflect the results and benefits of Phase Two, it is clear that the strategic planning process has achieved success.

# CHAPTER 11

# Essential Areas I:
# Enrollment Management
# and Program Planning

When an institution moves to the point where it needs to deal with the substance of the strategic planning process, it will have to determine which major areas to address and whether this work can be done centrally or whether it will require subcommittees in order to plan effectively. For small institutions, no subcommittee work may be indicated. However, for large or complex institutions, subcommittees are probably needed to provide leadership in major areas of concern to the strategic planning committee (SPC).

Regardless of the complexity or size of the institution, there are several areas that planning must consider. This chapter deals with two central areas: strategic enrollment management (SEM) and academic program planning (APP). Figure 11.1 emphasizes these two areas of the overall strategic planning process.

## Strategic Enrollment Management

In all likelihood, the first area of concern, and perhaps the first subcommittee in which planners may need to become involved,

Figure 11.1. Planning by the SEM and APP Subcommittees.

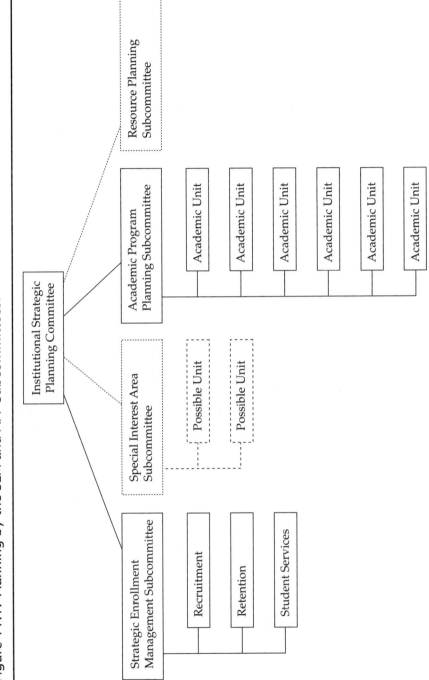

is the critical area of campuswide enrollments. Simply, if the institution does not have an adequate handle on its enrollments, in terms of both numbers and meeting student expectations, it is asking for trouble. As C. A. Green (1990) has suggested, it is important for the institution to target its desired student audience, guided by solid research and organizational needs, and by coordinating with other institutional activities. SEM is the strategic planning methodology that attempts to do this by developing control of the number of students who enroll and remain in various university or college programs, and by managing the several different characteristics that a student body needs to reflect in order to meet criteria put in place for the organization by itself or external constituencies.

It is important to have a handle on the nature of the student population on campus, as well as the nature of the population on its way, in order to better assess the fit between student needs and academic programs. As Bank, Biddle, and Slavings (1992) suggest, a surprisingly small amount of attention is paid to the expectations students have when they enter college, or to how the institution should respond to them. Further, Levine and Associates (1989) tell us that many colleges and universities have very little knowledge about the types and mixes of populations that are beginning to become a part of the campus environment. While institutions begin to move away from provider-driven methodologies and toward consumer-oriented education, it is important that they develop control methods that will allow them to understand better the needs and wants of their student population (present and future) as well as those of employers, graduate schools, and other end users of the institution's products. The results of this understanding will not only yield information about the emerging student body but will also provide valuable information to the academic departments that educate these students. This and the revenue impact of the student population are the major reasons that this aspect of campus life needs to be a primary area in the planning process.

## Building the SEM Planning Model

The student body mix has the greatest impact on the revenues of the institution. For public institutions in particular, the proportion of undergraduates, graduates, in-state, and out-of-state students in a focal body of students can significantly skew revenues one way or the other. Modeling this process is one of the primary contributions SEM can make to help the institution develop a revenue flow process that will allow the institution to control the specific enrollment mix that will maximize enrollment revenues. The implications of this information for the institution's long-term planning and yearly budgeting process is obvious.

*Elements of the Model.*  The elements of the model are dictated by the type of institution and the programs it offers. Exhibit 11.1

Exhibit 11.1. Common Elements of the SEM Model.

---

*Revenue/Student Types*

    Undergraduate students
    Graduate students
    In-state students
    Out-of-state students*
    International students*
    Minority students
    Nontraditional students
    Off-campus students
    Independent study students
    Special category students

*Collection Times/Methods*

    Fall semester**
    Spring semester**
    Summer term
    Payment when service is given

---

*Private institutions might not need to divide this particular category
**Or fall, winter, and spring quarters

lists several of the common elements that might be found on one campus or another. These elements can actually be divided several different ways. For example, both in-state and out-of-state students can be subdivided into undergraduate and graduate categories. Minority students and nonminority students can represent still another important criterion that will increase the analysis from four categories to eight.

*The Matrix of Element Interdependencies.* Table 11.1 shows what a SEM revenue model matrix might look like. Once the SEM subcommittee has identified all of the types of relevant student categories and defined them by revenue classification and/or special interest categories, it arranges these categories to form one dimension of the matrix, as depicted in Table 11.1. The payment times or methods form the second dimension of the matrix. The matrix model is then completed by inserting in the cells of the matrix the actual revenue amounts generated by category against time frame or source. Some cells in the matrix may not be filled, because a particular student group does not exist or such a transaction does not occur. For example, there may be no out-of-state students who take off-campus courses. Once the matrix has been completed, cells may be totaled to identify the revenue generated by enrollments. This becomes information that the strategic planning process can use to modulate and maximize revenues.

The example in Table 11.1 is fictitious, so the student numbers and dollar amounts do not represent any particular institution. Planners can easily obtain precise figures on their own institution and plug them into the table to determine the amounts for that institution. To exercise control, SEM planners can look at the various cells in the matrix and determine whether the amounts there are maximized under the various constraints the institution is facing. For example, in Colorado, there is a law that limits out-of-state FTE students to 33.3 percent. If the example in the table were based on a Colorado school, out-of-state students would represent approximately 16 percent of the population. One option available to the institution for improving tuition revenue yields over time would be to

Table 11.1. An Example of the SEM Revenue Model Matrix.

### Payment Times or Methods

| Revenue/Student Types | | | Fall Sem. | Spring Sem. | Summer Term | Payment When Service Given | Totals |
|---|---|---|---|---|---|---|---|
| Non-Minority | In-State | Undergraduate Students | 10,000@1,200<br>12,000,000 | 9,500@1,200<br>11,400,000 | 1,000@1,200<br>1,200,000 | | 24,600,000 |
| | | Graduate Students | 3,000@1,350<br>4,050,000 | 2,800@1,350<br>3,780,000 | 1,000@1,350<br>1,350,000 | | 9,180,000 |
| | Out-of-State | Undergraduate Students | 2,000@4,200<br>8,400,000 | 1,700@4,200<br>7,140,000 | 500@4,200<br>2,100,000 | | 17,640,000 |
| | | Graduate Students | 1,000@4,400<br>4,400,000 | 900@4,400<br>3,960,000 | 200@4,400<br>880,000 | | 9,240,000 |
| Minority | In-State | Undergraduate Students | 2,000@1,200<br>2,400,000 | 1,800@1,200<br>2,160,000 | 800@1,200<br>960,000 | | 5,520,000 |
| | | Graduate Students | 700@1,350<br>945,000 | 600@1,350<br>810,000 | 100@1,350<br>135,000 | | 1,890,000 |
| | Out-of-State | Undergraduate Students | 200@4,200<br>840,000 | 170@4,200<br>714,000 | 50@200<br>210,000 | | 1,764,000 |
| | | Graduate Students | 150@4,400<br>660,000 | 135@4,400<br>594,000 | 100@4,400<br>440,000 | | 1,694,000 |
| International Undergraduate Students | | | 500@4,200<br>2,100,000 | 450@4,200<br>1,890,000 | 90@4,200<br>378,000 | | 4,368,000 |
| International Graduate Students | | | 75@4,400<br>330,000 | 72@4,400<br>317,800 | 35@4,400<br>154,000 | | 800,800 |
| Off-Campus Students | | | 900@1,400<br>1,260,000 | 800@1,400<br>1,120,000 | 700@1,400<br>980,000 | | 3,360,000 |
| Independent Study Students | | | | | | 500@450<br>225,000 | 225,000 |
| Special Category Students | | | | | | 150@450<br>67,500 | 67,500 |
| Totals | | | 20,525 | 18,927 | 4,575 | 650 | $83,349,000 |

increase the percentages of out-of-state students as a percentage of the whole, assuming that the total number of students does not decline. A further examination of the example indicates that the percentage of minority students appears to be low, at 15 percent. This suggests another area on which the institution should concentrate in order to bring minority enrollment to a more acceptable level. That level could be the same as the percentage of minorities found in the statewide high school graduation rate.

Note that the matrix could be as complex or as simple as the planners would want. For example, if an institution believes that the number of nontraditional students will increase, it will want to view the first eight categories more specifically by adding "traditional students" and "nontraditional students" as additional categorical designations. This will result in creating sixteen different categories. In the case of private institutions, it might not be useful to look at in-state versus out-of-state categories. This would reduce the eight categories seen in the example to four.

While this example shows how planners can use the model to improve revenues, it also demonstrates how the model can be used to meet other objectives of the institution as well. Such models are extremely useful to both planners and managers of the institution in graphically demonstrating several specific performance areas and standings, which allows the strategic planning process to precisely target strategic areas for planning and control.

The development of strategies, which the SEM planning area will consider, will generally be done in two different categories: recruiting efforts to attract desired groupings of students, and retention activities to keep currently enrolled students (or perhaps previously enrolled students targeted for reenrollment) at the institution.

## The Strategic Planning and Management of Recruiting

Recruiting activities are found on every campus. Institutions are interested not only in attracting students, since any particular group of students will turn over in four to six years; they are also interested in the type or quality of student they hope to admit. However, while every college or university engages in recruiting, it may not be engaged in recruiting strategically. For this reason, with the use of a model such as the one described earlier, planners can begin to identify specific areas in which recruiting should be concentrated. By using this model along with the strategic elements that come from other areas of planning such as enrollment, the resources available to the recruiting efforts of the institution can now be addressed differently in order to begin the process of changing the mix of student populations entering the college or university. For example, if state revenues appropriated to the university are declining, that might imply the need for alternative revenue sources. On a per student basis, nonresident students pay more in tuition, so an increase in nonresidents would improve revenue to compensate for the shortfall. With this strategic reasoning in place, resources could be allocated to recruiting nonresidents and to scholarships designed to attract them. Dramatic results will not be evident immediately. But by the second or third years of enrollment management, differences resulting from the strategy should become evident.

## The Strategic Planning and Management of Retention

Once an institution has expended resources on attracting a particular student mix, it follows that the institution would then seek to retain that mix. Surprisingly, however, many colleges and universities do not actively put resources into programs or activities that do this. While there are institutions that do an excellent job of retention, others do little or nothing. This lack of retention activity makes little sense. Recruiting is expensive. For example, more scholarship dollars may be needed to attract specific target populations. Once a student begins a program in higher education, the student, family, and others will make an additional series of investments of money and time that suggest that the student will be successful. But if the student finds that the institutional environment is coarse, unhelpful, and unforgiving, that investment is wasted as the student looks elsewhere.

Traditionally, there has been a feeling that, as an adult, a student should be capable of adapting to the institutional environment, regardless of its costs, expectations, and educational methods. There is almost a sense that regardless of the efforts made to enroll a student, once the student has enrolled, it is a matter of the survival of the fittest. This view is patently unfair, and unrealistic on a variety of moral, ethical, and practical fronts.

Further, there is generally a lack of adequate bases of support that can provide substantive help to students in making adjustments to radically different cultures and to the expectations that often mark the academic experience. While some help groups do exist to serve particularly vocal or powerful constituencies, other student constituency groups are not served at all. Looking back at the minority example we described earlier, and recognizing that the institution is underrepresented in certain minority groups, little is accomplished when scarce resources are expended to attract such individuals only to have them leave soon after arriving because the institutional culture was unfamiliar and unwelcoming to them.

Retention strategies focus on problems such as these and develop target activities that anticipate the problems faced by students who want to be successful but who find the traditional college or university system difficult to acclimate to. In fact, SEM planning helps targeted units and programs of the institution acclimate better to the student body by developing a more comprehensive understanding of students' needs and by developing and providing viable options to help students overcome the difficulties they face and move toward a complete degree program. In devising these strategies, the SEM planners need to focus on a variety of areas, including financial aid, academic assistance, academic advising, housing concerns, cultural support, transportation needs, and even child care and counseling help.

## SEM KPIs, Goals, Strategies, and Policies

Once the SEM subcommittee has gathered its data and established (with the SPC) the general direction of the strategic planning process, it will develop its own KPIs, goals, strategies, and policies. With this data in place, it should be a fairly simple process to look at the two major areas of concern for SEM (recruitment and retention) and develop appropriate KPIs and policies.

For instance, using the example in Table 11.1, let us assume that the number of minority students presently enrolled in the university is far below the state high school graduation rates of minority students, and that minority enrollment in other like institutions in the state is also higher than at the focal institution. By devising some reasonable formula that matches the criteria the committee believes are strategically critical, the committee determines that in-state minority enrollment will be one of its SEM KPIs. The committee would at this point identify the current measure (current measures are provided in the table and in this case indicate that 13.2 percent of the current enrollment is represented by in-state minority students), and then determine five- and ten-year goals. Based on the data the committee has collected, the committee might set goals of 16 percent in five years and 20 percent in ten years as reasonable numbers that would raise the enrollment of minority groups to levels consistent with benchmark standards.

The committee might also propose several strategies, such as increasing scholarships for in-state minority students or adding additional recruiters to target and work to enroll the top academically qualified minority students in the state, as operational activities the university can use to help achieve its goals. In addition, the committee might propose for governing board approval a policy to set the context for this particular vein of activities. Such a policy might read, "The University will seek to enroll and retain highly academically qualified in-state minority students at at least the same rate as concurrent in-state high school graduation rates." The committee would develop similar KPIs, goals, strategies, and policies to cover the major strategic SEM activities of the institution.

## Integrating Strategic Enrollment Management with Academic Planning

In discussing the various areas of concern and the formation of appropriate strategy in SEM, it should be apparent that effective strategy formulation and implementation will involve the participation of people across the campus and beyond the administrative function of enrollment management. Clearly many of the issues surrounding recruitment and retention are deeply imbedded in the activities and programs of the academic departments and faculty. In developing a recruiting program for groups of individuals with whom the campus has little experience, SEM planners certainly need to establish an effective interface with those academics who will be most in contact with this incoming group, to assure that these students will have academic opportunities that match their needs for a higher educational experience.

Also, academics need to be involved in the development of effective retention strategies as they design advising activities and provide academic assistance, particularly for those individuals and groups for whom the institution previously has not established a pattern of providing targeted assistance. A fair amount of education of both the administration and academic participants may be in order to help assure that the academic processes and the SEM objectives coincide. The planning function needs to develop tactics to assure that these joint educational and planning opportunities occur at the proper time and in the proper manner.

## Academic Program Planning

The second essential area of strategic planning in higher education is academic program planning. APP may not get underway until after SEM has begun its work, because it usually takes more time to identify the specific approach the institution should use in reviewing its academic program mix, and to identify which individuals and groups should be involved with this particular planning phase. Also, it is useful to have at hand some idea of the student mix as planners begin to wrestle with the issues of providing a relevant and fulfilling academic program. Nonetheless, it is still one of the major areas that strategic planning needs to develop.

Strategic planning in the academic areas of the campus offers different types of activities and opportunities than we have suggested for SEM. APP has a different set of directions and operational realities to deal with. Of obvious primary consideration is that on most campuses academics are the purview of the faculty. Yet as Wood (1990) suggests, thoughtful and determined college or university leadership is also needed to help define the need for changes and to smooth the process. So APP requires an integrated approach that includes the faculty who provide the program, but also those in administrative areas that are responsible for the overall program mix of the institution.

A typical college or university academic mix is comprised of a variety of disciplines, most of which were in existence long before the physical entity of any focal college or university, and others that have been developed within a broad, more universal academic world. Also, the traditional development of new or different academic programs is a slow process, and changing them is burdensome. Generally, individual campuses make changes cautiously, in their approaches to a given discipline, in how a discipline is taught, or in contributing to a portion of the general growth of the discipline. Any college's or university's desire to make changes more substantively or to prioritize its program mix is severely threatening to most of the campus academic structure.

Strategic academic planning is designed to align the institution with its relevant environments in the most substantive way, meaning that evaluating and challenging the curriculum mix and the academic tradition of the institution may lead to change. Keller (1994–1995) calls planners to decide what constitutes the proper content of instruction as higher education moves into the challenges of the post–cold-war world. In such a world, Hambrick (1994) warns, "Any academic field that is a reluctant wallflower will wilt. Any academic field that exists to satisfy itself and only its own interests will soon have few resources" (p. 16).

Realistically, however, no campus concerned with its accreditation ever ventures too far from prevailing discipline standards, which it has little power to moderate. This is not to suggest that strategic planning cannot take place in the discipline areas of a college or university. It only suggests that this process is potentially threatening to some academic areas, and strategic planners need to be particularly sensitive to these concerns. Once again, the participative approach is vital in putting a successful strategic academic plan together.

## Major Questions APP Asks

Individual colleges, universities, schools, and departments should not look at the strategic planning process as a terminal threat to either the content or the methodologies of their disciplines. Rather, strategic planning in APP involves wrestling with a different set of issues and questions:

1. How well does the institution support its mix of disciplines?
2. What is the demand for the courses taught in the disciplines it supports?
3. Has there been major growth or decline in the demand for those courses?
4. Does the institution have the proper faculty to support the courses it offers or wishes to offer?
5. More globally, can the institution determine that interest in some disciplines is declining?
6. Also more globally, can the institution determine that interest in certain new disciplines is increasing?
7. How deeply embedded is the institution in declining disciplines, and how well-suited is it to support growing disciplines?
8. How well do the institution's course offerings match the demands of its present and future student base?

9. At what level of quality is the institution able to offer its programs, and how well are students prepared to enter the world following graduation?

10. Is the institution attempting to provide more programs than it should, which may affect the quality of these programs?

11. Which of its course and discipline offerings demand disproportionate shares of the institution's resource base?

12. Which disciplines help the institution attract new resources, and which do not?

Certainly there are other questions that institutions can and should ask regarding the nature and fit of their academic mix of programs. These are hard questions, but they do help provide a clearer picture of the current state of the academic structure of the institution and allow for the beginning of analysis.

Different institutions have attacked these issues in different ways. Eaton and Adams (1991) report that at Iowa State University, academic planners developed five specific criteria to evaluate academic programs: (1) relationship to the institution's mission, (2) quality, (3) demand, (4) comparative advantage and uniqueness, and (5) financial considerations. Foote (1988) writes that at the University of Miami three questions were asked: (1) Is a program part of the "universe" of knowledge? (2) Is the program directly related to higher learning? and (3) Is it essential that this institution offer it? As a result, the university eliminated programs that did not meet the criteria and transferred resources to programs that did. At The University of North Carolina at Asheville, President Brown (1988) instituted a "thrust program" and challenged units across the campus to submit proposals for major funding that would help them achieve national prominence. The program allowed the units to determine for themselves the best routes to take to update their programs, personnel, and scope and achieve excellence. In a similar strategy, West Texas State University created a venture fund to encourage academic innovations (Roach, 1988).

At the unit level, the business unit at National University puts major emphasis on assessing the effectiveness of its MBA program. It does this by soliciting feedback from program graduates, as well as from the employers of these graduates, and then compares this data with data from pretests given to students entering the program (Williams, 1995). The results tell National where the various components of their programs are meeting needs, and where they need to bring about improvements.

The objective of ΛPP is to develop and support a strategic mix of disciplines and courses, within identifiable discipline trends, that match the strengths of the institution with the needs of its most critical academic constituencies. These constituencies include students, their employers, and major funding sources.

Mayhew, Ford, and Hubbard (1990) tell us that, in a world of declining resources, educational quality may be attained only by reducing the number of programs offered and the corresponding courses that support them. This suggests that academic strategic planners need to establish academic priorities to develop a proper mix of courses that fit the strategic needs of the campus. Defining that mix involves several steps that may be uncomfortable, if not threatening, to many of the faculty and deans on any given campus. Gumport (1993) suggests that many in the faculty may become politically active as discussions of program reduction or elimination surface, and that the strength of that resistance can be a factor of where those faculty already perceive themselves within the pecking order of the institution.

One part of the process will be to determine the need for programs. This may or may not be an easy task for the college or university, depending on the quality of its process of assessing current academic programs. High-quality assessment tools reveal the currency of programs on the campus, national trends, the success rates of graduates, the match with employer expectations, and the state of the market the discipline serves. External surveys may also be used to help determine trends, needs, and satisfaction levels.

On the basis of internal assessments, external surveys, and other research methods, the institution will begin to develop a rather substantive picture of not only where a program presently stands but also where the program ought to go. Consider the case of the University of Kansas Division of Continuing Education. As part of the strategic planning process, the division uses marketing surveys and focus groups with students in its professional programs to determine how well their current offerings are meeting needs, and what new or ongoing topics in the profession should be added to university-run conferences, short courses, and credit courses. This allows students to maintain accreditation, licensure, or certification by keeping these activities and courses available. The division then negotiates with the appropriate academic department on campus either to provide the necessary courses or to develop new course offerings, depending on what is identified in the student survey. Similar methods can help determine the demand for current affairs courses in any discipline or profession, particularly since most of the hot topics are developed in higher education to begin with. This is as true for on-campus offerings as for off-campus programs.

While this may appear to be a ponderous undertaking for a committee, there should be no misperceptions regarding how these tools are measured or who measures them. APP is not intended to develop completely new reviews of the college's or university's entire academic program. Rather, APP should use tools that are already developed across the campus (for example, program assessment) to help it develop a position from which to begin an adequate process for identifying program priorities.

## Developing a Scheme for Priorities

Roach (1988) has observed that when institutions find themselves in a position where they need to do fewer things but at a high level, academic prioritization is a requirement. He observed that at West Texas State University the successful result of prioritization was a savings of almost $1 million, which gave the institution needed flexibility when the Texas state legislature sharply reduced all institutional budgets. However, the term *program priorities* can send shudders across the general campus and therefore the process of setting them should not be done before a large audience. Results may even have to be known only to a small group, and certainly not in any form that might identify top tiers and bottom tiers of programs. The impact on departmental morale can be devastating, regardless of the reasoning behind the decisions made. Yet in order to know how best to increase resources and where to reduce them, some type of prioritization is needed.

In fact, prioritization already occurs on most campuses. Most deans prioritize departments by some schema in order to decide how to spread around available resources. For example, a dean may not fill a faculty vacancy in a particular department because she or he has determined that enrollments in that department are declining—not only at this institution, but also nationally. Instead, the dean will use these dollars to add a faculty position in a department where the national trend is an increase in enrollment. Decentralizing the activities of prioritization to schools or colleges may be the least offensive way of developing a campuswide understanding of where resources ought to be reallocated. Even so, it is important to have an overall institutional sense of where priorities exist within the general framework of the strategic plan, in order to assure the long-term viability of the institution over the short-term concern for affronting a particular dean, department, or program. Plugging into such a prioritization process will help assure that strategic academic programming is not too intrusive and divisive, if at all.

## Developing the Institutional Academic Strategic Plan

Although the APP subcommittee must work with the deans and the faculty to develop this portion of the overall institutional plan, and although the APP process is different from the processes involved in other areas of planning, the planning outcomes will look essentially the same as the outcomes in other areas. The KPIs, goals, strategies, and policies will reflect different development techniques, but they will still present measures that can provide control over several years.

*KPIs and Goals.* The biggest difficulty in developing KPIs in APP is putting numbers to quality issues. Other planning areas have a similar problem, but none as acute as in academic planning. For example, developing KPIs that adequately measure "high quality education," "proficiency in learning," "ability to apply concepts," "quality faculty," "meeting the needs of the community," and other such areas of performance are critical to the academic outcomes of the institution. However, although the concepts are difficult to quantify, the APP process still needs to develop measures that will provide reliable information regarding the ability of the institution to perform at designated levels in each of the areas.

These measures are developed by establishing surrogates that approximate as closely as possible the quality measure the process is seeking to establish. For example, "faculty quality" might be measured by determining the proportion of the faculty who regularly publish in established scholarly journals, a measure more appropriate in a research institution than in a teaching institution. "Proficiency in learning" might be determined by standardized exit exams, a growing trend in some fields, and several accrediting bodies now require and often provide such tests. True, these measures may not provide a complete understanding of the quality the institution is seeking, but they do provide valuable insight that can be used to create a better measure. Further, if one surrogate measure is insufficient, two or even three measures can be used together to help develop a fuller understanding of the quality element.

With measures in place, measurement is then simply a process of determining current levels and comparing these measures against established benchmarks (again, for several of the disciplines, accreditation tests and other standards already exist). At this point the APP subcommittee can determine what direction is appropriate and establish goals. For example, if current measures are above standard, maintaining current levels may be appropriate; or if current measures are 10 percent below standards, then the APP group might establish performance increases of 2 percent a year as acceptable improvement levels over the next ten years, not only to meet standards but also to raise performance to a level where standards are exceeded.

*Strategy Development.* Performance strategies in APP are, again, more complex, time-consuming, and taxing than most strategies in the other areas of the planning process. For example, the tenured faculty, as a body, are usually well entrenched and politically strong. Major changes are not going to occur in the academic area if the faculty oppose them. So, successful strategy development can only occur with the faculty's compliance and participation.

However, by working steadfastly with and within faculty governance structures, APP planners can begin to build cooperation by sharing the issue with appropriate faculty bodies and then by asking them to propose solutions. For example, if exit exams showed that graduating students consistently scored 10 percent below the standard, the APP planners might ask the discipline faculty, chairs, and the dean to suggest ways that the scores could be improved. Though this dialogue might take a while to conclude, it is important to allow the solution to evolve from within the affected group. Once an acceptable strategy comes forward to the APP committee, and once that strategy is approved, implementation should be simplified due to the fact that those who the process expects to take responsibility for the movement of the indicator happen to be the same people who proposed it. Add to this the fact that faculty usually take great pride in the work they perform and in the students they graduate, and the fact that they honestly do want to have performance outcomes that can be judged as above average or even superior, the task is not as ponderous as it might at first seem.

In all of this, it is very likely that faculty will more than trifle with the planning vocabulary and structure. At the University of Northern Colorado, the provost and deans resisted the policies adopted by the trustees. In their place, the provost brought forward a plan that addressed priorities necessary for dealing with an accreditation focus visit due to occur in 1998, and including modest initiatives called "priorities" and "strategies," such as assessment and advising. Though modest and not cast in the vocabulary of planning, the plan gave the university planner priorities that could be linked to the university plan and tied to budgeting.

*Policy Development.* Discipline-specific policy is probably not a good idea. Policy that goes to the governing board for approval is meant to be general enough to cover the entire campus and not to micromanage specific areas of the campus structure. While there are some exceptions to this (for example, one particular campus might have built its reputation around a single program and will develop policies that maintain the primacy of that program), most comprehensive colleges and universities need to build flexibility into the directions that policy is designed to influence. As a result, academic policy should generally focus on the macro issues that affect the general direction of the academic programs of the campus. For example, developing a policy that establishes a comprehensive international component to the general education of all students is a good campuswide academic policy.

## Quality and Quantity: Interfacing with SEM

Partially because many academics may resent reducing their work to numbers, and partially because of the difficulty in measuring quality issues and outcomes, it is probable that a discussion may begin about how strategic planning appears to be more interested in numbers than in quality. This will be particularly true if the SEM process begins to suggest areas where the academic programs appear, based on interest surveys, to need to increase or decrease their student numbers.

In the final analysis, however, it truly is quality that strategic planning is designed to achieve, while it seeks to manage quantity. As external pressures on higher education continue to mount, those pressures are directed more at producing high-quality outcomes for the resources provided. Waste is a concern, but most states and governing boards that engage in the discussion of what is wrong with higher education are not truly suggesting that college and universities should do more for less. Rather, the concern is that institutions be accountable for the way they use resources, and that those resources be used to provide quality education. There is a significant difference in the two directives.

## Performance Control at the Institutional Level

Measuring outcomes of the academic plan will be more time-consuming and cumbersome than the methods we have suggested for other areas, such as SEM. This is true because most data gathering is done only on a periodic basis. Many program assessment processes work on a four- to seven-year cycle, for example. However, control of the process, once the data has been generated, works pretty much the same as in other areas. The central issue is what to measure and how to measure it. Once those issues can be put to rest, the data that come from the measures will provide academic planners with important information about what strategies have apparent effect on the measures and which do not.

With this information, the strategic management of the academic process is more straightforward. Deans, chairs, and their faculties can see firsthand what works and what does not. These academics can then make needed adjustments, if required, and over a period of time will begin to see the major shifts they had hoped for from the process.

# CHAPTER 12

# Essential Areas II: Resources, Technology, and Support Systems

Along with strategic enrollment management (SEM) and academic program planning (APP), there are other areas in which strategic planning occurs. Though resource planning will be something each campus needs to incorporate within its planning process during the first phase of planning, there are a variety of other areas that individual campuses may or may not choose to develop as part of their strategic plan. Figure 12.1 demonstrates how these other areas fit within the overall strategic planning process model.

## Resources

The third major area of strategic planning has to do with the resource base of the institution. As Schmidtlein (1990) points out, linking budgets to planning is difficult for most colleges and universities; yet as Roach (1988) indicates, such linking is a critical component of a conceptually complete and implementable plan. Mathews (1990) tells us that managing resources is the key to controlling organizational decline in colleges and universities, as well as the key to supporting meaningful

Figure 12.1. Resources and Other Areas in Which Subcommittee Planning Occurs.

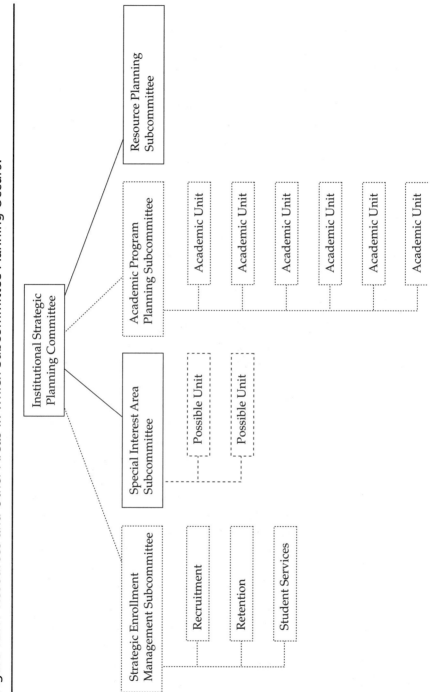

change. One way of integrating budgets so they will be compatible with one another, according to Canary (1992), is to build the budget as a *financial plan* that fits within the overall strategic plan. Dooris and Lozier (1990) report that The Pennsylvania State University helped secure its strategic planning process by directly tying the decision-making process of resource allocation to planning priorities. The University of San Francisco also ties strategic priorities to its annual budgeting cycle, and has a policy that allows the faculty budget to be moved among faculty salary categories or even nonsalary categories (with presidential approval), providing greater strategic flexibility (University of San Francisco, 1995). Another reason to engage in planning in this area is that some studies have shown that strategic planning can positively impact overall financial performance (Capon, Farley, and Hulbert, 1994).

It is important to understand that resources and budget control are considered *after* much of the rest of the plan has been explored, particularly after its enrollment and academic aspects are beginning to take shape. This is purposeful. In higher education, it is important to emphasize *what* we do as a prelude to developing *how* we will get it done. The planning around institutional resources is part of the *how*. However, the tendency in many planning exercises often is to put the issues of resources up front so that the planning process can be predicated on the resources that the institution will have available to it. This is a mistake. It puts constraints and limitations on the process before the central purpose of the college or university is considered.

The type of strategic planning we are outlining in this text is concerned first with determining *what* the institution is doing, or perhaps what it *should* be doing, and then with developing a plan for *how* best to do it. As a result, the central planning process is not limited or constrained, and the various planners throughout the institution can think more realistically and creatively about how best to shape their academic program to meet the needs of their most crucial strategic constituencies. With these central directions in mind, it is appropriate to look at the implications of the emerging plan for the resource base of the institution.

While we suggest that the SEM and APP areas need to develop at least the initial foundations of their portions of the plan prior to the development of the strategic resource plan, the ties between the three areas of planning will continue to grow and strengthen as more and more elements of all three portions of the plan become more clear. Once planners begin to look at the resources available to the institution, they may need to revisit some of the planning premises and either scale them back or reject them altogether.

Leslie and Fretwell (1996, p. 13) tell us that there are forces at work that portend the possibility of real structural change in the financial and resource foundations of higher education. But it may also be that new resource bases will become apparent. Grants, contracts, revenues generated from intellectual properties, increased giving, and several other sources and types of income might become reasonable possibilities for increasing the resource base of the institution. And as Mercer (1993) has observed, states and other entities are putting increasing pressure on public colleges and universities to keep tuition increases to a minimum. Mercer's conclusion is accurate, particularly if the reason for going after these new sources is tied to specific legitimate outcomes of the strategic plan.

Another objective of developing the resource plan is to see the limitations of the resource base. It is becoming more and more apparent that colleges and universities need to apply their resources with better justification relative to the academic priorities of the campus; and as Hyatt (1993) suggests, they also need to look at alternative approaches to revenue generation. As the academic plan continues to emerge, and as the programs that hold the greatest promise for the growth and success of the institution are identified, resources need to be found or moved to support them. Likewise, as the institution identifies elements of the academic program that are in decline or that no longer match its direction, it can begin to withdraw resources from those areas by making the resources available to support other areas. This is a threatening process to many, but if planners, administrators, and academic managers view these changes as emerging over time, much of the bite can be taken out of reductions while still providing additional support in those areas where the overall benefit to the institution will be more strategic.

## Determining the Institution's Current Resource Base

Resources come in a variety of shapes and sizes. They include money, people, facilities, equipment, investments, good will, and potential. Part of what strategic resource planners need to develop is a resource audit for the campus. This process involves placing value on all of the items in the list and beginning to determine the nature of these assets. Using methods such as straight accounting, human resource management accounting, and value assessments, resource planners can construct a fairly accurate picture of the resource base of the institution.

Beyond determining what the base is, however, resource planners need to look at how resources are presently used and how such use limits or maims opportunities. For example, much of the cash that is generated through a yearly fundraising drive by an institution's foundation may be earmarked for only specific purposes, such as the scholarship fund. Or to look at human resources, it is difficult or impossible to use a faculty member in biology to cover programs beyond biology. There also might be an old fieldhouse facility whose general purpose has been replaced by a new facility that can now be converted through a fundraising effort to support new computer laboratories for the campus's burgeoning technology programs. These examples are typical of the results a resource audit should obtain about the current resources of the campus.

## Determining the Strengths and Weaknesses of the Resource Base

A resource audit will reveal a great amount of information. Some of this information will be good news for planners while other information will be bad news. It is useful, then, for the planning process to begin to determine which resources are restricted or cannot be used beyond their present application, and which resources can be easily shifted from one use to another. It would be great if all the resources were unrestricted, but in most colleges and universities this is simply not the case. Testing the institution's resources against the list of KPIs is a very helpful methodology for differentiating and prioritizing resources to support the planning process.

For example, in some states, classified salaries are determined by the state, and the money to pay those salaries is specifically appropriated in the state budget. Even though the college or university pays its classified employees through its own payroll system, it has no right to use the appropriated fund in any way other than what the state has prescribed. In other states, the faculty are unionized and there are strict rules as to how faculty are paid—again, reducing the flexibility of the institution to maneuver resources in this area. And since approximately 80 percent of the costs of many public colleges and institutions can be their payroll costs, much of the flexibility of the cash budget may already be taken away.

Yet there are areas where resources can be freed. Not all of the allocation to an institution (by the state in a public institution or by the governing board in a private institution) will be pledged. Programs that no longer have an audience or meet a need can be shut down. Part of the annual giving campaign can concentrate on unrestricted giving. Retiring full professors can be replaced by tenure-track assistant professors or even instructors. In other words, events occur that begin to develop larger resource pots. Whatever the amount, these newly developed resource bases represent areas where the resource planning activity of the strategic planning process can begin to identify resources that can be reallocated over time to support strategic growth and development.

## Establishing the Groundwork for Broadening the Resource Base

Redistribution of current resources is an important outcome of the strategic resource planning activities. However, redistribution may not be enough. To develop an academic program mix that better meets the needs of the external environment, the institution may need to locate additional resources to build a high-quality program to meet those needs. As suggested earlier, there are a variety of sources for these additional resources, but since these resources are unlikely to come from the traditional resource base (though some may), they may prove to be more difficult to obtain. As more and more institutions that traditionally have depended on and gotten public funding to support growth and development begin to look for other sources, competition is increasing.

The strategic planning process must prove itself a very valuable partner in this search, since finances are a central concern of the strategic planning process. By bringing better definition and direction to the institution, and by developing a better sense of what the institution needs to do to develop a better fit with its environment, the planning process can develop a marketable commodity in the form of a proposal for a new or revised academic program, research project, or service. Potential funding agencies will respond better to a proposal that is grounded in a fundamentally sound strategic plan and that promises to develop into something that will potentially benefit the agency as well.

## Including Foundations, Alumni, Research Corporations, and Other Resource Bases

As the institutional strategic planning committee (SPC) begins to structure its efforts to develop its resource plan, it needs to include the principal players who oversee the institution's resource base. Based on their experience at The Pennsylvania State University, Dooris and Lozier (1990) provide good advice by telling us that it is important to build on existing resource allocation structures and procedures in tying resources to the strategic planning process. Further, given the importance of the groups these players represent, it might be useful to have them also engage in strategic planning as units, and then integrate what emanates from these plans into the overall resource plan. One key group is administrators who work with the budget and the human resource management activities of the college or university. Other players include those who are often seen as peripheral to the central administration of the institution—managers and decision makers from the institution's foundation, alumni office, research corporation, and any other body that functions to develop additional program and operational resources. Strategic planning will become a natural vehicle for aligning the activities of these important organizations with the institution, and will improve both communication about the process and dialogue among major campus constituents.

## Moving from Planning to Strategic Budget Control

As the overall strategic plan becomes more and more visible, and as those charged with the development of the resource plan are better able to tie resource allocation to developing priorities, inclusion of the tenets of the strategic plan within the budget process should be an inevitable outcome. Also, one of the most important ways that strategic planning is legitimized and incorporated into the ongoing strategic management of the institution is to make the elements of strategic planning an identifiable part of the budgeting process. This incorporation should occur through the strategic resource planning function, since it is an application of the results of the planning process by those whose major responsibilities within the institution include development, oversight, and control of the institution's budget on a year-to-year basis.

Further, many governing boards want to approve budgets that are built on a specific rationale consistent with the direction of the institution. The process of using the budget to support strategic priorities helps provide such rationale and allows the board to track how institutional resources are being used to achieve strategic objectives over time. At UNC, the governing board adopted strategic planning as the institution's primary planning and management activity to tie the budget to the strategic plan. The board hoped that this would allow them to understand on a year-to-year basis how the university's resources were being used to achieve its academic priorities.

The board then created a committee of its own to link planning to budgeting. This gave the university planner the legitimacy to bring planning priorities forward. It also led to the resources subcommittee becoming the university's budget advisory committee, which assists the administration in budget development. Ever since the establishment of the strategic planning process, each time a budget has been presented to the board the budget advisory committee has consistently wanted to know how the budget has been constructed specifically to meet strategic objectives.

## Other Areas of Planning

Strategic enrollment management, academic program planning, and resource planning are probably the three most common areas of strategic planning on any U.S. college or university campus. They are also, perhaps, the three most essential areas. Yet other areas of programming or operations may be significant enough in the life of the institution to also be designated as major areas, and as part of the institutional strategic plan. This section identifies some of these areas and discusses how the overall plan would incorporate them into the process.

### Information Technology

As we discussed in Chapter Two, we are moving out of the industrial age into the information age. This is a critical concern to campus strategic planners, because it means they can no longer develop plans for the campus based on traditional models that have their roots in the older way of doing things. This is not, however, a concern for only the academic side of the institution. While the academics of a college or university need to reflect the realities of the society it mirrors and serves, the campus itself must also move from the industrial model to the emerging information model. Noorda and Dallinga-Hunter (1992) and Raghunathan and Raghunathan (1991) point out that as we come to depend more and more on information and technological systems, strategic planning is becoming more and more critical, particularly because of the impact of these systems on overall organizational performance.

*The Impact of the Information Revolution.* Electronic technology and information technology are revolutionizing nearly everything done on the campus. Change is at hand in areas from marketing and registration to teaching chemistry; from athletics to campuswide energy savings; from the library to tracking the campus's human resources; and from worldwide satellite communication conferences in the business school to language laboratories. This revolution brings with it major challenges to everyone, from students to the governing board.

And not everyone is excited about these changes. The dean of faculty of a very small private college reacted to a recommendation to expand its presence internationally via a strategic information initiative by saying, "I just don't agree that technology will occupy the central role in future society. If we apply IT [information technology] here in this way, then we threaten the very basis of our institution. Faculty will be replaced by robots, our pastoral campus will be replaced by machines, and wires, and keypads, and video screens. We will be helping dehumanize our society—and I am against IT completely."

Others are not so negative. The strategic plan at Villanova University states that its approach to technology is that it can not only expand the university's resources but it can also become an enabling force to better serve both the internal and external constituencies of the university without increasing staff (Office for University Information Technologies, Villanova University, 1995). Nonetheless, and regardless of the internal concern and resistance the previous quote exemplifies, trends are becoming more and more clear. The campus must adapt in order to compete and to accurately reflect a leadership position in the information age. Further, as Carter, Nilakanta, and Norris (1991) tell us, "As information technology undergoes rapid changes, we need to continue to focus attention on stimulating innovation in teaching and research via the use of computer"

(p. 287). Students must be highly computer literate, campuses must be networked, classrooms need to accommodate new types of technology, laboratories need to adapt to new technological methods of analysis, the administrative systems need to be modernized and integrated onto a single platform, and the interface between the campus and the worldwide community needs to be reflective of the techniques now used in business and industry.

*Establishing Campuswide Standards for Growth and Development.* On certain campuses, information technology is becoming a major concern while on others it is not. For those campuses where it is an important issue, however, planning how information technology will be used within the institution presents problems. First, it is unlikely that the campus will be able to rely on discipline-developed guidelines to tell it how to build its systems. In other words, this is not necessarily an academic problem. Second, the campus will need to develop much of its system in cooperation with external vendors who have developed the administrative systems and the academic interface supports. Third, the movement toward an integrated, campuswide information technology system is costly and will require a major shifting of resources or the development of new resources.

Clearly, given the range of possibilities, it is conceivable that planning in this area could get out-of-hand and become unrealistic given the realities of the resources available to or acquirable by the institution. To give some guidelines to the planning process, then, it is useful to develop a set of standards the campus should aim for in developing its information technology system. These standards might reflect what is happening on other campuses across the country, or they might be based in expert opinion as to what levels of information technology would best serve the overall institution over the next several years. These standards should also be prioritized to help managers better understand the best application of resources for technological development on the campus.

*KPIs, Goals, Strategies, and Policies.*  In order to be effective, these standards need to be quantifiable as well as realistic, given the opportunities and constraints of the resource base. These standards then lend themselves easily to the development of KPIs, goals, strategies, and policies.

A caveat is appropriate here, however. The field is changing so dramatically that a fair amount of caution needs to be integrated into the plans to make major, highly expensive changes that might be obsolete in the relative short run. For example, as of this writing, many campuses are scrambling to put personal computers with Pentium technology on the desk of every faculty and staff member. The cost per machine is somewhere between $1,200 and $3,000. Yet within the next two years, the Pentium technology will be replaced, and within three to four years, the current computers will be obsolete. This example represents a significant challenge to the planning process, since adaption to today's standards may cost hundreds of thousands, perhaps millions of dollars—yet within three years these standards may be obsolete.

Perhaps a more thorough investigation of where the latest technology is needed on campus, as opposed to where less-sophisticated applications will work well, will allow planners to develop a plan that is current but more cost-effective. Strategic plans can and should mirror these challenges and constraints in setting different time frames for goals and strategies, and in developing a policy base that reflects the rapidly changing environment of information technology and sets the institution's direction as it seeks to interface with that environment.

*Innovative Methods of Growth.*  The increase of information technology and the other elements of the emerging information age represent a significant challenge to the campus. However, they also represent a tremendous opportunity. Students expect to learn what the world they are about to enter is like and what it will require of them. They also hope to learn where the trends are headed, and higher education can continue, through research and analysis, to maintain its traditional lead in this area. Strategic planning in this area can help an institution point the way toward the emerging world—an important and fascinating opportunity for the educational process.

## Operations and Administration

Operational and administrative activities are another area in which particular campuses might want to do some specific strategic planning. Though some strictly operational types of day-to-day activities (such as mail services or food stock purchasing) may not lend themselves well to long-term strategic planning, it is appropriate that the direction and purposes that college and university administrations pursue reflect strategic planning. Costs, efficiency, and effectiveness are common issues in the administration of many colleges and universities, and the strategic planning process needs to look at these areas much the same as it looks at the academic, student, resource, and other areas of planning. The demands to cut prices, the growing national problem of deferred maintenance, and other day-to-day management problems need to be addressed (Leslie and Fretwell, 1996). Also, much of the burden of implementing the plan and operating the campus within the framework of strategic management will fall to administrators, therefore requiring a planning premise that will guide the long-term outcomes of the strategic planning process.

Those involved in resolving planning need to have a thorough knowledge of what it takes to run an effective college or university. Many of the deans and faculty will view the administration as overpaid and overpowered bureaucrats who take away resources from the academic mission of the institution. While strategic planning is not going to change many of these perceptions, it can at least develop a rationale for what administrative services are needed on the campus and what resources are required to support them. Realistically, most of the faculty recognize the need for someone else to be in charge of the administrative functions of the campus, and they are not really anti-administration—they are simply uninformed and uninvolved.

The strategic planning process in this area should develop a basic planning rationale and then set out plans for administrative and operational standards, much the same as it has done in other areas. For example, because of uncertain market conditions and the emerging needs for recruiting, information gathering, and public relations dictated by recognition of the importance of developing solid external relationships, it may not be easy for campus managers or strategic planners to pinpoint specific administrative salary standards or travel guidelines. Yet standards can be determined, perhaps based on national benchmarks, that would keep administrative activities in line with national criteria.

Another issue is the need to change traditional thinking to strategic thinking, and traditional decision making to strategic decision making. We may have implied in this book that the transition might just happen on its own. In fact, it does not. The move toward thinking and making decisions strategically must be specifically planned out, practiced, reinforced, and monitored. Top administrators and academic leaders need to constantly remind themselves and others of the strategic significance of the issues they wrestle with. They need to tie results to strategic directions outlined in the original planning process, and be in a position to defend their actions based on strategic KPIs, goals, strategies, or policies. This is why several institutions have devoted a part of their planning process to this area of institutional life.

## Campuswide Operations

Beyond the administrative component, campuswide operations need to be included in certain institutional plans. Adequacy of facilities, maintenance of the capital plant, the accounting function, the personnel function (human resources management), and other critical operations of the campus are but a few of the subareas that particular colleges or universities might want to highlight in their strategic planning process. Several of these areas might already have an operational plan in place because of the more traditional bureaucratic or business setting in which they conduct their activities. Such plans should be reviewed in light of the general strategic direction of the institution. For example, it is not a bad idea to make sure that if the institution has an overall campus facilities master plan, that plan should be congruent with or perhaps, in reference form, even be a part of the developing institutional strategic plan. In this way, planning will continue to be effective in these areas, but it will also be consistent with the emerging college or university strategic plan.

## University Services

In many respects, residential campuses in particular must be almost as concerned about the activities and services that occur beyond the classroom as they are with academics. But even on nonresidential campuses, the contemporary college or university is faced with growing demands to assist the student, faculty, and staff in life issues. Again, however, service-type operations can be challenging to develop plans around because of the highly qualitative nature of their activities. Nonetheless, planners can still develop standards and surrogates for these subareas and devise KPIs, goals, strategies, and policies in much the same way we have described for other qualifiable activities of the campus.

*Student Services.* The subarea of student services may well need to reflect changes that are occurring in the general mix of students, and their needs to survive and compete for a college education. Single mothers may need child care; returning or nontraditional students may need assistance in redeveloping study habits; minority students may need support groups to help them adapt to the academic climate. As costs continue to increase, many students need significant help and counseling regarding the financing of their education. More and more campuses are recognizing their responsibilities relative to the health needs of their students; and housing and nutrition continue to be problematic for many. These and other examples reflect the growing need of the campus to respond more directly to the life-related needs of its student body. These services are costly, but they are also related to the ability of the institution to retain its students as well as to assure that the maximum opportunity exists for students to do well in their academic pursuits. The ties of planning in these areas to SEM are fairly straightforward.

*Administrative Services.* Faculty and staff also represent a significant set of needs. Health and life insurance, retirement, promotions, tenure, and a wide range of employee benefits are not simply a legal requirement of many colleges and universities, they are also competitive issues. Institutions compete nationally for faculty, staff, and administrators, and they need to make sure that their employment packages at least meet national standards.

Other administrative services beyond the human resource management function also lend themselves to the strategic planning process. Accounting, information processing, records, media support, and others are vital to the overall smooth running of both the administrative and academic functions of a campus. Once again, standards can be determined and appropriate KPIs, goals, strategies, and policies can be developed to reflect these important aspects of the inner workings of the campus.

*Community and Other Public Services.* One of the key areas of planning should be the interfacing of the college or university with the community, or communities, of which it is a part. In developing a strategic interface, today's college or university needs to understand that education of college students is not the only service their constituencies expect. Increasingly, local communities, states, and even national groups look to the college or university as a place to get certain types of help and/or advice. As gigantic storehouses of knowledge, colleges and universities also have a responsibility to be good and supportive neighbors.

Strategic planning presents an excellent opportunity for the institution to develop a focused understanding of just what its communities' needs are and what its abilities are to respond. Community and public services are not generally areas in which the college or university will provide rewards for the faculty, students, and staff who provide them. Yet in order to build a stronger relationship with the external environment and help assure its long-term viability, the institution needs to develop its capabilities in these areas. Thus, developing standards, appropriate interfaces, and perhaps even reward systems within the context of the strategic plan begins to make more and more sense.

### Other Area Concerns

There may be other areas in which the institution's strategic planners may determine there is enough activity or importance to warrant the development of a specific area for planning. While planners should not plan for the sake of planning, certain campuses may have specific areas of activity that it would be a serious error not to include in the central strategic planning process.

Once again, it may be that on a particular campus a single institutional SPC can adequately handle all of the critical areas involved in the planning process. On another campus, strategic planning might be much better served by a series of area subcommittees as well as unit committees. Clearly the safest and most prudent avenue would be to develop as simple a planning process as possible. The key is to understand what needs to be included—that is, what has strategic significance to the institution and what does not. With this understanding, the institution should be able to avoid making this process more difficult than it needs to be, and to streamline it to fit the strategic needs of the particular college or university.

## Relationships Among the Several Areas of Strategic Planning

Once planners have made a decision regarding which areas they will include in their plan, they then need to understand the relationships that occur among them. As we indicated at the beginning of this chapter, the interdependence of strategic

Figure 12.2. Integrating the Strategic Planning Process.

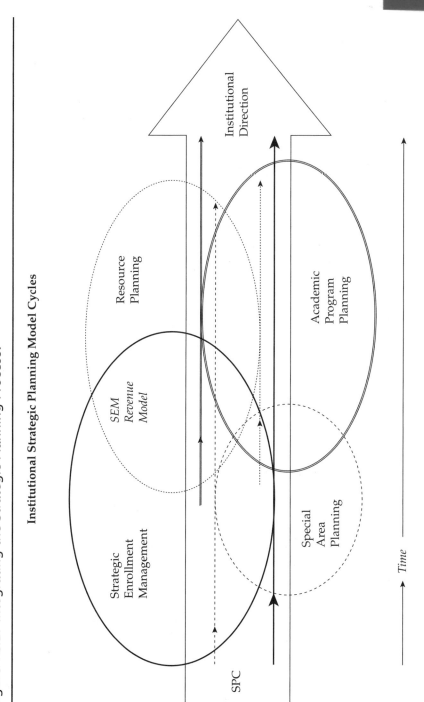

Institutional Strategic Planning Model Cycles

enrollment management, academic program planning, and resource planning is basic, and no single section of the plan can be developed successfully without congruence among all three areas. Figure 12.2 demonstrates these relationships, and also suggests that there may well be a logical order in which a particular college or university should undertake planning in the various areas.

Once again, *this is not a process in which resources should dominate the development of the plan in the other areas.* Creativity must come first, and then the issue of what is realistic or possible should follow. Also, the resource issue is not simply a discussion of how to allocate what is available. It is also an issue of how current resources are being used, and calls for making a decision to reallocate these resources to areas and programs that the strategic planning process has identified as priorities for the institution. In developing the basic three areas of the plan (after the initial stage, in which the SPC develops the central tenets of planning), planners will identify areas in which various planning elements from one area of planning need to be consolidated with those of another area.

The other areas of planning may be developed either concurrently or after the basic three areas have taken shape. In any event, the elements found in any area of the plan need to be consistent with what has been developed elsewhere. Resources will tend to be a focal point for determining this consistency, since most planning issues involve resources at one point or another.

Nonetheless, it is important that academic objectives be consistent with service objectives, that SEM objectives tie in with resource objectives. Institutional master plan objectives need to be consistent with academic directions. In other words, a comprehensive strategic plan needs to be tested rigorously for internal consistency. Once the institution's SPC can determine that this congruency exists, it can then move forward knowing that the basic plan is sound, and increase the probability that it will be successful.

# Acting on the Plan

# CHAPTER 13

# Implementing the Plan

Without a doubt, the processes and objectives we have described throughout this book up to this point are worthless if they are not properly implemented. Yet as one goes through the literature and reads what theorists and case writers have said about implementation, there is a general lack of specific tactical substance that gives adequate methods and advice to those who actually attempt to implement the results of strategic planning. Part Three of this book looks at several of the issues surrounding successful implementation of the strategic plan on a college or university campus.

In this chapter, we will attempt to fill the gap by presenting material helpful to the strategic planner that can be found in the literature, as well as useful advice that can be gleaned from both successful and unsuccessful implementation events in a variety of colleges and universities.

## The Basics: Fundamentally Required Elements

Gratch and Wood (1991) tell us that support must be generated at all levels as the plan is being developed, or trouble will result when the institution begins implementation—perhaps a simplistic view, but nonetheless fundamentally true. And as we have stated, strategic planning activities and implementation are incremental events. The impact of these statements is that campus strategic planners must worry about implementation at the very beginning of the planning process, and they must work within a participative process to begin implementation of the components of the plan as they emerge and pass through the required approval process. For example, during the University of Northern Colorado's (UNC) strategic enrollment management (SEM) planning, due to the immediacy of an impending enrollment shortfall in the fall of 1993 the SEM subcommittee worked overtime during the last part of spring and the early part of summer to develop the long-range perspective of a substantive SEM program, and then used that perspective to identify specific short-term activities it could engage in to address the impending problem. While there was not enough time to meet the enrollment problem head-on with complete success, enough activity was accomplished to lessen the potential impact and to set the university up to better meet its goals in upcoming years. This action was accomplished on a university-wide basis, with administrators working in student recruiting and enrollment with the institution's president, vice presidents, academic deans, and faculty representatives. When appropriate tactics were developed, they were immediately approved by the responsible groups and put into place by many of the people that had helped to develop them.

The example just presented also illustrates that as the process pinpoints and adopts certain desired outcomes, it also develops specific tactics for their implementation within the framework of long-term strategies. Further, when these tactics for implementation unfold, events and opportunities occur that lend legitimacy and give substance to how the plan can be implemented.

The most simplistic tactics for implementation found in the literature include the well-known theoretical issue of recreating or redesigning the organization's structure, which may lead to the serious problem of dealing with those who are highly resistant to change. But this is not the only problem many campus planners have discovered. Sandy (1991) has also pointed out that "planners can become frustrated because bold initiatives often remain lifeless prisoners in plan books that are rapidly filed away. Those who receive the plans can become frustrated because they don't perceive the initiatives as relevant to their real-world issues" (p. 30). Implementation is chronically beset with problems (Wilson, 1992). And when a reduction in force or elimination of programs is involved, implementation will be decidedly political and emotion-charged (Hardy, 1990).

Meredith (1993) has also suggested that the success or failure of strategic planning may well be institution-specific, which makes it even more difficult to understand how any particular campus can develop a successful implementation strategy. He also suggests that some of the most successful implementation tactics have included participative planning, institution-wide planning, making the planning in fact strategic as opposed to traditional, defining clear goals, linking planning and budgeting, involving the academic community, ensuring good communication, and creating a more effective facilities plan. Our position is a bit more straightforward: that in practice, team building, communication, top-leader commitment and direction, tying strategic priorities to the institution's budgeting process, and overcoming planning obstacles from the very beginning are specific tactics critical to effective implementation.

## Communication Issues

Several authors, particularly those who have done case studies in higher education, point to the need for comprehensive and appropriate patterns of communication between strategic planners and the rest of the campus community (Cline and Meringolo, 1991; Eaton and Adams, 1991; Morrill, 1988; Roach, 1988; and Aggarwal, 1987). Floyd and Wooldridge (1992) also found that one major problem in implementation was that middle managers often neither understood nor were committed to the strategies devised at the organizational level. Nebgen (1991) simply states that communication is the single most important element in successful strategic planning. Hanson and Henry (1993) suggest that developing a strategic marketing program in conjunction with the institutional strategic plan may be helpful in developing appropriate implementation tactics. At the University of Iowa, planners recognized the importance of ongoing and open participatory processes in making their plan successful, along with the necessity of making decisions about programmatic and resource allocations within the context of the university and units plans (University of Iowa Campus Communications, 1995).

How the community is involved with and informed about the strategic plan, how their opinions and concerns are taken into consideration, and how people throughout the campus believe the strategic plan has included them are all vital issues of communication. If communication is taken lightly by the strategic planners, the plan is doomed to failure. If it is taken seriously, and developed through truly collegial efforts, the implementation of the plan is much smoother. Chiarelott, Reed, and Russell (1991) reflect on the strategic planning process at Bowling Green State University and conclude that three important additional communication considerations include using language with which people on campus are familiar and comfortable, weighing the side effects of which group does the decision making, and making sure that as large a constituency group as possible is educated about the intricacies of the strategic planning process.

## Using Media with Caution

One-way communication devices, such as updates, newsletters, and news releases, are not in themselves particularly effective means of increasing participation. Two-way communication devices, such as open forums, focus groups, town meetings, and reports to major constituent groups, are much more effective in making sure that people understand what the process is leading to and accomplishing, and they provide the opportunity for those who are not directly involved in the process to make comments and voice concerns.

At UNC, we made most of the mistakes possible. We put out two professionally published newsletters toward the beginning of the process and asked people to write letters to the editor. No one did. The only demonstrable response we got was concern over how much it cost to publish the newsletters. We then went to memo-type letters to the campus community. This time the responses were characterized by confusion about language and the complexity of the process rather than adding anything constructive. Later we attempted to improve communication through open forums and "Lunch with the President" sessions but were extremely disappointed by the low turnout. Plus, the people who came to one such gathering seemed to be the same ones who came to the rest of them.

Though the faculty senate regularly scheduled reports on strategic planning, both the planning committee's inability to report the accomplishments of major objectives on a regular basis and the complexity of the process we had adopted proved to be sources of irritation rather than information. In time, the faculty senate decided to withdraw its support of the process (because results emerged slower than anticipated, and because a general political climate had developed that desired to kill the process altogether), and the planning committee was facing major credibility concerns as it attempted to bring the planning process to a demonstrable position. The authors have heard very similar stories from several other planning efforts on college and university campuses across the country. One particular faculty senate approved a plan developed over a three-year period, and then asked for a vote of "no confidence in the president" for elements contained in the plan. Another demanded to know how the budget was going to be affected before they would buy into what they assumed must be a Machiavellian process because it was an administrative one. A private university systematically shrunk from a student body of 25,000 to

12,000, periodically selling off real estate assets to cover a structural deficit, while fighting tooth and nail all attempts to "plan."

In regard to improving participation and communication, we soon learned that small informal groups, meetings with governance groups, personal politicking, and doggedly keeping the strategic planning activity simple and straightforward were better methods of discussing the process and improving communication. Also, our governing board went on record as heavily supporting the process, which also helped improve acceptance. As we began to ask specific standing committees across the campus to react to a specific issue or proposal, to test a particular recommendation against current practices and capabilities, and to recommend a course of action to the responsible strategic planning committee, the participatory process began to take hold. Eventually, after policies that we had routed through campus standing committees in this manner were approved by the board of trustees, the credibility of the process began to increase significantly.

In an important way, the last example shows how the process was actually beginning to move from Phase One (the planning stage) to Phase Two (the implementation stage). At UNC this began to occur in the second year of planning. By moving decision-making activity related to the strategic direction of the plan to the campus governance structure, we were able to move the elements of strategic thinking to an important operational position in the university. In the third year of planning, as we moved to wind down significantly our strategic planning phase, we also were able to decentralize much of the strategic decision making in this manner, keeping only the university's SPC intact to continuously monitor the effects of strategies over time.

## Making the Planning Document Public

Many people believe that strategic planning has no substance to it until a document is produced. After all, what good is a plan unless it is written down and shared with the campus as a whole? As a consequence, attention focuses on the liturgy surrounding the document rather than on the dynamic unfolding of planning activities that lead to desired outcomes or resolve important issues.

As we described in Chapter Seven, we believe that an effective strategic planning document needs to be kept simple and in a format that can be easily rewritten as new elements of the plan emerge over time, as Brown (1988) has also suggested. Such a document might contain the elements included in Exhibit 7.1.

## The Process Is More Important than the Document

One of the most important outcomes of strategic planning is the decision-making process for shaping change that it creates. This process is characterized by the strategic thinking and strategic decision making that are developed early in strategic planning. As enrollment issues are addressed and key performance indicators are identified, approaches for shaping change emerge from the assessment and analysis of strengths, weaknesses, opportunities, and threats. Enrollment strategies spawn ideas about the curriculum that is needed to serve those enrolled, thus triggering academic program planning. Shifts in academic programs have budgetary effects, so budget and resource planning evolves. As implementation institutionalizes these activities, the document of the plan evolves to contain the residue of the planning process, with little of the flavor of the work that went into its creation. While the document can signal a coming together of each phase of the process, it cannot become the sole basis for planning. More important than the document are the insights its development triggered, the understandings created among participants about how to accomplish desired outcomes, and the exposure it gives to the strategic thinking that underpins the plan. Certainly the participative process underscores these outcomes.

The process has been important in preparing planners at a variety of levels to produce a document, and the process also goes beyond the document that signals whether or not strategic planning has been effective or successful. Process is a bridge that educates those involved in planning about how to link planning with actual governance and decision making to solve real problems. This is an outcome that over time helps to sell planning to those who are skeptical about it or who see it as a threat to previous and accepted practice. Through involvement in the strategic planning exercise, participants broaden their vistas of the state of the institution, as well as their views of the state of the environments within which it operates. These perspectives enable them to understand why doing business the old-fashioned way is no longer suitable or acceptable in the changing world in which they live and in which the university functions.

## The Essential Role of Team Building

Neumann (1991) strongly supports the proposition that the development of a team is essential, including those from the top administrative leadership of the campus to those throughout the organization who are charged with implementation. Team participants eventually become ambassadors. Ideally, those who plan represent major constituents, and also represent the process that links strategic planning back to those same groups. We do not suggest that as ambassadors they should begin to proselytize their constituents into a "new religion" of strategic planning. But they can perform the task of being well-informed participants in campus discussions about the elements of strategic planning and strategic management.

More often than not, people who have gone through the strategic planning we describe in this book tell us that they understand much more about the direction and purpose of the institution as a result of their participation. Cross (1987) tells us that implementation is dependent upon effective communication among planning constituents, and Akkermans and Van Aken (1992) call for broad-based involvement of faculty, administrators, staff, and students. Those we have talked with also tell us that because of their involvement in strategic planning they feel more a part of the institution, and empowered to do something that will benefit the institution and, as a consequence, themselves. These are clearly the benefits of good team building.

## Campuswide Leadership Involvement

These important effects of the process need to be emphasized by those who lead the campus. Involvement gives people firsthand knowledge of the issues, problems, and shortcomings associated with planning. As the process solves real problems, such as enrollment shortfalls, the utility of strategic planning gradually takes shape. For example, as enrollment management strategies affect present practice and improve it, the link between planning and decision making becomes evident. In these incremental ways, the opponents, the doubters, the tenuous supporters, and the enthusiasts begin to share a sense of what strategic planning entails and how it can affect management.

For all the good that process can achieve, process can also bring with it certain obstacles that should be avoided. Morgan and Piercy (1993) suggest that effective planning avoids staff-directed planning, concentrates more on planning rather than on budgets or fantasies, develops planning skills among all those involved in the process, ties resources to planning, rewards the planning activities and outcomes, develops teams, keeps the process simple (particularly at the beginning), is iterative, demands specific implementation tactics, and recognizes that strategic planning is a continuous process. Newport, Dess, and Rasheet (1991) warn that the plan should be checked against itself internally prior to implementation to be sure that there are no inconsistencies. And Kaufman and Herman (1991) warn that unless the vision under which planning proceeds is of the world in which we want to live now and in the future—if it concentrates instead on courses and their content (believing that societally beneficial results will be the outcome)—nothing but short-term, stopgap objectives will be achieved. These are all issues that planning leadership must keep its eyes on, and without the continuing support and vigilance of top-level leadership, many of the pitfalls will easily develop.

The evolution of gradual understanding and familiarity with how planning solves problems helps campus leaders explain the benefits of the strategic planning process to the constituents they represent. Once people who have helped develop the initial document understand this, the discussions between committee members and other people and groups across the campus will spread and broaden the understanding of planning. Particularly with strong campus leadership support, sooner or later most campus constituents will come to learn that the campus turned a corner at some point and is now managing itself in a different way, a way that, it is hoped, more and more people will come to understand is beneficial in one way or another to everyone involved.

## Overcoming Campus Obstacles to Planning

Resistance to change is common and is clearly a major part of the campus environment, as we have discussed throughout this book. It is helpful, therefore, for those involved in strategic planning to understand some of the characteristics of change that cause individuals or groups to respond as they do.

### Change Chills

Strategic planning challenges current practice. In the academy, where process is primary, this challenge has a chilling effect. University faculty and staff must be prepared for both the slow pace of change and the uncertainty that surrounds it.

Failure to prepare the campus for the participative and incremental ways in which results will emerge leads first to skepticism about strategic planning, and gradually to opposition. Because the strategic planning process is complex, people will wonder, Why go through the effort if the results are not clear or immediate? Since other committee structures are already in place, people may also wonder why these cannot be the vessels for planning. If these committees are codified in the institution's handbook or codes, people will directly challenge the legitimacy of those planning activities and entities that appear to interfere with present practice and codified jurisdictions. Regardless of the campus scenario, preparation should be carefully made to warm the chill of opposition and skepticism before the legitimacy of planning is seriously undermined.

Planners can lay groundwork by describing the process that will be followed, identifying the major phases of the process, specifying the committee structure and how it will initially relate to existing structures, clarifying any jurisdictional issues as early as possible, and then bracing themselves for opposition anyway. Since colleges and universities are composed primarily of people, and since budgets are heavily weighted toward salaries, the great fear is that planning will lead to layoffs. Particularly to minimize deleterious events, leadership must be honest about these probabilities and indicate how they intend to use the results of planning. Planners cannot be effective if they bear the burden of being the hatchets of change. Refuge should be found and rooted in the participatory nature of the process. But fundamentally, if people fear change, the constructive alternative is to help shape it.

Because of the chill of fear, strategic planning must move incrementally and slowly, trying to clarify what is happening at each new step. This is why we recommend that the proper sequence for demand-driven planning is enrollment management, solving some special campus need (at UNC and at the California State University at Los Angeles it was technology), academic program planning, and finally resources planning.

As we indicated in Chapter Ten, of these planning areas, the most difficult to explain, conduct, and legitimize is academic program planning. For this reason, it is important to show some success in planning before undertaking academic program planning. Because the resistance to program change is endemic and fierce, the need for such change must be clearly argued, even if that need is not clearly seen. And it must be argued consistently and persistently until some results occur from academic planning. Finally, it is imperative that governing boards insist on change and are steadfast about their expectation. This is another reason that campuswide leadership must be part of the process from the very beginning and must communicate on a substantive and ongoing basis with its various constituencies.

## Empowering the Campus to Change Itself

There are some real problems in dealing with the normal campus expectations. Traditionally, campuses expect that first a vision will be set forth to guide change. Often, campus constituents will look to two sources for this vision. First, the president or chancellor is expected to have a vision for change and to espouse it. Second, the institution's mission statement is usually already set forth. Even if it is somewhat current, it is often outmoded and has largely been made so by the expectations of those who accredit the campus every ten years. For the purposes of strategic planning, such a mission statement cannot be the font of strategic change.

Further, if the president or chancellor puts forth a vision, whose vision is it? With presidential turnover in institutions of higher education in the United States at currently less than five years of tenure, and with planning likely to take nearly that long to mature, how is continuity achieved? And how are the important long-range effects of planning turned into reality based on what the president has described as her or his vision? Likewise, the mission statement is always an academic Christmas tree of sorts, where each constituency gets to hang its bauble of little substance. How do strategic elements for change emerge from a turf-protective entity? The plain truth is that the "vision thing" must come out of strategic planning at the point when those involved in it as well as those in opposition to it see the need for a uniting theme and for attributes that give a character to the institution, thereby helping to identify the institution's priorities. For it is only when priorities overlay finances that strategies for achieving desirable and effective change can emerge.

The hard reality is that the campus will want a vision from its president or chancellor, will call for it, and will criticize that individual for lack of leadership if no vision emerges. And just as bad, even if one does emerge, it will be criticized unless it is an inclusive Christmas tree with an ornament on it for everyone. Similarly, if strategic planning begins with the mission statement, an approach we have argued against, the statement will also likely have an ornament for everyone. In either case, present preferences will drive the strategy for the future. The resulting misfit will be painfully obvious when finances, politics, or external forces refuse to provide support or funding.

What presidents or chancellors, along with other campus leaders, can do is consistently call for program priorities as essential for effective academic planning. If trustees or regents have ideas about such things, those ideas should be deliberately and carefully surfaced to drive home the need for campus empowerment. This empowerment should take the form of identifying and shaping academic priorities through academic program planning, using the process described in Chapter Eleven. Effective campuswide leadership under these conditions takes the form of resisting the temptation to provide "the official vision," reinforcing how priorities must precede strategic change, and enlisting the firm support of the governing board members for a set of priorities as major budgetary decisions are made.

To help the process along, it may be permissible for a president or chancellor to set forth her or his ideas as catalysts for thought or to encourage those who seem willing to take up the task. Such advocacy, coupled with praise for those who assume the mantle of strategic planning, can encourage others to become empowered and to join in the effort to share in the ownership of shaping change.

## Joining to Obstruct

As we identified in Chapter Five, campus politics is a force to contend with in the development of a college or university strategic plan, and it has both its positive and negative attributes. Because participation drives the model of strategic planning that we prefer and that is generally supported in the literature, as planning gets a head of steam, opponents will realize that planning might just succeed. Rather than joining the process to help shape change constructively, they may now join to help derail it. Ploys will vary with the nature of campus politics, but they will be aimed at slowing change by delaying successes and attacking proponents as violators of shared governance or underminers of quality already in place. Since process is so central, process will be the tool to overcome this resistance.

Opponents will want the review of every relevant group "before we can move ahead." The relation of planning to governance and its committees will become a prerequisite for the giving of legitimacy to any strategic planning results. Often opponents will charge that strategic planning is too vague or too ambitious or theoretic and should be held at bay "until we can solve the immediate problems of concern." The tendency will be to come up with present-oriented problem-rooted management plans as prerequisites to or substitutes for strategic planning. By keeping the horizon to the current year—usually the current budget cycle—strategic planning can be both put off and made subject to the criticism that it is not of practical use or is not working. This is because, as a long-term tool, strategic planning usually cannot adequately serve as a short-term device. Regardless of the technique, the intent will be to slow or veto planning, especially academic program planning.

The antidote to these tactics for planners and institutional administrators is to stay the course with strategic planning, being sure to link planning activities to the resolution of real and important issues. Also, governing board support has proved to be a useful ally. This is why an incremental strategy that focuses first on visible things like enrollment or technology and that can be implemented to produce early results is so important. It gives the lie to the impracticality of strategic planning, while also laying the foundation for demand-driven academic program planning that comes later.

## Strategic Planning Works

Because strategic planning addresses the future, it is always vulnerable to the wisdom of hindsight. Persistence is the antidote to hindsight. Strategic planning will work if planners stay the course but also adjust to the realities of the day. The point is that persistence rather than rigidity makes strategic planning successful. Unfortunately, the tendency among many planners is to stay with the idealized structures and processes with which planning began. This will ensure failure. If academic program planning, in order to gain legitimacy, must go through review by existing governance committees, let it happen; but planners and administrators must structure the review process so as to avoid deadlock or unnegotiable conflict. Also, approval of academic program change is necessary from particular faculty bodies, it is somewhat imperative that representatives of those bodies be active in the development of the plans from the beginning.

## Structural Ramifications of the Change Process

Strategic planning is designed to develop change. Since a college or university is primarily a human services institution, most of this change is going to affect the people who are associated with those services. As strategic planners begin to think about moving from Phase One to Phase Two, they need to deal with the issue of merging the new operations of strategic planning with the ongoing operational processes of the campus, as demonstrated in Figure 13.1.

Structural changes in the process itself will occur as the strategic planning process gives way to strategic management. Certain committees or functions that were a part of the landscape before strategic planning began, as well as those additional committees that were created by the strategic planning process, will need to merge, wither away, or give rise to new organizational entities. However, even though the changes brought about by strategic planning may be extremely beneficial to the institution, certain individuals or groups within the organization may not fare as well or may perceive that they will not fare as well as a result of change. This is the main impetus for resisting change.

### Dealing With Resistance

Resistance to change is a perfectly natural human response, particularly if people view those changes as actually or potentially damaging to their well-being. Nonetheless, what many in higher education feel is actually or potentially damaging to

Figure 13.1. Merging Strategic Planning with the Ongoing Organization.

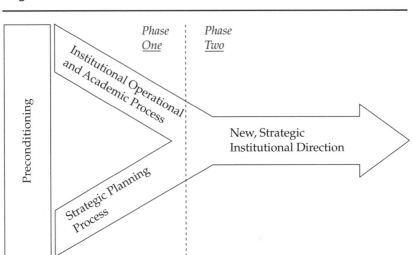

their well-being is usually something that challenges the way they are used to doing things. Also, those in the academic segment of the institution are accustomed to having a high degree of autonomy and control over the work they do, and they deeply resent the institution suggesting to them or forcing them to do things differently, or to do different things.

These are essentially structural issues. Structure in this context is the pattern of how people are arranged within the organization to do its work. Structure also involves patterns of communication, power distribution, and control methods that are used to help provide the stability and order that are necessary to allow the organization to operate as efficiently and effectively as possible. Doing things differently disrupts these familiar patterns of activity and causes dissonance among the affected members of the organization.

Strategic planning can determine, for example, that one element of the structure (a particular program area) has too many people located in an area where demand for services has decreased over time. Curing this situation not only alters the configuration of people in the affected area but also modifies the pattern of activities that go on in that area. This makes the change felt more widely throughout the organization. This also helps explain why the changes that come about through strategic planning often lead to resistance. This resistance can come from both the part of the areas that are heavily affected and from larger segments that are either partially affected by the change or that fear the same thing could happen to them.

## Collaboration and Participation

We have continuously stressed the need for participation, communication, and cooperation in the development of the strategic plan, in the implementation stages, and in Phase Two, when planning gives way to strategic thinking and strategic decision making. One of the reasons these actions are needed is to anticipate and help reduce the development of the resistance to change that will occur once people begin to feel the structural ramifications of that change. As we stated earlier, if people are involved in helping to shape the change, or if they believe that the change will actually benefit them, they are less likely to resist and can be effective in reducing resistance among others. For example, Cline and Meringolo (1991) tell us that at The Pennsylvania State University their bottom-up approach provided an important vehicle for institutionalizing a participative management system.

It would be imprudent to let it be thought that strategic planning can lead to little or no disruption of an institution's structure—that somehow planners can write the plan in such a way that everyone is accommodated and real change takes place somewhere outside the boundaries of the campus. In fact, the changes required may be so revolutionary that entire departments and campus operations could be targeted for closure or for major expansion. Keeping in mind that it is the survival of the institution that is important here, not the well-being of specific elements of its faculty, staff, and administrators, optimum changes that strengthen the institution could well be seen as catastrophic by parts of the organization.

## Humane Strategic Planning

Ideally, an institution has not allowed itself to get to the state where catastrophic structural change is necessary. Moreover, if strategic planning can identify structural problems before they are causing the institution great difficulties, planners can chart a course for change over time that provides a humane and relatively nondisruptive means of overcoming those problems. This should be the preferred goal, and it should override the desires of those campus constituents who see what they believe to be problems and demand quick and decisive action. The pain of change flows from the severity of a problem and the impact it has on the strategic direction of the institution.

Essentially, strategic planning can be both a humane and a revolutionary tool for institutional administrators, faculty, staff, and governing boards. This is an important guideline, because external environments, especially the business sector, do not tend to be humane in their approaches to fixing what is wrong. As state legislatures manipulate budget allocations, as grant providers juggle requests to cut out overhead and other costs of doing business, and as foundation donors put limitations on how their money can be used by the institution, the potential for cuts exists. None of these resource providers take responsibility for the structural havoc that might be caused by their actions. Some even think that the institution is fat anyway and could use some trimming. Strategic planning can include strategies for altering the structure in a humane fashion, especially since it can do so over time.

Time is really the focus. The process of strategic planning provides the institution with a different perspective on its situation, problems, and environments over the long term. By taking the entire operation out of a pattern of doing things in the short run to achieve short-term results, an institution buys time. With time, downsizing or eliminating a department can be done through attrition or through retraining, so that job incumbents can remain with the institution but in a different and more useful capacity. With time, new opportunities, now obscured, can emerge, allowing the institution to live out a growth scenario instead of a scheme of retrenchment. With time, people can learn to trust and not fear change, becoming more flexible as inevitable changes occur.

## Overcoming the Hurdles of Tradition Binding and Lack of Creativity

Colleges and universities are heavily tradition bound. Much of their character and nature comes from the development of a proud tradition of academic excellence and societal contributions. Tradition brings with it a pride that is evident not only on the campus but also among its alumni, donors, and the community in which it is located. For these reasons, tradition is a valuable asset to a college or university and is one strength on which strategic planning can build.

Tradition can also be a weakness, however. From a structural point of view, tradition may well mean that a college or university has been successful with the programs and faculty it has developed over the years, so there is little reason to change. This attitude is one of the most difficult to contradict, even in the face of massive problems that the current structure is incapable of addressing.

*Digging In.* In their discussion of some of the strategic choices organizations make, Miles and Snow (1978) talk about the choice of being a "defender." A defender is an organization that has invested heavily in its current operations and does not believe that the changes occurring all around it are substantive enough to accommodate. Such an organization believes that the changes they see are temporary or even faddish and by sticking to their traditional methods of operation they will be successful in the long term. The defender wins if the change goes away. However, the defender loses if the change becomes the institutional norm and in order to compete, and therefore survive, the organization makes the change at a later stage and finds itself in a negative competitive position.

This is the real problem with being tradition bound inside the institution. Conducting the academic program of the college or university in the future based on the successes of the past is betting that the world of today is an aberration, that if one digs in and holds steady, this madness will go away and society will continue to expect the institution to provide what it has always provided.

We are suggesting in this book that this is a bet not worth making. Further, we are suggesting that the changes that are occurring all around education are substantive enough that colleges and universities have no choice but to adapt and forge new relationships. While it is painful to change traditional academic and operational methods on the campus, perhaps the real choice is to change now or lose the chance to be around later to make the change.

*The Issue of Creativity.* Another structural issue that tends to create problems for strategic planning is a lack of creativity and the will to risk. This is not to suggest that creativity does not exist on a college or university campus. It does, and it is an attribute of higher education. Yet this creativity appears to be constrained within the disciplines. A professor who might be responsible for developing a new vaccine to fight a particularly vicious infectious disease may also be in the forefront of the resistance to restructuring her or his college, because she or he cannot see or understand that there are benefits in changing the program mix of the unit.

Tradition in the institution of higher education is marked by stability in the administrative setting within which academics create and flourish. Nearly all changes in the academy over the centuries have been evolutionary rather than revolutionary. Consequently, the structure that most academics, staff, administrators, and students are familiar with does not represent a highly creative organization. Since this stable structure has served academia well in the past, there is the perception that it can probably do so in the future. However, as the context within which teaching, research, and service occur changes, most academics do not want the structure of the university to change.

At UNC, it took a while for planners to realize this. As we

attempted to develop scenarios for change and began a discussion of how these changes would affect the institution, it was initially a surprise to encounter a high level of resistance, primarily from the academic community. That resistance was predicated on the proposition that there was no real need to change things. Discussions, which often evolved into arguments, about who would actually benefit from the change led nowhere. The notion of the university as a public liberal arts college that also prepared teachers was a legacy from its past that stuck. While being tradition bound in this particular way and basically resistant to change was an evident part of the resistance, it was also true that many people just could not see what planners were talking about.

A small public college in a small northeastern town was distanced from external forces. The stability of a large tenured faculty coupled with a history of previous public acceptance as a prominent teacher's college further shaded how many viewed the forces of change. Few saw an imperative for change, even though most sensed a growing disaffection between the public and higher education. Together this melange of forces translated into a concern for the unknown, for which the convenient remedy was a greater level of resistance to planning.

*New Ground.* The problem facing the campus strategic planner is overcoming the lack of a sense of the need for change and the lack of a willingness to risk on the part of the several constituency groups in a university community. This resistance is made more difficult by the fact that there are so few examples of success in strategic planning by universities. Planners therefore cannot *show* campus constituents how a process occurs, or what the results should look like. When the only model most individuals and groups on campus have is the old structure and its old operations, it can be extremely difficult to ask them to accept new methods of doing things, or to convince them that altering the configuration of the university will bring more benefit than harm. Many people simply cannot believe that change will be better. To overcome this, leadership must be involved.

On some campuses, perennial skepticism and lack of trust among administrators, faculty, and staff contribute to the problem. There may be a feeling among various groups that somehow this strategic planning process is really a sinister smoke screen covering the true intent of the central administration or the governing board. Others will simply not trust the process, regardless of the circumstances (Mayer, Davis, and Schoorman, 1995). Many will sit back and wait for the other shoe to drop, convinced that somehow doom is just around the corner. These attitudes simply make the planning process much more difficult to legitimize.

*One Step at a Time.* One of the true benefits of the strategic process is the incremental nature of planning and implementation. It can be very helpful in dealing with negativity, skepticism, and resistance to be able to point to early successes or structural results associated with the planning. For example, if SEM is able to demonstrate improved control over out-of-state recruiting or success in its efforts to better recruit minority students, some evidence is then provided that allows planners to show changes and results to the campus community. As more and more results occur, they can add to the general case planners are building. Such a tactic may not dispel the overall distrust and fear that may exist, but it can certainly decrease it. With time, as the entire process continues to solidify and no dire disasters occur, planners should be able to invite and build support for their activities.

We began this chapter by arguing that the planning process was more important than the planning document. If there is an imperative in strategic planning, it is that the process be carefully thought out, that it be flexible, and that it result in expanding participation to broaden the base for acceptance.

# CHAPTER 14

# Adjusting the Plan
# to Institutional Needs

The previous chapter talked about many of the issues of implementation that face college and universities, without particular regard for the fact that within the genre of institutions of higher education there are clear classifications that impact the character of strategic planning as well as the implementation of the products of planning on individual campuses. This chapter looks at some of the concerns that affect strategic planning on different types of campuses: the issues that face public institutions versus those that face private institutions; the issues that impact small colleges and universities versus those that face large colleges and universities; and the issues that influence planning in research institutions versus those that influence planning in primarily teaching institutions. The various states and conditions of these several types of colleges and universities present particular challenges as well as opportunities. As strategic planning goes forward on each campus, planners need to take these differentiating factors into account.

## Public Versus Private Institutions

Because the catalyst for strategic planning comes from the rapidly changing private sector, private institutions may have some significant assets that enable them to be more effective planners than public institutions. For one thing, private colleges and universities have had to be concerned with the external environment for a much longer period of their histories, simply because of their need for private support. Embedded in this tradition and instinct is a concern for the driving constituencies, those who by virtue of ideals, values, and dollars have given impetus to the evolution of the private university. When it became cheaper for the private corporation to invest in research rather than carry the overhead of proprietary laboratories, some private colleges and universities became major research universities through this kind of corporate investment. Sponsor support, broad private-giving requirements, and selectivity in admissions have all forced the private college or university to serve the needs of the private sector during the beginnings of this the postindustrial age, and these institutions have been rewarded in the form of gifts and investments. Harvard does not have the largest endowment among U.S. colleges and universities by accident. The instinct for reading the private sector economy and its educational needs, coupled with the ability to respond to the specific needs of sponsoring constituencies, gives the private institution an advantage over the public institution in reading and reacting to external change.

Another asset of private institutions is that concern for external environmental constituents has made them familiar with market niches and the notion of new markets. Historically, private colleges have dominated the liberal arts, using them as a market niche to sustain their programs. Also, private institutions such as Stanford and Harvard, among others, recognized the market niche for bringing excluded groups such as minorities into higher education when environmental forces made that an issue.

Because of the vital role enrollment plays in funding private institutions, they already have a working knowledge of how to develop market strategies to exploit niches and new markets. Using alumni to recruit, developing attractive scholarships, and balancing academic preparation with potential for social contribution are strategies that have been successful and that have sustained the growth of private higher education. For strategic planners in private colleges and universities, the issue is less learning how to carry out such strategies and more identifying and defining the new market niches for which strategies are required.

Size and the flexibility associated with it are artifacts of the early elitism of many private institutions. Today these characteristics can be valuable assets in planning for change. For example, it is easier to make substantive changes at the smaller institutions, such as Harvard or Stanford, than to make major changes within the multicampus and heavily enrolled University of California system. Many of the innovations in new fields have come out of the small private colleges and universities, which have encouraged interaction between disciplines that has led to new knowledge. Fields like political science grew out of the extension of political philosophy and political economy in institutions such as Columbia and the University of Chicago, where the discipline was redefined for the twentieth century.

Values have also played a prominent role in the development of private education, a fallout of its origin in sectarian education. Values have infused purpose in ways that have kept private institutions less influenced by the fads that periodically sweep higher education. The need to redirect values rather than having to define them and then nourish loyalty to them enables some private institutions to pursue market opportunities without sacrificing their endemic character.

Then there is the asset of the need to be different. This need has several origins: religion, the institution's need to compete for students by distinguishing itself from other institutions, and the opportunities attendant to size and affluence that encourage being selective. Comfortable with using difference as a means of charting a course, private institutions are more nimble than their public peers in the ability to devise an exclusive or dominant market strategy that differentiates.

Private colleges and universities also have their weaknesses, however. Foremost among them is the tradition of the liberal arts core. Conflict over the canon and the rooting of private education in the Anglo-European tradition have their source in the notions of excellence and competency that collide with the reality of economic restructuring for a global marketplace. When reinforced by sectarianism, nimble can turn to numb and adaptation can thereby be limited.

Some private institutions, most notably seminaries or their descendants, have a niche as narrow-purpose institutions. Women's and men's colleges are examples of this kind of narrowing, a trait that, in today's competitive educational marketplace, constrains strategic opportunities. Having resisted the trend toward homogeneity in much of higher education since World War II, these institutions have an instinct for highly specialized niches that may be increasingly limiting or anachronistic. In such circumstances, the challenge for strategic planners is to offer revenue-inducing approaches to exploring new markets—approaches that entice support and welcome new ideas. But the effort to broaden perspectives will cause as much conflict in the narrow-purpose institution as the effort to find a niche by narrowing the focus of the all-purpose university.

Strategic planners must modulate this conflict through focus groups and other forms of discussion that gradually lend acceptance, if not legitimacy, to the consideration of necessary change. Linking a broadened mission to strategic enrollment management or treating the mission as a special campus need is one way to fit the matter into strategic planning. As earlier discussions point out, considering mission to clarify matters at some midpoint in the planning process is preferable to undertaking a discussion of mission at the outset of planning. Should the latter happen, the discussion will be ponderously theoretical, or constrained by the preemptive limits of founding values so that the mission will deal with "shoulds" rather than "doables." If broadened opportunities becomes a mission-

related topic as a consequence of strategic enrollment management, then its consideration will likely be productive in both a
value-legitimizing and a practical sense.

In the post–Sputnik decades, some private institutions
have become multipurpose universities, extending their
growth well beyond their early intent. In these cases, focus
must be brought to educational sprawl. Conflict will arise in a
number of ways, including between the younger faculty
attracted by the "mini-university" environment and the older
faculty who prefer earlier traditions. That is not the argument
to engage. The better effort is to give shape and character to
what can be done well, and then to move that dialogue to some
common ground within the college culture.

Occidental College, for example, created a new market
niche by positioning itself as a specialized research college
(Slaughter, 1988–1989). The trick in these endeavors is to keep
the dialogue focused on anchor points that will differentiate the
individual institution from the pack. Given the economic,
demographic, and competitive pressures it faced, Illinois Benedictine College used revenue, enrollment, and curriculum planning to construct rational strategic opportunities for the future
(Dolence and Norris, 1994).

Last, but no less limiting among weaknesses, is the problem of value rigidity alluded to earlier. Values can limit as well
as expand the definition of problems, and thereby specify their
resolution. When old values prevail in the face of a contradictory environment, effective planning is difficult. For example,
if the Citadel insists on keeping women out while society
expects the opposite, the conflict may resolve itself only outside
of the rubrics of the strategic planning process. Rigid stances
remove many options from consideration, stymieing strategic
planning and leading to increasingly outdated priorities. And
yet, if private institutions keep focused and concentrate on their
sharply defined purposes, they can develop effective strategic
plans (J. S. Green, 1990).

The issue of change in private education is especially complicated when rigid values and limited funding coexist. This is

not uncommon. And today, as Blumenstyk (1993) tells us, private colleges are scrambling to meet new financial challenges as they find that student financial aid is the fastest growing item in their budgets. For strategic planners, the initial step for coping with this challenge is to raise the revenue aspects of survival through strategic enrollment management and by slowly letting the process pose the Hobson's choice of old values or survival. Where the trustees or regents are a source of realism, they should be invited into the discussions to help legitimize the need to refocus values toward strategic innovation. Where they are an obstacle, the avenue to their attention is the effect on revenue of an atrophying mission.

## Large Versus Small Institutions

According to Martinsons (1993), effective strategic planning does not depend on the size of an organization. Though differences exist, both small and large institutions can engage in strategic planning successfully. One key differentiator between the two is the variety that exists in the base of support. For example, it is not uncommon for large public research universities to receive less than 20 percent of their support from the state. Over the years, these institutions have diversified their funding with large doses of research support from the federal government and private corporations; significant auxiliary enterprises, including research parks; and vastly broadened private giving. As one element has diminished, other parts of the revenue portfolio have picked up the slack, allowing not only growth but also significant improvements in quality and constructive reflexes to change. At the University of Washington, Seattle, for example, a world-class program in molecular biotechnology was put together with support from a single donor, in spite of declining state support for the overall university budget. This ability to find revenue substitutes that improve program quality is an important adapter and a key technique for strategic planning in large universities.

Another differentiator is that workload and productivity

also vary between large and small institutions in ways that impact strategic planning. The workload mix in the large university, where there are graduate programs and where graduate students often support the teaching load, varies significantly from that of the small institution. In land grant universities, extension programs and other forms of outreach enable mixed strategies for coping with new demand other than absorbing growth on the campus. In the professional schools, where internships are customary practicums and support licensure, people in the professions can assist in supervising placements, freeing the campus faculty for other things. Linked with technology, large institutions have more options available than small institutions for devising strategies to cope with external forces and expectations.

The faculty culture in the large institution is different from the faculty in the small institution in important ways. With lighter teaching loads and more assistance available in classrooms both on and off the campus, faculty at large schools have more time to be entrepreneurs. This means that they are more likely to be revenue generators in ways that relieve the institution from the full burden of their individual compensation. In the large universities, it is more common for summers to be times for projects, grants, and other nonteaching activities that support not only the faculty member but also other members of the campus, usually graduate or advanced undergraduate students. These options open faculty experience to activities outside of the campus. Often these are collaborative activities with colleagues and students from other campuses, so the faculty member has a better sense of how external forces affect the institution as well as the individual faculty member.

This exposure to scholarly development has interesting side effects for campus governance and politics. Attracted and kept busy by scholarly concerns for greater periods of time than faculty in small institutions, the faculty members at large institutions are less preoccupied with the mechanics of faculty governance. Sometimes they have to be recruited to serve, for their attention and instincts are attracted elsewhere. Less invested in personal gain through institutional means, these faculty do not become preoccupied as easily with the politics and bureaucracy of faculty rights, governance, committee life, and faculty political leadership. As a consequence, faculty processes, rules, and codes are less Hammurabic, and governance is conducted more out of a sense of shared responsibility and less by a rubric of control.

Faculty relations with regents or trustees also vary. In the large university, the board is often large and physically remote. In the small institution, the board is more likely small and proximate. Hometown regents are always familiar and available, so faculty use this access frequently. For smaller institutions, the result of direct access can often become micromanagement by the regents. Even if that extreme is not operative, the consequence is an undermining of the ability to make and sustain the tough decisions often associated with strategic planning.

In the large university, proximity is unusual and the preoccupation with faculty politics is less compelling. Distance, size, complexity, and faculty proclivity combine to mute meddling and to move those politics that do occur to higher ground.

In spite of their many differences, small colleges or universities need to engage in strategic planning for many of the same reasons that larger institutions have decided to develop their strategic planning processes (Thompson, Johnson, Warren, and Williams, 1990). Yet often the challenges are quite different. For example, in the small institution the small funding base offers the institution fewer options. In most public institutions, state funding often accounts for more than 50 percent of revenue, making the campus dependent on state dollars. This means that strategic planning is constrained by fluctuations in state issues and taxes. Further, administrators must heavily cultivate legislative relations, often in spite of lesser influence due to size and mission. Always in the shadow of the flagship and land grant universities, small public colleges and universities must tag along financially, with overall state largess driven by the large institutions. Unless alumni happen to be in leadership positions and can influence legislators, the toil is tough and the reward modest.

This preoccupation with legislative and executive behavior complicates adaptation to change. For one thing, political leadership must be accepting of, or tacit about, initiatives born through strategic planning. The ability to anticipate whether they will be or not is important. So is the need to devise a marketing strategy that sufficiently reflects state priorities so that those things the university desires to do can receive legitimacy by being part of a larger responsive package.

The workload mix is a key constraint in the small institution. Teaching tends to be a major mission, and this is often accompanied by few graduate programs, most of which are at the master's level. So efficiencies are not easily found. The option of increasing teaching loads is there, but it is a faculty hot button. Furthermore, it is hard to demand active scholarship while providing little opportunity and even less research support to do anything of strategic consequence.

All of these constraints limit opportunities for flexible response to external demands. Collaboration with other institutions is one antidote. Linking with community colleges through transfer and articulation agreements is another. This allows the four-year partner to keep lower-division classes small and to differentiate from other competitors what can be done in them. It also establishes a stream of remediated upper-division students, which helps address issues of inadequate preparation at the secondary level. One strategy that Appleby and Carrillo (1990) suggest to help alleviate these problems in smaller institutions is to concentrate on specialized programs, which help attract qualified students, improve educational standards, and facilitate program review. Their research has shown that this strategy is particularly well received by accrediting boards. But as Jaschik (1992) reports on the reaction of Worcester State College's faculty to state-imposed specialization, a collegial agreement between the faculty and the external control may not come easily. He also points out that in other states, such as Mississippi, specializing through reduction has been done to try to improve quality. And even further, specialization is not a panacea. As Zakrajsek and Pierce (1993) point out, many new doctorates are *too* specialized, and potential employers are sometimes unable to find people with broad enough backgrounds to fill departmental positions requiring a broad base of preparation. This becomes a problem particularly for small colleges or universities, even those who have pared down their programs to a handful of specialties.

Because in smaller institutions everyone knows almost everyone else, preoccupation with faculty governance is likely, as is the control of faculty politics by a long-time network. When this preoccupation exists, rules and regulations can be cumbersome in their size and specific content. If there is tension between faculty and the administration, content can smother change and the flexibility it requires. For example, at the University of Northern Colorado, codification became the Hammurabic code of governance. It included more than two volumes and contained great specificity, mixing rules and regulations with trustee policies in a melange of directives, including a detailed salary model that allocated salaries without regard to merit. This hampered efforts to recognize innovation and scholarly leadership, and coupled with small legislative appropriations, vacuumed revenue into lockstep salaries, which starved program improvements and did not recognize quality.

This preoccupation with detail, the control it engendered, and the jealous control of prerogative led to conflictual and negative politics. Faculty felt that they possessed veto power over university policy. Fifty-five faculty members sued to get back pay on grounds that their salaries violated the salary model. The faculty senate debated and passed a no-confidence vote on the board of trustees. Leadership refused to help sort out policies from rules in codification as the trustees had requested. And the senate opposed strategic planning every step of the way. These details are less worth noting than the posture toward change that this behavior reflects. When heels dig in so politically and righteously, options for strategic change diminish significantly and planning becomes a major political exercise. It can only go forward if it is widely inclusive, and expected by the trustees. Without the clear message from the board that planning must occur or it will be imposed, strategic planning will flounder in the governance process.

At small institutions, the temptation to go directly to the board of trustees is endemic. It is also an easy tactic for undermining strategic planning and resisting change. If the board is so weak that members can speak openly as individuals and espouse personal agendas, and if this is accompanied by the board's inability to routinely rise above special interests for the good of the entire institution, strategic planning will be inhibited and lack legitimacy. If, however, the board is strong and its members tend to speak with one voice, the board can become a counter to campus resistance. Since board members come from off campus, and because their terms are usually staggered, their familiarity with external expectations can be a real asset for planners as they devise ways to address the resistance to change.

Finally, smaller institutions are heavily interpersonal. The old guard can directly affect the lives of newer faculty, not only in promotion and tenure but also in everyday life—from committee work to menial tasks within a department. Rumor is also likely to be a main telegraph system on the campus. This Peyton Place atmosphere can strangle new ideas and the willingness to become active for change. When combined with a tradition of a heavily controlling faculty governance committee that recycles itself, the politics of resistance thrive. Where fact and overt behavior can be countered by innuendo and pointed faculty governance resolutions, strategic planners must be skilled politicians.

One significant possible solution is to build strategic planning leadership around respected and open-minded faculty members whom the old network cannot delegitimize or openly attack. This reliance on visible leadership by respected faculty can insulate strategic planning from the accusation that it really is an administration Trojan Horse, and it can mute the use of personal attack, either overt or covert, on planning leadership.

## Research Institutions Versus Teaching Institutions

One of the greatest distinguishing features of colleges or universities is their designation as either a research or a teaching institution. Though similarities exist, they are markedly different institutions. Strategic planners at these two types of institutions must consider different circumstances, faculties, and philosophies as they develop their particular campus plans.

### The Research University

Excellence drives the research university. The capacity to survive and adapt is a storehouse of options as the research institution faces change. Take the land grant research university as an example. Heavily dependent on governmental agencies such as the U.S. Departments of Agriculture, Energy, and Defense, and the National Aeronautics and Space Administration, all of which are undergoing reduction and restructuring, and subject to the severe forces of economic change that challenge the future of rural America, the land grant universities are under severe pressure. But because of a long history of excellence in agriculture, technology, and community service through extension, past practices are cues for future directions.

For this reason, strategic planning at a land grant college or university has a good grounding on which to begin. In his address celebrating the 125th anniversary of Colorado State University, C. Peter MaGrath (1995) of the National Association of State University and Land Grant Colleges argued that the land grant colleges and universities should

1. Emphasize food, nutrition, and agricultural profitability, coupled with better use of engineering, technology, and business, to relate effectively to the needs of urban America.
2. Link to education and the public schools as part of an approach to refurbish the social infrastructure of rural and urban America.

3. Meet the needs of small and medium-sized businesses as restructuring of the global economy unfolds.
4. Revive undergraduate education in the research environment.
5. Tie undergraduate education to international languages, cultures, and issues.
6. Enhance diversity in this nation of immigrants.

The particular recipe for change is not the point. The point is that a record of accomplishment accented by excellence can help define key elements for strategic planning as the research university addresses the external environment.

To continue the land grant example, excellence can also be tied to change by extending high-quality past practices. For the land grant institution, extension can lead to the refocusing of outreach on the human needs of rural life. Rural development in the form of a focus on agribusiness can be redirected toward the small business and competitive infrastructure made possible by technology and the selling of information and services as clean ways to revitalize rural economic development. Issues like clean air, clean water, and soil conservation can refocus the conservation tradition on current national concerns. These ideas reflect the kinds of strategic thinking that planning can trigger in the research environment.

The commitment to research and graduate study can breed open-mindedness to counter habit and tradition. Barnett (1992) writes that research is the fulcrum of the academic community. While research universities have their embedded traditions, the scholarly interest in change serves as a counter to resistance bound by traditionalism. More important, research faculty interacting with graduate students have much to deter them from a preoccupation with faculty politics, though as Marshall and Palca (1992) tell us, research institutions are feeling pressure from governments and industrial partners to be more responsive and relevant to their needs.

On some research campuses, faculty senate activism is not infrequently the domain of the less-scholarly faculty, arguably because some may use their time for faculty governance rather than for research. Because they are not active scholars, these leaders often are less prestigious in their own disciplines; they command less respect and are therefore less effective. Their ideas and issues are not ipso facto self-legitimizing. The result is more use of the faculty bureaucracy to thwart strategic planning and change.

Conversely, a faculty of active researchers is also a faculty of risk takers. Regularly competing for grants breeds a willingness to risk, as does the challenge of making the great discovery. Basic research also stimulates the need to think the unthinkable, to speculate and hypothesize, to push the envelope of knowledge, and never to assume one has all the answers. The inquiring mind becomes a mind more willing to engage in and challenge strategic planning options. This similarity between scholarship and the planning process is a resource that planners in the research environment can use to keep the issues of change on the table.

Also worth noting is the tendency among research university faculty to see themselves as entrepreneurs linked first to the academy and their disciplinary peers and then to the college or university where they are employed. Because they are mobile and, for scholarly reasons, must stay informed about external matters, they are more likely to consider initiative, creative change, and getting the university apace of external realities important activities of which to be a part. In response, the college or university must maintain an incubative and enabling environment in order to keep these faculty. Lagging behind the state of the art will drive away rather than keep such faculty. In sum, the research university is a seedbed for change and strategic planning; it must be open and challenging, and it must encourage the high-level thinking that is necessary for the institution to succeed over the long term. These, of course, are the attributes that encourage strategic thinking.

## The Teaching University

A fair amount of controversy has grown up about the relative importance of research and teaching institutions. While both serve an important function for academia and society, Barnett (1992) has concluded that the essence of higher education is in the function of teaching, and Crase and Crase (1991) suggest that competent instructors benefit the institution because they promote continuity and can enhance both the social and academic climates. And yet, in teaching institutions, whether excellent programs exist is arguable (Perelman, 1992). They are not easy to define, because good teaching is not easy to define. They are not obvious to everyone, because their leading-edge attributes are not evident. This means that debate and argument can keep strategic planning from achieving any working consensus. Nevertheless, as a necessary precursor to identifying where quality and excellence can be found, debate and argument ensure a more thorough dialogue about what constitutes quality and excellence. In this environment, it is especially important to keep the mission statement from being the venue for that argument, because such an argument will not be grounded in an experiential sense of excellence and will likely turn on theoretic descriptors that are abstract and uninstructive about real programs and real degrees.

Teaching institutions also have a proclivity for undergraduate study. This implies, among other things, that resources, operational activities, and priorities will focus on undergraduate education. Undergraduate studies are a kind of leveling force in the university. At this level, covering material and basics takes precedence over discovery, leading-edge activity, and the breaking of new ground. An English degree is described and designed to be not better than but as good as a degree in math or dance. This leveling under the rubric of basic competency turns attention to the minimum rather than the maximum achievement. When coverage supersedes depth of knowledge, expertise and excellence suffer by taking second place. Leveling has the effect of satisfying the democratic sense of equality, but it does little to help differentiate and focus, activities that take on real significance as revenues fall.

Because dialogue and discussion are hallmarks of teaching, they also lead to the strongly felt need for interaction. In the environment of the teaching college or university, committees, governance structures, and governance itself, as contributors to the great legitimizing discussion, become ends in themselves. Unless an issue is properly talked through, it is at least illegitimate and at most incomplete. Either way, when applied to the strategic planning process, lack of discussion becomes an instrument of sabotage.

A focus on minimum competence has the side effect of resisting risk, being skeptical of innovation, and preferring the tried and true, the basics or the core. This becomes a kind of common-denominator requirement that inhibits any ordering or preference among programs that may imply more or less importance. This also means that an attack on one program is an attack on all programs and has the effect of putting strategic planners in a most precarious environment, for unless they can show that change will benefit all equally, the argument will be that change is to be avoided. The only viable antidotes are a strong governing board that demands change and is willing to take the heat that demand engenders, or the ability to get a few prestigious or widely respected faculty members to provide the public impetus for and leadership in strategic planning.

The most debilitating attribute in the teaching institution is an innate belief in the primacy of teaching and its imperative to convey excellence and truth. Those engaged in the enterprise of truth can be rigid and self-assured, and can possess a sense of imprimatur that is preemptive, if not self-righteous. High priestesses and priests of truth are pharisaic. This puts strategic planners, as advocates of change, on the defensive from the very beginning and gives them the burden of proving that what they might strategically espouse will not corrupt or undermine good teaching. Since the teachers define good teaching, planners are clearly disadvantaged.

When this self-defined role is coupled with a lack of active scholarly inquiry, a sense of dependency emerges. Not used to vying for grants on a regular basis and thereby supporting themselves in some way, such faculty become institutionally dependent. They expect progressive salaries, look to summer school to tide them over between academic years, and see their personal self-interest as the self-interest of the institution. This dependency smothers any urge to deal realistically with the future. By being institution-centered and by seeing the institution as a proper buffer from the realities of the external world, their ivory-tower minds are cocooned. Sometimes this combines with a kind of intellectual superiority that plays down the need to pay any attention to the views of the less qualified. When pride partners with special interest, the result is a stubborn resistance to change.

For the research university, the prerequisites for planning and institutional change are reconnecting with the public; reconnecting research and teaching, because the former informs the latter; becoming adept at adjusting to changes in federal research priorities; and helping to shape a new relationship of research support from both public and private sources. For teaching institutions, the challenge is to develop a new valued role by addressing the intellectual and social needs of a changing society, to keep from getting outdated by practicing active scholarship to stay informed, and to fashion a niche-based strategy for using shrinking public resources effectively while finding alternate sources for revenue. In these cases, the key is for institutions to reconnect with their attentive publics and serve real needs while expanding basic human knowledge.

## Institutional Combinations

Obviously some classes of institutions combine two or more of the various types of institution described in this chapter. There are small, private, research institutions; there are large, public, teaching universities; and there are other combinations that describe particular focal colleges and universities. In the discussion presented in this chapter, we have attempted to offer a perspective on a variety of aspects that strategic planners on any campus need to take into account when putting together a regimen of strategic planning.

The considerations presented here are important, because as we have argued throughout the book, each institution needs to identify itself and its environmental sets *uniquely*. In building a general theory of how strategic planning can be effectively accomplished in institutions of higher education, the resulting model becomes more complex as it becomes possible to discern the various aspects that make each institution unique regardless of any general tendencies toward sameness in programs or disciplines from one locale to the next. The ideas presented in this chapter provide additional suggestions that will help strategic planners build a more effective and realistic strategic plan and then move toward implementation through effective strategic management and decision making.

# CHAPTER 15

# Moving from Strategic Planning to Strategic Management

One of the unsettling realities of life today is that everything is subject to change. Since the central point of strategic planning is to align the institution with its environment, it is important to understand that that environment is constantly changing. This means that the strategic planning process goes on long after the initial plans are agreed upon and implemented. Strategic planning continues to survey the various changes that occur in both the internal and external environments, and continuously seeks optimal alignment conditions. This last chapter looks a bit ahead, and lays the groundwork for continuing the process well into the future as a means of surviving and prospering over the long term.

## Time to Move Forward

The first step in facing the future is to confront the status quo. In a tradition-based culture, the instinct is to look to the past and to defend the preserve. The yearning to have the environment of education do what it always has done in recent memory, regardless of how much times have changed, ironically underscores how time bound a simplistic sense of tradition can be. After all, universities have not always been what they are today. Even tradition includes change, and this argues in favor of facing the present in relation to the future.

It is probably a fair statement that, in spite of the increasing homogeneity that one finds among colleges and universities, each institution of higher education is different in some way from other institutions of higher education, requiring each institution, to some degree, to define its own particular strategic planning system (Haiss, 1993). As a result, works that attempt to develop models for practitioners need to address these differences. While there may be no exact matches among institutions of higher education, significant similarities do exist in classes of institutions. A recognition of these commonalities can help strategic planners adapt the planning models we have developed in this book to meet the needs of particular campuses. This chapter identifies several of these classes of colleges and universities, and attempts to provide some ideas about how planners can design approaches that consider the special needs of their individual campuses.

## The Inevitable Presence of Change

The children of the baby boomers are packing their bags for college. For the first time in a generation, the number of eighteen-to-twenty-year-olds is on the rise (National Center for Higher Educational Management Systems, 1995, p. 2). At the same time, the economy is recreating itself in a global way while technology is creating the information age. So, as we described at length in Chapter One, while traditionally trained college graduates cannot find jobs easily, policy makers face the need to broaden access to education in order to assure the widespread expertise needed to create and use information in ways required by the information age.

The immediacy of this restructuring plays nicely to the instinct common in most higher education settings, which is to plan for the short term. For this reason, present policy issues are defined simplistically: (1) reduce demand or limit capacity through the implementation of enrollment caps, higher tuition, requirements for better preparation of incoming students, and time limits for program completion; or (2) increase capacity by creating new campuses, improving interinstitutional and inter-sector collaboration, increasing efficiency, expanding technology, and perhaps even shipping students to other states that have excess capacity. Administrators are openly challenged to do more with less by tinkering with class size, increasing teaching loads, cutting sections with low enrollments, starting three-year degrees, redefining the core curriculum, modifying the reward system, and improving assessment (National Center for Higher Educational Management Systems, 1995, pp. 2–4). Most of these potential polices are basically stopgap measures, however, designed to change the look but keep the core university.

In this book, we place repeated emphasis on the importance of recognizing the impact of the external environment on strategic planning, because scanning the environment to understand it is an absolutely essential first step in effective planning. How strategic planners scan the external environment is the key to understanding it. In certain areas, colleges and universities already scan portions of their environments regularly, in their recruitment activities, development work, alumni communications, and other routine linkages with the off-campus world.

But as one examines current practices, the problem that one discovers with this type of scanning is that it is embedded in tradition and habit. Put another way, colleges and universities do not have good instincts about innovation at the institutional level. As an example of this, in a recent study Siegfried, Getz, and Anderson (1995, p. A56) of Vanderbilt University point out that change in higher education is so short term in perspective and so heavily conditioned by present practice that innovation comes at a snail's pace. Citing a survey of more than two hundred institutions about thirty specific innovations, they report that on the average it took more than twenty-five years for just half of these institutions to adopt these innovations. This was true regardless of the cost. Moreover, financial innovations took even longer—forty years for half of the public institutions to adopt just five innovations studied in the survey. Private institutions moved no faster, except to adopt fixed payouts from endowments. On the basis of this particular study, as well as several other similar studies, it is clear that the capacity for change in colleges and universities is minimal because tradition and habit fundamentally condition responses to external forces.

In remarks prepared for a general faculty meeting, Clemson's acting president Phil Prince (1995, p. 1) makes a persuasive case for coping with this inertia by keeping plans simple. His argument is that it is necessary to state the obvious in order to understand and cope with the underlying complex issues or problems. By focusing on the obvious, he argues, planning can be kept from becoming an academic preoccupation with, and preference for, the theoretically complex or the intellectually integrated approaches to planning, both of which sacrifice clarity for elegance or completeness. For a strategic plan to be effective and adequately affect policy, it must avoid the pitfalls discussed in Chapter Fourteen; it must state the obvious directly, address the resulting issues simply and understandably, and identify the niche of opportunities within the grasp of the institution, given its role and capacity. To restate the obvious planning principle, a strategic plan must gradually become an instrument that, in spite of its inelegance, unites rather than divides the campus.

An effective strategic plan must overcome initial resistance by seeking the common ground that describes succinctly the community of talent and resources an institution must enlist to survive and flourish. For example, if the mission statement is written after the campus has experienced some appreciable success from its strategic planning process but while confusion about the value or role of strategic planning still persists, the mission statement can become a mechanism for finding this much-needed common ground. At this point, the mission state-ment may help clarify the shared attributes essential to shaping the character of the institution, and included in it can be those common interests strongly held by the campus. As an illustra-tion of this, if strategic planners develop the mission statement after enrollment management successes are evident, the state-ment will be grounded more realistically by the enrollment poli-cies and KPIs that identify the niches and markets that increase enrollments. This helps the institution respond more practically to the imperatives of the external environment that these poli-cies and KPIs reflect. Using mission statements in this way helps assure that the mission is not a wish list but an appropri-ate platform for launching the institution into its future envi-ronment. To accomplish this fit with the environment, strategic planners must navigate with a pragmatic sense of shared des-tiny, negotiate toward that destiny, state the case for it in ways that emphasize gains, and elude as well as withstand the nega-tive politics of resistance. This is no small chore, but it is neces-sary for planning to work in the face of opposition.

Once some sense of community emerges about the attrib-utes of strategic change, institutional strategic planners can more effectively address the significant forces in the external environment. Presently, those obvious external forces include fiscal austerity, global competition, technology, and repairing the disconnection between the tax-paying public and public institutions, and between the diminishing constituencies for private higher education and private institutions. In both are-nas, the required linkage is student learning that is relevant to the times and that ensures meaningful and defining interac-tions between institutions and their crucial external constituen-cies. This new relationship will shape the information age to better serve humankind.

The focal concern here is student learning rather than fac-ulty workload, routine accreditation, traditional claims of qual-ity, or any of the headline-grabbing parlance of politicians or education leaders about "what must be done" to improve or save higher education. These political panaceas reflect present perceptions and assume things such as the stability of existing campuses, credit hours, contact hours, test scores and other traditional measures, classrooms as the perpetual sites of learning, and other current practices that ignore what the information age will do to learning. None of these remedies necessarily assesses or summarizes effectively what colleges and universities must do to enhance student learning.

The old factory model of education, in which process validates, is out-of-date. If nothing else, the cost of doing business as usual is increasingly prohibitive. Howard Bowen, economist and former university president, puts it in theoretical terms. He has derived a "revenue theory of costs," which argues that higher education institutions spend all of the money they can raise. The only limit in this circumstance is cost (Breneman, 1994, p. 5). Thus, if costs rise, more revenue is the instinctive solution. Based on this theory, it seems reasonable to argue that the transformation of colleges and universities in this time of economic restructuring is imperative. The Hobson's choice for higher education is either to transform or implode when revenues diminish.

Enter Bill "Trey" Gates, founder of Microsoft. By combining everything from ideas to a worldwide information networking service in his basic operating software, Gates is challenging everything from banking to mailing to education, forcing all providers to face the issue of how they develop and make available their operations and services. He is also global in his focus, helping to lead the revolution in information technology on a worldwide scale.

In education, if faculty can provide knowledge through technology and students can surf the system for what they need, what is the fate of the capital-intensive campus filled with asbestos and languishing without dollars for deferred maintenance? Put another way, what will happen to the central city of higher education when the suburbs of information networks grow? When businesses do more of their own skills instruction? When technology brings Harvard to the home? When faculty can actually teach anywhere through technology and basically work out of their homes? When laboratories are displaced with simulations?

What will tenure mean if knowledge is available in Prodigy-like bytes? Why will students bother to enroll if they can get their information through Microsoft? Will Microsoft-type companies become universities because of their ability to transmit and offer interactive learning with expert-based information? What will happen to colleges and universities when the emphasis is on student learning that is more effectively assessable externally in a variety of ways than completing a certifiable process in a college or university?

Already, some universities are responding in a positive way. For example, Anglia Polytechnic University in Great Britain has identified through its strategic planning process that the university needs to maximize flexibility of staff; to move away from contact hours as the sole management tool for how classes should be taught and, instead, move toward new measurement methods based on quality, innovation, and effective learning; and to allow students to determine for themselves the optimal place and timing of their fixed meeting points to allow them to organize their own learning more effectively. These policy changes were endorsed by Anglia's faculty senate in 1994 (Kitching, 1994).

Will research universities be attracted by the problem to be solved rather than by a shared discipline or profession? If faculty are more the guide on the side or the knowledge navigator, what will the classroom entail? If the administration is a developer and general contractor, what will happen to governance and present routine relationships? Will Microsoft run the equivalent of universities to feed its information appetite and capacity much like Ma Bell ran laboratories and programs to sustain its telephonic empire? These issues, and many, many more, make up the context within which the future will develop. Much of what constitutes the appropriate answers to these questions depends on how classes of institutions identify their market niches and become dissimilar as they turn away from the present tendency to be like the top universities in the search for strategies to survive. The role of strategic planning and strategic management in higher education is to identify where appropriate connections can be made and how the strengths and values of the academy can help lead the world into the next century and beyond.

## Transformation in Higher Education

Up to this point we have concentrated our discussion on the processes and practices that can help a college or university do substantive and effective strategic planning. Lurking out there, however, is the future. While strategic planning's main premise is to align the institution with its environment, it must also take into account what it can learn of the future. Of course, no one can accurately predict the future, but there are those who identify and monitor trends, and it is useful to review what such people are identifying as some of the relevant forces that will shape the academy over the next several years. The impact of these trends is dramatic, and as any campus develops its own strategic plan, many of these thoughts present a critical perspective within which campus strategic planners need to develop their own scenarios.

Dolence and Norris (1995) discuss some of the present trends that are impacting higher education as a whole, and tie the strategic planning process to the ability of a campus to meet the challenges and threats of the future in a logical, calculated, and responsive manner. We felt that a summary of these ideas would be useful to the reader, as an exclamation point on the strategic planning process we have developed throughout this book.

### The Transformation Process

First, it will be useful to develop a description of what we mean by the term *transformation*. As we use it, transformation is more than simply change; it is a process that has four interrelated and intertwined subprocesses within it. Transformation is fundamentally substantive and basic in nature. It challenges the central tenets of what we have become comfortable with as the rubrics of how colleges and universities operate and what they offer their student body and community base in the way of both education and research.

Though our view of transformation is specific to higher education, it is very important to understand that change is not simply an issue being faced by educational institutions. Virtually every sector of society, business, and government is facing the need to reorient their purposes and directions as they move from the industrial age to the information age. As a result, all organizations are undergoing some form of transformation. The forces driving these changes are basic, endemic, and relentless.

Unfortunately, higher education is lagging behind many other societal and economic sectors in responding to these forces. Yet as these changes play themselves out, colleges and universities lag behind at their own peril. According to Dolence and Norris (1995), futurists estimate that beginning in the year 2000, every seven years each individual in the workforce will need to accumulate learning equivalent to that currently associated with thirty credit hours of instruction, just to keep up with growing demand. At a minimum, this level of learning will be needed by every member of the information age workforce in order to remain competitive and productive—perhaps even to maintain basic employment.

This translates into the full-time equivalent enrollment of one-seventh of the workforce at any point in time. Further, Dolence and Norris tell us that since there will be an estimated 141 million workers in the United States in the year 2000, this could amount to more than twenty million full-time-equivalent learners. This contrasts with the approximately twelve million full-time equivalent students enrolled in U.S. higher education today. Based on the existing model of the number of campuses needed to support these new students, these learners will require an additional 672 campuses with an enrollment of thirty thousand students each. Dolence and Norris further estimate that at $350 million each, the 672 campuses would cost $235 billion to build and an additional $217 billion per year to operate. To meet the full potential demand by the year 2010, a new campus would have to be opened every eight days.

The demand for new learning systems, new tools, and new approaches is building, along with a growing demand for dramatically different and innovative curricula. In demonstrating these demands, it is useful to imagine the product development (curriculum) momentum that can build behind a potential market of twenty million people in the United States alone. And this is not merely a projection of the future; it is a phenomenon that has already begun to build. The growth of on-line services and the plethora of educational software and multimedia software pouring into the marketplace every day are all significant. As one foreign-language faculty lamented to one of the authors recently, "How can I attract students to an introductory French class for which we charge well over $1,000 when the student can buy a complete French course from the computer store for less than $200? On top of that, the Foreign Service does not use my course to train diplomats when they use this other method."

As higher education is being forced to respond to changes in the technological and general educational environments, it is becoming obvious that the needs and economics of the information age and its potential learner clients are not going to just go away. Already, commercial providers are penetrating the fringe of the learning marketplace, and once they take root, which they already may have, they will potentially change the learning marketplace forever.

## The Reorientation from "Teaching" to "Learning"

One of the dominant differentiating forces of the information age is emerging: *learning*. A new lexicon is even being invented as the information age unfolds and shapes the future. Already, new concepts are taking hold, such as "learning organizations," "perpetual learning," "knowledge workers," "knowledge industries," and "knowledge networks." Learning is the central focus of each concept—learning at a faster rate, learning a wider range of subjects, learning in new ways from new intermediaries.

Formal learning processes that span a person's entire lifetime are now commonly accepted as a logical competitive course of action. Learning while working, compensation plans that recognize and reward learning, and investments in learning are programs already in place that lead to the systematic removal of barriers to learning. Further, consumer demand has spawned the development of a free market in learning ware, knowledge bases, knowledge navigation tools, and knowledge synthesis infrastructures. The "business of learning" is a dominant business in the information age.

To respond adequately, colleges and universities are facing the need to transform themselves to adequately meet these challenges. That transformation is achieved through four interrelated and inexorably intertwined subprocesses:

1. Realigning the organization with the environment
2. Redesigning the organization to achieve the new intent
3. Redefining the roles and responsibilities within the realigned, redesigned organization
4. Reengineering organizational processes to achieve dramatically higher productivity and quality

*Realignment.* To transform our institutions of higher education, strategic planners need to develop plans that realign their organizational intent with a substantive understanding of the following:

1. The demands of the information age
2. The emergent needs for individualized learning
3. The growing mandate for barrier-free, lifelong learning
4. The evident need for high-quality and flexible enabling services.

It is becoming increasingly apparent that these environmentally related realignment activities are critical to meeting the learning challenges of the twenty-first century. These forces require higher education leaders to reconsider all of their basic conceptions and metaphors for how, when, and where learning occurs, and the roles of providers and facilitators of learning.

The colleges and universities we know today will not disappear. Rather, transformation will progress relentlessly as the information age advances, bringing with it incremental change as it develops. This change will be necessitated by the emergent information explosion, the increase of "network scholarship" (the development of scholarship within a network, including electronic media that can serve as a lab, a forum for debate, and a new arena for testing and disseminating ideas), "knowledge navigators" (those who develop the capacity to work with the overwhelming universe of information), and "knowledge workers" (the savvy users of technology who are not intimidated by complexity). One clear implication here is the emergence of the student as a "learner," someone who takes responsibility for her or his own education. The role of a professor will move from being the source of all knowledge to being the mentor, synthesizer, evaluator, and certifier of mastery. As Pascarella and Terenzini (1991) have suggested, the goals of instruction must become more associated with motivation, attitudes, and higher-level cognitive processes. This is simply a different sort of learning environment. There is a challenge here to the institution because, as Rowley and Lujan (1995) have observed, the current mode and mind-set of those in higher education is not programmed to accommodate the type of change we describe here.

*Redesigning, Redefining, and Reengineering.* The impact of the emergence of these forces will necessitate structural changes in today's colleges and universities. Old paradigms will give way to new external demands. For example, "open access" is already a demand of the modern learner, forcing higher education to rethink traditional degree programs in favor of a more cafeteria-style approach to learning.

Further, as the phenomenon of networking continues to spread, campuses will have to redesign their operations to accommodate it, or risk losing an edge in the growing competitive economy. Likewise, colleges and universities may need to develop hybrid disciplines to create the capacity for learners to reshape disciplines to fit individual needs. And they may also need to develop ways of allowing something called "just-in-time learning," which moves education away from the factory model of delivery to the customized demands of the workers in the information age. Also, Dolence and Norris (1995) suggest that colleges and universities may well need to restructure to provide for a fusion of learning systems, information-age service standards, personal learning diagnostics, point-of-access pay plans, and a seamless, personalized set of services to accompany a seamless educational system.

## Implications for the Academy

In imaging a world in which demand-driven education is the norm, the college's or university's strategic planning process is embarking on a new road, a perilous journey, one that promises to be as dangerous as it is exciting. The challenges are great. In redesigning the organization to achieve a new set of directions and methodologies, planners must wrestle with fundamental issues such as the role of the classroom, the allocation of resources, the direction of research agendas, and how institutions will pay for the changes they are about to make. It will also be necessary to redefine the roles and responsibilities within the realigned, redesigned organization, which can only be done humanely if it is done over time, with care, and with broad-based education and support. *There is no feasible way of doing this outside of the strategic planning process.*

In its development, any well-conceived strategic planning process should address how the campus will reengineer organizational processes to achieve dramatically higher productivity and quality. Incorporating new technologies, instituting new curricula, inventing new means of interaction between faculty and students, reinventing the student enrollment management processes of the campus, addressing the substantive capital needs of the new academic systems, and forming more meaningful alliances between the institution and its most critical environments are all part of the reengineering demands that will come with transformation.

Several institutions that do strategic planning are beginning to include major strategies related to this need for transformation and reengineering. Iowa State University has three specific university-wide strategy sets that (1) develop an understanding for the implications of emerging science and technology, (2) expand technology transfer, and (3) ensure the proper use of information technology and computational services (Iowa State University President's Office, 1995). Fort Lewis College (Burns, Peters, and Young, 1994) is using its strategic planning process to "enable Fort Lewis College to create an organizational structure that is less departmentally oriented, in terms of administrative, student services, and academic functions, and which could approximate what has been called a 'seamless' institution, with fewer boundaries and edges, and which is more holistic, integrated and accessible" (p. 7). Northeastern University's strategic plan has specific strategies to serve the lifelong learner and to develop strategic alliances with other institutions to share knowledge and resources (Northeastern University Strategic Planning Steering Committee, 1994). And the Ohio Board of Regents states in its system strategic plan that "if information technology is to be a tool for transforming higher education, Ohio's college and university facilities must become the pioneers of change" (Gauthier, 1995, p. 2). Apparently, some colleges and universities are well on the way, while others lag behind.

While we have focused on higher education in much of this discussion, there is also the daunting matter of the current "seamless system" from K-12 to community colleges to the comprehensives and major universities. Dropout rates are climbing, casualties of the present system. The contemporary role of the community college is generally unaddressed, while more freshmen go through the gates of such institutions than through the gates of colleges and universities. For higher education, the challenge is to plan more effectively by considering the need for a better fit from high school to college.

Responsible strategic planning must address this systemic issue, and given technology and the rising cost of education at all levels, consider how efficiencies may be realized while improving retention throughout the system. This suggests that major reform might be needed as, for example, high schools link themselves more effectively to community colleges, and perhaps as K-12 becomes K-n (where "n" is a number more or less than 12), giving community colleges a larger role to play for traditional students between school and work, and for the older students, between work and academics. This will require good articulation and wise use of technology, especially in handling the transfer of information endemic to lower-division education and freeing up the upper-division classroom for developing greater thinking skills and encouraging experimentation and exploration. This, of course, is a topic ripe for further research and discussion.

## Closing Thoughts

This book has attempted to develop a model of strategic planning in colleges and universities that uniquely fits the characteristics of modern institutions of higher education. This model differs in several substantial ways from the more traditional business model, but it is nonetheless firmly based on the importance of developing a long-term strategy to align the institution with its environment, in order to ensure long-term survival. While many within the academy continue to rebel against the notion that substantive change is inevitable, others are beginning to look for models of change that will help lead their institution through the troubled times ahead. We believe that the strategic planning model we have outlined here presents a method of change that is humane, environmentally sensitive, innovative, and keenly adaptable to the idiosyncrasies of higher education.

## Two Central Themes

Successful transformation requires successful preparation. Strategic planning holds the promise of developing a firm foundation for change based on an increase of self-knowledge and of the knowledge of external changes that impact the academy. As we have discussed throughout, the transformation we are referring to is the change in thinking and decision-making patterns that exemplify the management of institutions of higher education at all levels. Through the growth of knowledge, administrators, faculty, and staff need to begin to see that the parochial view of what needs to be done and how to do it are issues that can most effectively be addressed through a long-term understanding of what is best for the institution. To address this transformation, this book has developed two particular, central themes, as it has built the foundation of a successful model of strategic planning.

*Change the Way People Think and Make Decisions.* One of the major themes of this book has been the move from traditional thinking and decision making to strategic thinking and strategic decision making. Zabriskie and Huellmantel (1991) suggest that strategic thinking occurs when decision makers are able to visualize what they want their organization to become, and when they are able to align their resources to compete successfully. Such managers are able to assesses the risks, revenues, and costs of the strategy alternatives available to them, and to identify the questions they want answered strategically. These managers can think logically and systematically about the planning steps and model they will use to activate their strategic thinking on the organization's operations. Further, as Suutari (1993) suggests, while strategic thinking is necessary at all levels of an organization, it is particularly important that it be instilled at the functional levels, or within defined departments, where the day-to-day decisions are made. These are powerful forces that shape significant and meaningful change when they all come together in a college or university setting.

In the academy, one should expect the heart and soul of the institution—the faculty—to be preoccupied with what is taking place in their particular fields of study. They help develop and interpret the advancements that occur in their disciplines, and are heavily rewarded for those activities. As a result, their focus for change and innovation is logically directed toward their disciplines—they expect the institution within which they are housed to provide resources, opportunities, and stability. This parochial view is understandable, and helps explain why faculty tend to resist change with such fervor when the institution begins to question the course it is taking and how it is utilizing its resource base.

However, parochialism is not simply a characteristic of the faculty. Administrators and staff have become very comfortable and familiar with the ivory-tower way of doing business. To a large degree, those who manage colleges and universities are as tied to the unique qualities of their institutions as are the faculty. They dislike change just as much as those who teach and do research.

But the world of today and tomorrow is changing, and that change is dramatic. Today's world is no longer tolerating the academy; it is beginning to expect more and more responsiveness to the ills and opportunities that mark the world. In order to respond adequately, colleges and universities have got to do more than simply pay attention; they need to partner more with those critical environmental elements that provide long-term opportunities and support. This requires a whole new way of thinking.

"Business as usual," or "the same old same old," does not exemplify the type of decision making and managerial thinking that the new environmental forces are looking for. Rather, they are looking for decision-making and managerial activities that meet *their* needs. From an internal perspective, this requires that thinking and decision making be done within the context of this emerging relationship. College and university programs, business practices, and the basic interface between the institution and its critical environmental set must become more aligned, or the institution runs the risk of becoming irrelevant.

This is perhaps the greatest challenge, but also the greatest benefit of the strategic planning process. And it cannot be done in the short term. Faculty, staff, and administrators must all learn the benefits of thinking strategically, and without a major and immediate crisis, this may be difficult to achieve. Nonetheless, with time and persistence, substantive change can occur in the institution. That is why the process, although it can be successful only if it is truly participative, needs the strong and unwavering support of top administrators and governing bodies. As these bodies and other leaders of the college or university continuously practice strategic thinking and strategic decision making in their areas of responsibility, the model can extend throughout the institution, particularly if key members of the campus are part of the overall strategic planning initiative. Over time, the change will occur.

*Change Provider-Driven Education.* Another central theme involves the impetus for the development or support of academic programming. The luxury of the provider model of education is coming to an end. While the development of knowledge has been the purview of college and university faculty, that development has been more self-directed than it has been sensitive to the actual needs and wants of the external environment.

For centuries this has been alright, because society was behind where the academy said it could go. This is no longer the case. With the development of the information age, with the unimaginable advances in transportation and communication coming much more quickly and substantively than anyone has been prepared to deal with, colleges and universities find themselves in a catch-up position. They can no longer decide what programs to offer based on what they think the world will need. The world is now making that decision, and expects the institutions of higher education to be responsive.

For those institutions that are developing means of interacting appropriately with those elements of their environments that need their expertise and innovation, the result is a partnership that benefits everyone. Those institutions that insist on providing programs that they feel are best for society to take advantage of risk death, or worse, irrelevancy.

Instead, understanding who the student is and what the student needs is a central tenet of successful strategic planning. This student comes from and represents a society that is changing daily. This student will enter a work world that will demand skills and knowledge based on the complex needs of emerging technologies. The academy is the knowledge service station that helps the student get from where she or he has been to where she or he needs to go. If the academy cannot adequately provide the student with the skills and knowledge bases he or she needs, then the universal student will begin to seek out other sources of preparation that will do it.

The environments that require this type of service and linkage go beyond the environment of the student, however. For state-supported colleges and universities, the cries for relevancy from legislatures to tax payers are becoming legion. For private colleges and universities, the concern of alumni and governing boards are just as pronounced and severe (perhaps more so, because their resource base is more fragile). Strategic planning provides bridges to meet these challenges.

## Reinforcing the Short Term with the Long Term

Part of the transformation process we have described is setting the context of administrative action and academic programming within the long-term framework of where the institution is headed. Two positive benefits come from this. First, it becomes much easier to develop short-term priorities because a referent is now in place that helps administrators, staff, and faculty decide where resources should be concentrated or where innovation should be encouraged. This is important because in a world where resources are already precious, the future appears to promise many fewer resources to do the work colleges and universities are asked to do. It is already important for the institution to choose wisely in deciding how to allocate its resources, but in an increasingly hostile environmental setting, using today's resources to help sustain tomorrow's institution becomes an even more critical responsibility. *Strategic planning is the only logical way of helping to ensure that those long-term successful factors have been properly identified.* With these in place, it is then much easier to prioritize in the short run to help assure the longer run.

Second, administrators, staff, and faculty must make decisions from an institutional perspective, rather than from their traditional parochial views. As we have acknowledged throughout, this is difficult. Colleges and universities are parochial by nature. Since allegiance to the institution is less strong than allegiance to one's own discipline, it is not unusual for faculty on most campuses to think narrowly. This condition may have been alright for the college and university of yesterday. Today, the institution needs the allegiance and support of all its human resources if it is going to be successful. When the good of the whole becomes a necessary part of the academic equation, loyalty to the institution may begin to emerge and compete successfully with loyalty to the discipline or profession.

Of course, the accepted reward structure has nothing in it that rewards faculty for loyalty to the institution. Rewards are based on research and teaching. Yet, the emerging environment may make it time to look at the reward system in higher education and make new decisions based on new realities. Already, the issue of tenure has moved from sacred ground to public whispers in legislative places. Perhaps the wisest course of action is for colleges and universities to face these issues and devise adequate moderations themselves, rather than risk having those on the outside make these decisions for them. A successful strategic planning effort can help institutions shape these decisions. If they do not take the initiative, the danger is real.

## Planning to Survive and Prosper

While the overwhelming reason for strategic planning is to survive by better aligning the institution with its most critical environments, planning can also help the institution to prosper. We have only hinted at this outcome throughout this book, but it is perhaps as important as simply ensuring that the college or university will be around for the next several years.

Prosperity in higher education means many things on many fronts. Administratively, prosperity may mean more than balanced budgets. It can mean burgeoning endowments and positive public relations. From a staff perspective, prosperity may mean salary parity (or better, somewhere above parity) and positive working conditions. For faculty, prosperity may mean rich new discoveries, exciting new ways of interacting with students, quality publications, and recognition within a discipline. For students, prosperity may mean a meaningful and useful education that properly prepares them for the world they are about to enter. For the community and beyond, prosperity in higher education should mean that the people in the ivory tower are listening and responding in a manner that helps improve the quality and productivity of life. In other words, prosperity should mean that everyone wins.

Because the definition of prosperity changes from one campus to the next, the strategic planning process should incorporate the tenets of prosperity as planned outcomes. Along with the other planned outcomes—increased relevance, and partnerships with strategic stakeholders—planners can also design a future that is rewarding. While the academy may no longer enjoy the privileges and status it had in the past, it now has the opportunity to define a niche in society that is still as strong, viable, progressive, and necessary for prosperity as education always has been. Each college and university has the opportunity to develop its own part of that niche, and to do so in such a way that everyone benefits. This is the choice made by those who do substantive strategic planning.

The future need not be the dark world of the unknown. Certainly, as the tempo of change increases and the complexity of life accelerates, the future can be cruel and unforgiving. Conversely, the future always contains opportunities and challenges that will reward those who understand them and take advantage of them. Strategic planning in business has held this promise for well over thirty years. For today's colleges and universities, no longer immune from the world in which they live, strategic planning can be a logical and effective method of intervention, defining an appropriate direction toward a future in which they will flourish.

Ackoff, R. L. *Concepts of Corporate Strategy.* New York: Wiley, 1970.

Aggarwal, R. "Systematic Strategic Planning at a State University: A Case Study of Adapting Corporate Planning Techniques." *Innovative Higher Education,* 1987, *11*(2), 123–135.

Akkermans, H. A., and Van Aken, J. E. "Process-Related Problems in Operations Strategy." *International Studies of Management and Organization,* 1992, *22*(4), 6–20.

Allen, G. "Defining the Mission Is Crucial to Long-Term Success." *Manufactured Home MERCHANDISER,* Aug. 1993, pp. 24–25.

Ansoff, H. I., Avenr, J., Brandenberg, R. G., Portner, F. E., and Radosevich, R. "Does Planning Pay? The Effect of Planning on Success of Acquisition in American Firms." *Long-Range Planning,* Dec. 1970, p. 207.

Appleby, D., and Carrillo, E. "The Specialized Program in the Small Liberal Arts College." *Educational Research Quarterly,* 1990, *14*(1), 21–28.

Bank, B. J., Biddle, B. J., and Slavings, R. L. "What Do Students Want? Expectations and Undergraduate Persistence." *The Sociological Quarterly,* 1992, *33*(3), 321–355.

Barnett, R. "Linking Teaching and Research." *Journal of Higher Education,* 1992, *63*(6), 618–636.

Bedian, A. G., and Zammuto, R. F. *Organizational Theory and Design.* Orlando: Dryden Press, 1991.

Birnbaum, R. "The Latent Organizational Functions of the Academic Senate: Why Senates Do Not Work but Will Not Go Away." In R. Birnbaum (ed.), *Faculty in Governance: The Role of Senates and Joint Committees in Academic Decision Making.* New Directions for Higher Education, no. 75. San Francisco: Jossey-Bass, 1991.

Blaisdell, M. L. "Academic Integration: Going Beyond Disciplinary Boundaries." New Directions for Higher Education, no. 54. San Francisco: Jossey-Bass, 1993.

Blumenstyk, G. "Private Colleges Scramble to Deal with Rising Costs of

Financial Aid." *The Chronicle of Higher Education,* Apr. 21, 1993, pp. A33–A35.

Bollinger, J. G. "Strategic Planning in an Academic Environment." *Engineering Education,* 1990, *80,* 19–22.

Botstein, L. "Structuring Specialization as a Form of General Education." *Liberal Education,* 1991, 77(2), 10–19.

Bottrill, K. V., and Borden, V.M.H. "Appendix: Examples from the Literature." In V.M.H. Borden and T. W. Banta (eds.), *Performance Indicators: Guides for Strategic Decision Making.* New Directions for Institutional Research, no. 82. San Francisco: Jossey-Bass, 1994.

Brady, J. "The Search for Mission Control." *Folio,* 1993, *22,* 42, 51.

Brandt, R. "On Strategic Management: A Conversation with George Wilkinson." *Educational Leadership,* Apr. 1991, pp. 22–25.

Breneman, D. W. "Higher Education: On a Collision Course with New Realities." *Association of Governing Boards Occasional Paper no. 22.* Washington, D.C.: Association of Governing Boards, 1994.

Broad, W. J. "Top Quark, Last Piece in Puzzle of Matter, Appears to Be in Place." *The New York Times,* Apr. 26, 1994, pp. A1, B10.

Brown, D. G. "The University of North Carolina at Asheville." In D. W. Steeples (ed.), *Successful Strategic Planning: Case Studies.* New Directions for Higher Education, no. 64. San Francisco: Jossey-Bass, 1988.

Bruton, G. D., and Hildreth, W. B. "Strategic Public Planning: External Orientations and Strategic Planning Team Members." *American Review of Public Administration,* 1993, 23(4), 307–317.

Bryson, J. M. *Strategic Planning for Public and Nonprofit Organizations: A Guide to Strengthening and Sustaining Organizational Achievement.* San Francisco: Jossey-Bass, 1989.

Bryson, J. M. *Strategic Planning for Public and Nonprofit Organizations: A Guide to Strengthening and Sustaining Organizational Achievement.* (Rev. ed.) San Francisco: Jossey- Bass, 1995.

Bryson, J. M., and Bromiley, P. "Critical Factors Affecting the Planning and Implementation of Major Projects." *Strategic Management Journal,* 1993, *14,* 319–337.

Burke, W. W. *Organization Development: Principles and Practices.* New York: Little, Brown, 1982.

Burns, S., Peters, P., and Young, C. "Fort Lewis College: Strategic Plan for Instructional Technology." [http://www.fortlewis.edu/comtel/develop/etsplan.html]. 1994.

Byars, L. L. *Strategic Management.* (3rd ed.) New York: HarperCollins, 1991.

Byrne, J. A. "Virtual B-Schools." *Business Week,* Oct. 23, 1995, pp. 64–68.

Calfee, D. L. "Get Your Mission Statement Working!" *Management Review,* Jan. 1993, pp. 54–57.

Campbell, A. "The Power of Mission: Aligning Strategy and Culture."

*Planning Review Special Issue: Conference Executive Summary,* Sept./Oct. 1992, pp. 10–12, 63.

Canary, H. W., Jr. " Linking Strategic Plans with Budgets." *Government Finance Review,* Apr. 1992, pp. 21–25.

Candy, P. C., and Crebert, R. G. "Ivory Tower to Concrete Jungle." *Journal of Higher Education,* 1991, *62*(5), 570–592.

Capon, N., Farley, J. U., and Hulbert, J. M. "Strategic Planning and Financial Performance: More Evidence." *Journal of Management Studies,* 1994, *31*(1), 105–110.

Carroll, S. J., and Tosi, H. L. *Organizational Behavior.* Chicago: St. Clair Press, 1977.

Carter, D. J., and Wilson, R. *Minorities in Higher Education, 1994, Thirteenth Annual Report.* Washington, D.C.: American Council on Education, 1995.

Carter, R. B., Nilakanta, S., and Norris, D. "Strategic Planning for Information Systems: The Evidence from a Successful Implementation in an Academic Setting." *Journal on Research on Computing in Education,* 1991, *24*(2), 280–288.

Chaffee, E. E., and Sherr, L. A. *Quality: Transforming Postsecondary Education.* Washington, D.C.: George Washington University Press, 1992. (ED 351922)

Chiarelott, L., Reed, P., and Russell, S. C. "Lessons in Strategic Planning Learned the Hard Way." *Educational Leadership,* Apr. 1991, pp. 36–39.

Chickering, A. W., and Gamson, Z. F. "Seven Principles for Good Practices in Undergraduate Education." In A. W. Chickering and Z. F. Gamson (eds.), *Applying the Seven Principles for Good Practice in Undergraduate Education.* New Directions in Teaching and Learning, no. 47. San Francisco: Jossey-Bass, 1991.

Chorn, N. H. "The 'Alignment' Theory: Creating Strategic Fit." *Management Decisions,* 1991, *29*(1), 20–24.

Clinchy, E. "Higher Education: The Albatross Around the Neck of Our Public Schools." *Phi Beta Kappan,* 1994, *75*(10), 745–751.

Cline, N. M., and Meringolo, S. M. "A Strategic Planning Imperative: The Penn State Experience." In J. F. Williams II (ed.), *Strategic Planning in Higher Education.* Binghamton, N.Y.: Haworth Press, 1991.

Collins, J. C., and Porras, J. I. "Organizational Vision and Visionary Organizations." *California Management Review,* Fall 1991, pp. 31–52.

Cope, R. G. *High Involvement Strategic Planning: When People and Their Ideas Really Matter.* Oxford, Ohio: The Planning Forum, 1989.

Crase, D. R., and Crase, D. "Tenure Decisions in an Era of Specialization." *Journal of Home Economics,* Fall 1991, pp. 40–43.

Cross, R. H. III. "Strategic Planning: What It Can and Can't Do." *SAM Advanced Management Journal,* 1987, *53*, 13–16.

Cyert, R. M. "Carnegie Mellon University." In D. W. Steeples (ed.), *Successful Strategic Planning: Case Studies*. New Directions for Higher Education, no. 64. San Francisco: Jossey- Bass, 1988.

Daly, W. T. "Teaching and Scholarship." *Journal of Higher Education*, 1994, 65(1), 45–57.

Das, T. K. "Time: The Hidden Dimension in Strategic Planning." *Long Range Planning*, 1991, 24(3), 49–57.

David, F. R. *Strategic Management*. (3rd ed.) Old Tappan, N.J.: Macmillan, 1991.

Dean, J. W., Jr., and Sharfman, M. P. "Does Decision Process Matter? A Study of Strategic Decision-Making Effectiveness." *The Academy of Management Journal*, 1996, 39(2), 368–396.

Detomasi, D. "Mission Statements: One More Time." *Planning in Higher Education*, 1995, 24(1), 31–35.

Dill, D. "Rethinking the Planning Process." *Planning for Higher Education*, 1991, 22(2), 8–13.

Dodd, J. L. "President's Page: Strategic Thinking, Strategic Action." *Journal of the American Dietetic Association*, 1992, 92(6), 750–751.

Doerle, C. "Strategic Planning Is for Everybody." *Institutional Distribution*, Dec. 1991, pp. 16, 158.

Dolence, M. G., and Norris, D. M. "Using Key Performance Indicators to Drive Strategic Decision Making." In V. Borden and T. Banta (eds.), *Performance Indicators: Guides for Strategic Decision Making*. New Directions for Institutional Research, no. 82. San Francisco: Jossey-Bass, 1994.

Dolence, M. G., and Norris, D. M. *Transforming Higher Education*. Ann Arbor, Mich.: Society for College and University Planning, 1995.

Dominick, C. A. "Revising the Institutional Mission." In D. W. Steeples (ed.), *Managing Change in Higher Education*. New Directions for Higher Education, no. 71. San Francisco: Jossey-Bass, 1990.

Dooris, M. J., and Lozier, G. G. "Adapting Formal Planning Approaches: The Pennsylvania State University." In F. A. Schmidtlein and T. H. Milton (eds.), *Adapting Strategic Planning to Campus Realities*. New Directions for Institutional Research, no. 67. San Francisco: Jossey-Bass, 1990.

Eaton, G. P., and Adams, J. W. "Strategic Planning at Iowa State University: Affirmation and Expectations." In J. F. Williams II (ed.), *Strategic Planning in Higher Education*. Binghamton, N.Y.: Haworth Press, 1991.

Eddy, E. D., Jr. "The First Hundred Years, in Retrospect and Prospect." In E. J. Nesius (ed.), *Development of Land-Grant Colleges and Universities and Their Influence in the Economic and Social Life of People*. Morgantown, W.V.: Office of Publications, West Virginia University, 1963.

Ehrlich, E. M. "Firms of the Future." *Executive Denver*, May 1995, pp. 9–28.

Etzioni, A. *Modern Organizations*. Englewood Cliffs, N.J.: Prentice Hall, 1964.

Farmer, D. W. "Strategies for Change." In D. W. Steeples (ed.), *Managing Change in Higher Education.* New Directions for Higher Education, no. 71. San Francisco: Jossey-Bass, 1990.

Flack, H. "Three Critical Elements in Strategic Planning." *Planning for Higher Education,* 1994, 23(1), 24–31.

Floyd, S. W., and Wooldridge, B. "Managing Strategic Consensus: The Foundation of Effective Implementation." *Academy of Management Executive,* 1992, 6(4), 27–39.

Foote, E. T. II. "The University of Miami." In D. W. Steeples (ed.), *Successful Strategic Planning: Case Studies.* New Directions for Higher Education, no. 64. San Francisco: Jossey-Bass, 1988.

Fountoukidis, D., Hahn, M., and Voos, J. "Planning in Academic Departments." *Planning in Higher Education,* 1995, 23(3), 49–56.

Frank, D. "Faculty Take Charge of Planning Process." *FOCUS Articles.* [http://www.rutgers.edu/University/Focus/articlesfeb23/volume.1.shtml]. Feb. 23, 1996.

French, W. M. *America's Educational Tradition.* Lexington, Mass.: Heath, 1964.

Gardner, D. P. "Managing Transitions in a Time of Acute Modernity." *Trusteeship,* 1995, 3(4), 10–15.

Gauthier, H. "The Challenge is Change: Moving from Teaching to Learning." [http://www.bor.ohio.gov/plandocs/newsletter_oct95.html]. Oct. 1995.

Gilbert, J. T. "'Faster! Newer!' Is Not a Strategy." *SAM Advanced Management Journal,* 1993, 58, 4–8.

Gilmour, J. E., Jr. "Participative Governance Bodies in Higher Education: Report of a National Study." In R. Birnbaum (ed.), *Faculty in Governance: The Role of Senates and Joint Committees in Academic Decision Making.* New Directions for Higher Education, no. 75. San Francisco: Jossey-Bass, 1991.

Gratch, B., and Wood, E. "Strategic Planning: Implementation and First-Year Appraisal." *The Journal of Academic Librarianship,* 1991, 17(1), 10–15.

Green, C. A. "Targeting New Markets." In D. W. Steeples (ed.), *Managing Change in Higher Education.* New Directions for Higher Education, no. 71. San Francisco: Jossey-Bass, 1990.

Green, J. S. "Planning at a Small Institution: Bradford College." In F. A. Schmidtlein and T. H. Milton (eds.), *Adapting Strategic Planning to Campus Realities.* New Directions for Institutional Research, no. 67. San Francisco: Jossey-Bass, 1990.

Green University Institute for the Environment. "About the Green University Initiative." [http://gwis2.circ.gwu.edu/~greenu/gfp.html]. 1996.

Gumport, P. "The Contested Terrain of Academic Program Reduction." *Journal of Higher Education,* 1993, 64(3), 283–311.

Guskin, A. E. "Restructuring the Role of Faculty." *Change,* Sept./Oct. 1994, pp. 16–25.

Haiss, P. R. "The Evolution of Strategy and Strategy as Evolution." *World Futures*, 1993, *36*, 21–29.

Hall, M. C., and Elliott, K. M. "Strategic Planning for Academic Departments: A Model and Methodology." *Journal of Marketing for Higher Education*, 1993, *4*(1/2), pp. 295–308.

Hambrick, D. C. "What If the Academy Actually Mattered?" *The Academy of Management Review*, 1994, *19*(1), 11–16.

Hanson, E. M., and Henry, W. "Strategic Marketing for Educational Systems." *NASSP Bulletin*, Nov. 1993, pp. 79–88.

Hardy, C. "The Cultural Politics of Retrenchment." *Planning in Higher Education*, 1990, *21*(4), 16–20.

Hardy, C. "Configuration and Strategy Making in Universities." *Journal of Higher Education*, 1991, *62*(4), 363–393.

Harrison, J. S., and St. John, C. H. *Strategic Management of Organizations and Stakeholders*. St. Paul: West, 1994.

Herbert, T. T. *Dimensions of Organizational Behavior*. (2nd ed.) Old Tappan, N.J.: Macmillan, 1981.

Herold, D. M. "Long-Range Planning and Organizational Performance." *Academy of Management Journal*, Mar. 1973, pp. 91–102.

Hersey, P., and Blanchard, K. H. *Management of Organizational Behavior: Utilizing Human Resources*. Englewood Cliffs, N.J.: Prentice Hall, 1988.

Hinsdale, B. A. "Horace Mann and the Common School Revival in the United States." In N. M. Butler (ed.), *The Great Educators*. New York: Scribner, 1898.

Honan, J. P. "Monitoring Institutional Performance." *AGB Priorities*, 1995, *5*, 1–15.

Horne, E. V. "The Diploma: Time Card or Stamp of Approval?" *Trusteeship*, 1995, *3*(2), 5.

Houston, P. D., and Schneider, J. "Drive-By Critics and Silver Bullets." *Phi Beta Kappan*, 1994, *75*(10), 779–782.

Hunger, J. D. and Wheelen, T. L. *Strategic Management*. (5th ed.) Reading, Mass.: Addison-Wesley, 1996.

Hussar, W. J. *Projections of Education Statistics to 2005: Pocket Projections*. Washington, D.C.: National Center for Education Statistics, Feb. 1995.

Hyatt, J. A. "Strategic Restructuring: A Case Study." In W. E. Vandament and D. P. Jones (eds.), *Financial Management: Progress and Challenges*. New Directions for Higher Education, no. 83. San Francisco: Jossey-Bass, 1993.

Iowa State University President's Office. "The Strategic Plan for 1995–2000: Iowa State's Aspiration." [http://www.iastate.edu/~pres_info/2000/aspire.html]. Apr. 1995.

Ireland, R. D., and Hitt, M. A. "Mission Statements: Importance, Challenge, and Recommendations for Development." *Business Horizons,* May-June 1992, pp. 34–42.

Jaschik, S. "Regional Public Colleges Resist Their States' Demands That They Specialize." *The Chronicle of Higher Education,* Apr. 22, 1992, pp. A31–A32.

Johnstone, D. B. "College at Work: Partnerships and the Rebuilding of American Competence." *Journal of Higher Education,* 1994, *65*(2), 168–182.

Jones, L. W. "Strategic Planning: The Unrealized Potential of the 1980s and the Promise of the 1990s." In L. W. Jones and F. A. Nowotny (eds.), *An Agenda for the New Decade.* New Directions for Higher Education, no. 70. San Francisco: Jossey-Bass, 1990.

Jonsen, R. W. "The Environmental Context for Postsecondary Education." In Callom, P. M. (ed.), *Environmental Scanning for Strategic Leadership.* New Directions for Institutional Research, no. 52. San Francisco: Jossey-Bass, 1986.

Kanter, R. M., Stein, B. A., and Jick, T. D. *The Challenge of Organizational Change.* New York: Free Press, 1992.

Kaufman, R. "Beyond Tinkering: Education Restructuring That Will Work." *International Journal of Educational Reform,* 1993, *2*(2), 154–165.

Kaufman, R., and Herman, J. "Strategic Planning for a Better Society." *Educational Leadership,* Apr. 1991, pp. 8–14.

Keller, G. *Academic Strategy.* Baltimore: Johns Hopkins University Press, 1983.

Keller, G. "The Changing Milieu of Education Planning." *Planning in Higher Education,* 1994–1995, *23*(2), 23–26.

Keller, G. "The Vision Thing in Higher Education." *Planning in Higher Education,* 1995, *23*(4), 8.

Kember, D., and Gow, L. "Orientations to Teaching and Their Effect on the Quality of Student Learning." *Journal of Higher Education,* 1994, *65*(1), 58–74.

Kenny, S. S. "Using Business Leaders for Academic Planning." *Planning for Higher Education,* 1993, *21*(3), 21–26.

Kerr, C. *The Uses of the University.* (3rd ed.) Cambridge, Mass.: Harvard University Press, 1982.

Kitching, I. "A History of Anglia Polytechnic University 1858–1994." [http://bridge.anglia.ac.uk/~systimk/five_years/index.html]. Dec. 1994.

Klimoski, V. J. "Recapturing the Value of Mission." *Adult Learning,* Oct. 1991, pp. 19, 20, 27.

Knights, D., and Morgan, G. "Corporate Strategy, Organizations, and Subjectivity: A Critique." *Organization Studies,* 1991, *12*(2), 251–273.

Kuhn, T. S. *The Structure of Scientific Revolutions.* Chicago: University of Chicago Press, 1962.

Kukalis, S. "Determinants of Strategic Planning Systems in Large Organizations: A Contingency Approach." *Journal of Management Studies,* 1991, *28*(2), 143–160.

Lammers, T. "The Effective and Indispensable Mission Statement." *INC.,* Aug. 1992, pp. 75–77.

Langeler, G. H. "The Vision Trap." *Harvard Business Review,* Mar./Apr. 1992, pp. 46–55.

Lee, B. A. "Campus Leaders and Campus Senates." In R. Birnbaum (ed.), *Faculty in Governance: The Role of Senates and Joint Committees in Academic Decision Making.* New Directions for Higher Education, no. 75. San Francisco: Jossey-Bass, 1991.

Lee, C. "The Vision Thing." *Training,* Feb. 1993, pp. 25–34.

Leontiades, M. "The Confusing Words of Business Policy." *The Academy of Management Review,* 1982, *7*(1), 45–48.

Leslie, D. W., and Fretwell, E. K. *Wise Moves in Hard Times: Creating and Managing Resilient Colleges and Universities.* San Francisco: Jossey-Bass, 1996.

Levine, A., and Associates. *Shaping Higher Education's Future: Demographic Realities and Opportunities, 1990–2000.* San Francisco: Jossey-Bass, 1989.

Lipset, S. M. *Rebellion in the University.* New Brunswick, N.J.: Transaction Publishers, 1993.

Lively, K. "Anatomy, at a Price." *The Chronicle of Higher Education,* 1995, *41*(14), A20–A26.

Lovett, C. "How to Start Restructuring Our Colleges." *Planning in Higher Education,* 1996, *24*(3), 18–22.

Luft, R. L., and Noll, C. L. "The Changing Profile of Business Education at NABTE Institutions." *Business Education Forum,* 1993, *47*(4), 8–11.

MacTaggart, T. J. "Restructuring and the Failure of Reform." In T. J. MacTaggart and Associates, *Restructuring Higher Education.* San Francisco: Jossey-Bass, 1996.

MaGrath, C. P. "Looking Forward: The Twenty-First Century Land-Grant University." Speech delivered in Ft. Collins, Colorado, Feb. 7, 1995.

Marshall, E., and Palca, J. "Cracks in the Ivory Tower." *Science,* 1992, *257,* 1196–1201.

Martinsons, M. G. "Strategic Innovation: A Lifeboat for Planning in Turbulent Waters." *Management Decisions,* 1993, *31*(8), 4–11.

Mathews, K. W. "Allocating Resources as a Means of Inducing and Responding to Change." In D. W. Steeples (ed.), *Managing Change in Higher Education.* New Directions for Higher Education, no. 71. San Francisco: Jossey-Bass, 1990.

Matthes, K. "Strategic Planning: Define Your Mission." *HR Focus,* 1993, *70,* 11–12.

Mayer, R. C., Davis, J. H., and Schoorman, F. D. "An Integrative Model of Organizational Trust." *The Academy of Management Review,* 1995, *20*(3), 709–734.

Mayhew, L. B., Ford, P. J., and Hubbard, D. L. *The Quest for Quality: The Challenge for Undergraduate Education in the 1990s.* San Francisco: Jossey-Bass, 1990.

McCloskey, D. N. "Invisible Colleges and Economics: An Unacknowledged Crisis in Academic Life." *Change,* Nov./Dec. 1991, pp. 10–11, 54.

McSherry, J. "Mission Statements Galore." *Business Quarterly,* Spring 1994, pp. 9–10.

Menand, L. "What Are Universities for?" *Harper's,* Dec. 1991, pp. 47–56.

Mercer, J. "Public-College Officials Grope for Ways to Keep a Lid on Tuition." *The Chronicle of Higher Education,* Jan. 27, 1993, pp. A32–A33.

Meredith, M. "What Works (and Doesn't) in Planning." *Planning for Higher Education,* 1993, *22*(1), 28–30.

Miles, R. E., and Snow, C. C. *Organizational Strategy, Structure, and Process.* New York: McGraw-Hill, 1978.

Mintzberg, H. "The Fall and Rise of Strategic Planning." *Harvard Business Review,* 1994a, *72*(1), 107–114.

Mintzberg, H. *The Rise and Fall of Strategic Planning.* New York: Free Press, 1994b.

Morgan, N. A., and Piercy, N. F. "Increasing Planning Effectiveness." *Management Decisions,* 1993, *31*(4), 55–58.

Morrill, R. L. "Centre College of Kentucky." In D. W. Steeples (ed.), *Successful Strategic Planning: Case Studies.* New Directions for Higher Education, no. 64. San Francisco: Jossey-Bass, 1988.

Morrison, J. L., and Brock, D. M. "Organizational Planning and Policy Analysis: Combining Theory with Experiential Learning." *Innovative Higher Education,* 1991, *15*(2), 137–151.

Morrison, J. L., Renfro, W. L., and Boucher, W. I. *Futures Research and the Strategic Planning Process: Implications for Higher Education.* Washington, D.C.: Association for the Study of Higher Education–Educational Resources Information Center, 1984.

Munitz, B. "Wanted: New Leadership for Higher Education." *Planning in Higher Education,* 1995, *24*(1), 9–16.

National Center for Higher Educational Management Systems. *News,* May 1995.

National Commission on Excellence in Education. *A Nation at Risk.* Washington, D.C.: U.S. Government Printing Office, 1983.

Nebgen, M. "The Key to Success in Strategic Planning Is Communication." *Educational Leadership,* Apr. 1991, pp. 26–28.

Nelton, S. "Put Your Purpose in Writing." *Nation's Business,* Feb. 1994, pp. 61–64.

Neumann, A. "The Thinking Team: Toward a Cognitive Model of Administrative Teamwork in Higher Education." *Journal of Higher Education,* 1991, *62*(5), 485–513.

Newman, G. "Worried About Vision? See an Optometrist." *Across the Board,* Oct. 1992, pp. 7–8.

Newport, S., Dess, G. G., and Rasheet, A.M.A. "Nurturing Strategic Coherency." *Planning Review,* Nov./Dec. 1991, pp. 18–22, 26, 27, 47.

Newton, R. "The Two Cultures of Academe: An Overlooked Planning Hurdle." *Planning in Higher Education,* 1992, *21*(1), 8–14.

Noorda, S. J., and Dallinga-Hunter, C. E. "Information in Support of Decision Makers in Higher Education." *Higher Education Management,* 1992, *4*(3), 271–283.

Northeastern University Strategic Planning Steering Committee. "The Connected Community: A Strategic Plan for Northeastern's Second Century." [http://iris.acs.neu.edu:8080/provost/stplan/welcome.html]. 1994.

Nutt, P. (ed.). *Strategic Management of Public and Third Sector Organizations: A Handbook for Leaders.* San Francisco: Jossey- Bass, 1992.

Nutt, P. C., and Backoff, R. W. *Strategic Management of Public and Third Sector Organizations: A Handbook for Leaders.* San Francisco: Jossey-Bass, 1992.

Office for University Information Technologies, Villanova University. "Relationships of Goals to 'A Future of Promise': The Villanova University Strategic Plan." [http://153.104.1.8/admin.unit/polproc/future.htm]. 1995.

Ohio Board of Regents. "The Concept and Preparation of a Functional Mission." [http://www.bor.ohio.gov/plandocs/functmiss.html]. Apr. 1993.

Ohio Board of Regents. "Kent State University Functional Mission Statement." [http://www.bor.ohio.gov/fms/fmksu.html]. 1995.

Pascarella, E. T., and Terenzini, P. T. *How College Affects Students: Findings and Insights from Twenty Years of Research.* San Francisco: Jossey-Bass, 1991.

Perelman, L. J. *School's out.* New York: Avon, 1992.

Pfeffer, J. *Managing with Power.* Boston, Mass.: Harvard Business School Press, 1992.

Philpott, M. "Business Beyond Our Borders: An Integrated Approach." *Business Education Forum,* 1994, *48*(3), 21–23.

Pickert, S. M. *Preparing for a Global Community: Achieving an International Perspective in Higher Education.* Washington, D.C.: George Washington University Press, 1992. (ED 350971)

Pilon, D. H. "Emerging Needs for Consultants in Higher Education." In J. F. Wergin (ed.), *Using Consultants Successfully.* New Directions for Higher Education, no. 73. San Francisco: Jossey-Bass, 1991.

Placenti, F. M. "Firm Must First Know Its Mission." *The National Law Journal*, Jan. 13, 1992, pp. 23, 26.

Porter, M. E. *Competitive Strategy.* New York: Free Press, 1980.

Porter, M. E. *Competitive Advantage.* New York: Free Press, 1985.

Prince, P. "The Case for Restructuring." Clemson University faculty meeting, 1995.

Pulliam, J. D. *The History of Education in America.* (4th ed.) Columbus, Ohio: Merrill, 1988.

Quinn, J. B. *Strategies for Change: Logical Incrementalism.* Burr Ridge, Ill.: Irwin, 1980.

Raghunathan, B., and Raghunathan, T. S. "Information Systems Planning and Effectiveness: An Empirical Analysis." *OMEGA International Journal of Management Science,* 1991, *19*(2/3), 125–135.

Ray, S. "B. C. Pavilion Corpis. Buckley: Keep Mission Statement Simple." *Amusement Business,* 1993, *105*, 74, 83.

Richards, D. "Is Strategic Decision Making Chaotic?" *Behavioral Science,* 1990, *35*, 219–232.

Roach, E. D. "West Texas State University." In D. W. Steeples (ed.), *Successful Strategic Planning: Case Studies.* New Directions for Higher Education, no. 64. San Francisco: Jossey-Bass, 1988.

Roessner, J. D. "Incentives to Innovate in Public and Private Organizations: Implications for Public Policy." *Administration and Society,* 1977, *9*, 341–365.

Rosser, J. M., and Penrod, J. I. "Strategic Planning and Management: A Methodology for Responsible Change." In J. F. Williams II (ed.), *Strategic Planning in Higher Education.* Binghamton, N.Y.: Haworth Press, 1991.

Rothschild, W. E. "Avoid the Mismatch Between Strategy and Strategic Leaders." *Journal of Business Strategy,* 1992, *14*(1), 37–42.

Rowley, D. J., and Lujan, H. D. "From Provider-Driven to Consumer-Driven Higher Education: Transforming Directions, Strategically." In Rowley, D. J. (ed.), *Proceedings of the Institute of Behavioral and Applied Management, Seattle, Washington.* Madison, Wis.: Omni Press, 1995.

St. John, E. P. "A Framework for Reexamining State Resource-Management Strategies in Higher Education." *Journal of Higher Education,* 1991, *62*(3), 263–287.

Sandy, W. "Avoid the Breakdown Between Planning and Implementation." *The Journal of Business Strategy,* Sept./Oct. 1991, pp. 30–33.

Schmidtlein, F. A. "Responding to Diverse Institutional Issues: Adapting Strategic Planning Concepts." In F. A. Schmidtlein and T. H. Milton (eds.), *Adapting Strategic Planning to Campus Realities.* New Directions for Institutional Research, no. 67. San Francisco: Jossey-Bass, 1990.

Schön, D. A. *The Reflective Practitioner.* New York: Basic Books, 1983.

Shirley, R. C. "Strategic Planning: An Overview." In D. W. Steeples (ed.), *Successful Strategic Planning: Case Studies.* New Directions for Higher Education, no. 64. San Francisco: Jossey-Bass, 1988.

Siegfried, J. J., Getz, M., and Anderson, K. H. "The Snail's Pace of Innovation in Higher Education." *The Chronicle of Higher Education,* 1995, *41*(36), A56.

Skok, J. E. "Toward a Definition of Strategic Management for the Public Sector." *American Review of Public Administration,* 1989, *19*(2), 133–147.

Skoldberg, K. "Strategic Change in Swedish Higher Education." *Higher Education,* 1991, *21*, 551–572.

Slaughter, J. Early speech in Western Accreditation Association Self-Study Report, 1988–1989.

Smith, F. "Let's Declare Education a Disaster and Get on with Our Lives." *Phi Beta Kappan,* 1994, *76*(8), 584–590.

Society for College and University Planning. *SCUP News,* 1994–1995, *24*(1), 1, 6.

Sowell, T. *Inside American Education.* New York: Free Press, 1993.

Starr, S. F. "A President's Message to Planners." *Planning for Higher Education,* 1993, *22*(1), 16–22.

Steeples, D. W. "Concluding Observations." In D. W. Steeples (ed.), *Managing Change in Higher Education.* New Directions for Higher Education, no. 71. San Francisco: Jossey-Bass, 1990.

Steiner, G. A., Miner, J. B., and Gray, E. R. *Management Policy and Strategy.* (2nd ed.) Old Tappan, N.J.: Macmillan, 1982.

Stott, K., and Walker, A. "The Nature and Use of Mission Statements in Singaporean Schools." *Educational Management and Administration,* 1992, *20*(1), 49–57.

Suutari, R. "The Case for Strategic Thinking." *CMA Magazine,* June 1993, pp. 17–21.

Swain, D. C. "The University of Louisville." In D. W. Steeples (ed.), *Successful Strategic Planning: Case Studies.* New Directions for Higher Education, no. 64. San Francisco: Jossey-Bass, 1988.

Taylor, B. E., Meyerson, J. M., and Massy, W. F. *Strategic Indicators for Higher Education: Improving Performance.* Princeton, N.J.: Peterson's Guides, 1993.

Thomas, A. S., Litschert, R. J., and Ramaswamy, K. "The Performance Impact of Strategy-Manager Coalignment: An Empirical Examination." *Strategic Management Journal,* 1991, *12*, 509–522.

Thompson, A. A., Jr., and Strickland, A. J. III. *Strategic Management.* (9th ed.) Burr Ridge, Ill.: Irwin, 1996.

Thompson, C. F., Jr., Johnson, A. B., Warren, C., and Williams, C. "Facilitating Growth and Leadership Development at Small Colleges

Through the Interactive Approach to Strategic Planning." *Innovative Higher Education,* 1990, *15*(1), 55–64.

Tornquist, K. M., and Kallsen, L. A. "Out of the Ivory Tower: Characteristics of Institutions Meeting the Research Needs of Industry." *Journal of Higher Education,* 1994, *65*(5), 523–539.

Tremblay, W. "Determining Value in Higher Education: The Future of Instructional Technology in a Wal-Mart Economy." *Educational Technology,* Oct. 1992, pp. 49–51.

Tully, S. "Finally, Colleges Start to Cut Their Crazy Costs." *Fortune,* May 1, 1995, pp. 110–114.

University of Iowa Campus Communications. "Achieving Distinction 2000: A Strategic Plan for The University of Iowa." [http://www.uiowa.edu/home-page/news/strategic-plan/ADTOC.html]. June 1995.

University of San Francisco. *University of San Francisco Planning and Budgeting Guide, 1995.* [http://www.usfca.edu/usf/budget/budcontents.html]. Sept. 1995.

Veliyath, R., and Shortell, S. M. "Strategic Orientation: Strategic Planning System Characteristics and Performance." *Journal of Management Studies,* 1993, *30*(3), 359–381.

Veysey, L. *The Emergence of the American University.* Chicago: University of Chicago Press, 1965.

Vinzant, D. H, and Vinzant, J. C. "TQM and Strategic Management Issues." *The Public Manager,* 1993, *22,* 76–78.

Warner, W. K. "Problems in Measuring the Goal Attainment of Voluntary Organizations." *Adult Education,* 1967, *18*(1), 3–14.

Weaver, G. A. "A Board's Primary Sin of Omission." *Trusteeship,* 1995, *3*(3), 5.

Wergin, J. F. "Do You Really Need a Consultant?" In J. F. Wergin (ed.), *Using Consultants Successfully.* New Directions for Higher Education, no. 73. San Francisco: Jossey-Bass, 1991.

Western Governors' Association. "Governors' Goals for a Western Virtual University." *From Vision to Reality.* Denver: Western Governors' Association, 1996.

Williams, R. K., Jr. "Employer-Based Outcome Assessment of Value-Added Performance for the MBA." [http://nuntlc.nu.edu/~nuri/llconf/conf1995/williams.html]. 1995.

Wilson, B. G. "The University of Queensland: Strategic Plan 1996– 2000." [http://uqadminserver.jdstory.uq.e. . .dminWWW/UQstratplan/stp laN96.html]. Jan. 12, 1995.

Wilson, I. "Teaching Decision Makers to Learn from Scenarios: A Blueprint for Implementation." *Planning Review,* May/June 1992, pp. 18–23.

Wood, R. J. "Changing the Educational Program." In D. W. Steeples (ed.),

*Managing Change in Higher Education.* New Directions for Higher Education, no. 71. San Francisco: Jossey-Bass, 1990.

Zabriskie, N. B., and Huellmantel, A. B. "Developing Strategic Thinking in Senior Management." *Long Range Planning,* 1991, 24(6), 25–32.

Zakrajsek, D., and Pierce, W. "Academic Preparation and the Academic Consumer." *Journal of Physical Education, Recreation, and Dance,* May–June 1993, pp. 20–23, 31.

Zemsky, R., Massy, W. F., and Oedel, P. "On Reversing the Ratchet." *Change,* May/June 1993, pp. 56–62.